ABOUT TURN:

the life and loss of a soldier.

by Jonathon Appelbe-Wootton

COPYRIGHT

For my family and friends who stuck by me through the hard times.

For my Fusilier family that I hold so dear to my heart.

For the fallen who never made it back. We will always remember you and everything you sacrificed. Remember; we are the lucky ones who made it home and saw our families again.

Foreword

"Don't suffer in silence" is something that people say all the time, but the silence is sometimes all you know and can't escape. When the silence is broken, it can be with aggressive or violent outbursts. With inappropriate anger and emotional responses that wildly differ from what is 'normal'.

But it is true, and it is true for everyone whether they are the ones suffering or they can sense the subtle signs that their mate, their brother, their child, is just... *off.*

Ask for help. Tell someone how you are feeling. Admit that you are having a hard time because that does not make you weak.

It makes you human.

If just one person reads this and reaches out for help, in any form, then it has done its job.

J A-W

Prologue

Nowzad, Afghanistan

I was watching on through a pair of binoculars while Dan was on the gun, preparing himself for me to give a fire control order. Suddenly, as if on cue, the hidden man stood up with a weapon slung across his chest and started moving at speed towards a small wall on the far side of the roof. Probably only ten metres away from safety, Dan squeezed his index finger and a swarm of angry 7.62 machine-gun rounds headed in the unlucky bloke's direction. Somehow, none of the hot metal slugs hit the target and the man now hit the accelerator, trying to escape the next burst.

I watched as the roof and surrounding buildings were turned into a dust cloud, as bullets ripped through hundred-year-old mud walls and metal corrugated sheeting. The GPMG did what it did best: put a huge number of rounds on a target quickly. But somehow, the lucky man was still moving, and he headed for cover behind a small wall, desperately trying to live for another day. I shouted for Dan to make adjustments and fire right.

I carried on watching in disbelief as rounds seemed to hit everything but the target. Fortunately, with the last burst of machine-gun fire before the man escaped to safety, his luck finally ran out. A well-aimed group of five to eight red-tipped rounds ripped through the insurgent's body, taking him clean off his feet and through a cloud of red speckled dust, I watched him collapse in a heap, probably a metre from his exit.

"Did I get him? Did I?" Dan asked.

"Yeah, yeah you got him," I answered.

"Do you think he's dead?"

"There's no way he survived that. No way," I responded.

It's a weird thing, seeing stuff like that and even though it hadn't been me firing the gun that time, it seemed to affect me more than it did when it was *my* finger squeezing the trigger. I think maybe because I could see the desperate look in the guy's face as he frantically sought survival, and maybe a part of me hoped he would succeed. It's like when you watch a wildlife documentary and a lion is chasing down a deer or something. Most people want the deer to escape, don't they? That's what it was kind of like. But he put himself in that situation and how would the enemy treat me if I was stupid enough to be out in the open?

But I'd like to take you back to the start now.

Hi, my name is Jonathon Appelbe-Wootton, and after being diagnosed with Myeloproliferative disorder, a condition that causes your blood cells, platelets, white blood cells and red blood cells, to grow abnormally in the bone marrow, I decided I needed to write a book about the things I've experienced in my life. This book is for my daughter Isabella, just in case the worst thing happens. I wanted her to know about all the things, both good and bad, that I have done during my eventful thirty-four years on this planet.

I enrolled on an English GCSE course, and one day the teacher got us to write a short piece of creative writing based upon a travel event. I obviously had many to choose from, but finally decided on one that took place in Afghanistan. On finishing the story, I wanted my Mom to see what she thought and her reaction, along with my sister Kathryn's, kind of shook me. With tears running down their faces, my Mom said that I should definitely start trying to write a book about everything I had been through. And I suppose, along with my health issues, this was the motivation I needed to start telling my story.

Now, everything I have put into this book is the truth. No embellishments. Just how things played out, and to be really honest, maybe I could have gone into more detail on some events. But that wouldn't have been in the best interests of some of the great friends I have made along the way. Just to get a few things clear right away, I know that some subjects in this book are going to upset a few people, but I had to be completely truthful with everyone. So please don't change your feelings towards me too much. There have been times in my life that I have gone through absolute hell and needed things to help me through them, but I'm happy to say that now I no longer need those things in my life. I have my amazing wife, Emma, and my beautiful daughter Isabella, and another child on the way, which has helped suppress the bad memories within me.

For as long as I can remember I always wanted to be a soldier. My Dad was always telling me stories about the great battles the British Army had been involved in, and stories of the Special Air Services, with their involvement in Northern Ireland, and the siege of the Iranian embassy that took place in London in 1980. I suppose I have to thank him for opening my eyes to this future career path; to be a soldier is a great experience, to serve and protect your country while maybe one day laying your life down for it. In my eyes it's like representing your country at football or any other sport, but a soldier has to be respected more for the things he does, gets paid crap money and takes loads more risks than one of those girly footballers who rolls around on the floor after the slightest touch.

I don't want to go into too much detail about my childhood, as the memories are sometimes too painful to disclose, and I will keep them buried deep inside, only to be relived in my dreams. But I will tell you I was born on September 2nd, 1981 to parents Ian and Stephanie, who also have three other children; Richard, my older brother, and two younger sisters, Elizabeth and Kathryn. We lived in a three-bedroomed house on Reddings Lane in Birmingham, just over the road from a small park, where I spent most of my free time playing football and cricket with my friends, completely oblivious to the troubles my parents were having in their marriage.

My Dad worked for the blood transfusion service driving the HGVs, which I always thought was pretty cool, and he would sometimes let Richard and me come to work with him during the holidays. We would sit alongside him while he drove all over the Midlands. In his spare time he would fix up old motorbikes and I will always remember Mom giving him grief about bike parts strewn all around the house, some even finding their way to the family bathroom, which especially made my Mom's blood boil. As a child I always looked up to my Dad. We would play war games in the garden, shooting each other with air pistols and throwing home-made grenades that Dad had spent hours painstakingly making, constructed out of bangers and individual pieces of cardboard. We would spend ages running up and down the garden using upturned sun loungers as cover, until Richard or I would end up in tears after getting shot in the face by Dad's eerily good aim, or Mom coming home and reading him the riot act.

My Mom. I could write forever about Mom, the strongest, most amazing woman you could ever have the privilege to meet. She has survived everything life has thrown at her, an absolute soldier. Ask anybody who knows me and they will testify the same. After my Dad had been caught having an affair and he moved out of the family home, she was our rock. Mom raised four children while working all the hours God sent, and while doing a university degree at the same time.

Chapter two – The pain

During this time Richard went completely off the rails, with drug and alcohol abuse, fighting, and stealing from strangers and even from the very people that loved him the most, it didn't matter that you were related to him. In my later teens I remember having to hide my wallet under my pillow while I slept. Richard once stole my Giro and denied it until I threatened to ring the police, and then it conveniently turned up. He did everything, he was known locally by every police officer at the height of his criminal enterprise. I could have killed him for what he did to my Mom and sisters. I remember one night when I was about sixteen, he had pissed someone off and was keeping an axe by his side for protection. I kept thinking to myself that if I smacked it over his head, the pain and heartache would all be over. For about ten years he ruined our lives until thankfully, a long spell at her Majesty's pleasure released us from his vicious and evil grip. Even though we were in a living hell, Mom was always there for us, strong and committed, and in a way this made us all strong for the difficult times ahead. And there would be many.

On one such occasion Richard had pissed off some lads who didn't live too far from us, and on one alcohol-fuelled evening they thought it would be a good idea to come to our house and try to get retribution for something he had or hadn't done. We never actually got the truth. At the time I was only fifteen and still at school. The first thing I recall of this terrifying evening was when Richard woke me and explained that some lads were at the door and not to answer it as they would beat the shit out of him.

I stood at the top of the stairs shaking in fear, just hoping they would get bored and leave, but they didn't. They just kept banging on the door and it was this that woke my two sisters, eleven and eight respectively. Then the unmistakable sound of breaking glass reverberated around the house and I shouted at my sisters to get back into bed and hide under their blankets. I nervously made my way down the creaking staircase and peeped my head round the corner just in time to see the two trespassers smashing their way through the second glass door. Fear now made way for self-preservation, and the reality that I had to protect my sisters from the monsters that had forced their way into my home.

At first there was a stand-off, one standing there armed with a hammer, the other with a small baseball bat, and they demanded to know the whereabouts of my cowardly brother, who at this point was hiding away upstairs. I told them that he wasn't here, and they should leave before someone called the police, which made them even more angry. They moved towards me and tried to force their way upstairs, but there was no way as long as I was breathing that this was going to happen. I would protect my sisters to the death, obviously something my brother had different views on, leaving me to handle two guys ten years my senior. The first strike I didn't even feel, the hammer just bounced off my arm, and fortunately my adrenalin masked the pain. We then got embroiled in a furious battle over the stairs and as hammer and baseball bat strikes rained down, I just keep pushing them back until we all ended up in a heap on the floor with both guys on top. With all my strength I kept a grip of the two bloody weapons.

Suddenly the shouts of police officers echoed down the long hallway and I was rescued from this dire situation. The two offenders tried to blag their way out of their impending doom, but they were quickly rumbled by my statement. They went on to spend the next couple of years locked away at her Majesty's pleasure, while I slowly moved on with my life and tried to forget this life-changing event and what might have happened if they had made their way upstairs.

Another time that left deep scars was when I was about fourteen. Richard had been involved in a car-stealing ring, where cars were stolen to order and then taken to lock-ups and broken down into parts for either quick cash or to go to cars that had been involved in heavy accidents and not been written off. He got himself involved through a third party with a couple of really unsavoury characters, who you really wouldn't want to get on the wrong side of, if you know what I mean; the sort of guys that would take you to Earls Wood lakes and threaten to shoot your kneecaps out.

But Richard, as ever, would stupidly try and rip them off and leave someone else to try and clean up his mess. One night I was upstairs finishing off some homework when the doorbell rang. Not thinking anything of it, I made my way downstairs and opened the door. I was greeted by the barrel of a loaded rifle pointed straight at my face. I was forced backwards down the hallway by this big scary mountain of a man, and with a deep rough voice he told me if I liked the use of my feet I should tell him where my brother was. Although I knew of his location, I felt it a must to keep this secret, even though I was absolutely shitting myself.

His next response was to point the rifle at my head and repeat the same question about Richard's whereabouts. I again responded that I didn't know where he had gone. I was then forced into the living room where he tried to change tack and went with the nicely, nicely approach, but I was in too deep now to change my story. I started to fear what this guy was capable of and with good reason as my two sisters were asleep upstairs, unaware. I started to try and formulate a plan in my head. Then suddenly he stood up and walked towards the door, saying he would find Richard and when he did, it wasn't going to be good for him. I was just about to close the door behind him when he turned around, angrily pushing me aside and forcing his way back in.

"Where's your house phone?" he yelled.

"Over there behind the chair," I nervously replied, and in a fit of rage he ripped it out of the wall and left. I took a big sigh of relief, but I wasn't sure how I was going to explain to Mom about the phone, because until this point she was completely unaware of Richard's stupidity. After a few hours of me playing dumb about the whereabouts of the phone, I finally came clean and spilled everything.

As you can expect, Mom was furious about this and gave Richard hell. My Mom worried for the safety of her children and spoke to someone she knew from her work at the local pub who knew these guys. She asked them to put a stop to the men scaring her family. Which they did!

I went to Hall Green Secondary School and started my first year in the top class, but as none of my friends from York Mead, my first school, were with me, I started to lose focus and ended up dropping down to be with them. I had known my friends since I'd started York Mead when I was five, and I still class them as best mates now. Firstly, there is Marc H., a fellow Villa fan. We would spend ages together as kids, staying at each other's houses, playing video games. And when not doing that, it was football that was our common friend. Over the years we seem to have fallen out with each more often probably than with anybody else, with both of us stepping over the line on more than one occasion; maybe I pushed the limits of friendship to the absolute limits, but more on that later. I will forever remember a time that will always crack me up. It was New Year's Eve and we had just been hanging round the streets drinking cheap cider. We knew a few girls who lived just around the corner, and we went over to see what they were doing. One thing led to another and we both ended up with a girl. Funnily enough, they turned out to be sisters. We spent half the night with the first sister we'd been introduced to, but then later we swapped and then both of us ended up seeing them for a while.

Mark M. lived just around the corner from me and we would end up spending a lot of our late teenage years and early twenties hanging round together, drinking, smoking and every now and again taking the odd drugs. We would spend hours at my house playing on the PlayStation and when the pair of us got on Pro Evolution Soccer, the games were epic; especially true on one of the versions where I would play as Nigeria and he would use Ukraine. No one could touch us, it was always us two in the final.

Lee is Marc's cousin and even though I have known Lee the same time, it probably wasn't until our mid-teens that we became best mates, and after leaving school we were inseparable, with him sometimes spending weeks at a time at my house, while we tried to complete epic games such as Gran Turismo. He was definitely my biggest smoking buddy and I'll always remember the good old squidgy black that he could get from one of mates, the stuff was wicked. I will always remember hiding his drugs from him when we were stoned, and I would have him search all over in a desperate state, trying to locate them. Out of all my mates from the old days, we have never come to blows, even though I probably deserved it one drunken night. Ah, Lee, what you reckon?

I have known Mat T. since we moved to Reddings Lane at the age of five, and his family lived next door. Again, we spent most of our time together playing on the computer or over on the green playing cricket or football. One time will always stay with me and that was when he worked at a video rental shop called Titles, and he'd come over to my house one night after work. He'd had a massive argument with his manager and quit there and then.

To get revenge for this I came up with a sick but funny plan of posting what looked like a normal video through the night box. But it was, in fact, a box full of human shit. Mat, of course, agreed to this plan. I went to the bathroom and took the biggest, stinkiest shit I have ever delivered into this world into a plastic bag. I then spread it across two pieces of bread and made a kind of sandwich out of it. The smell was utterly revolting, to the point where the pair of us were heaving at the slightest whiff. After regaining our composure and luckily keeping the contents of our stomachs inside, we headed over the road to put our dastardly plan into action. As I neared the night box, I thought it would be even funnier to open the lid as I dropped it in.

The following morning, we walked over to see the outcome of our disgusting prank. To our delight, the place smelt out of this world. No words could describe the vile smell that now infested every inch of the place. We spoke to one of the guys there who had opened up, and he told us that the manager had been physically sick when he had to clean the contents of the night box out.

I enjoyed school in some ways but that was maybe due to the fact that I was around my friends. In truth, though, and especially in my later years, school just bored me and I knew I would leave as soon as I got the chance. When it was time to do my work experience, the school offered us a look at a life-course with the Army and after talking it through with Dave, Marc and a few others, it sounded like a great laugh, so we signed up. We spent a week at a base on the outskirts of Nuneaton, learning basic field craft, team building and how far our bodies could go before breaking down and collapsing into a shaking and sweaty mess. Despite this last element, I enjoyed myself immensely and thought I would join the Army as soon as I was old enough, and I pretty much gave up on schoolwork at that point.

Losing any family member is difficult, but when Poppa died it hit the family hard. It was like knocking a giant pillar out from the footing of a building and knowing it wouldn't take long for the building to come crashing down around it, and that was like what happened with us. With Dad now moved out of the family home and only seeing him every couple of weeks, Pop was like another father figure. We were always close, but after Dad had left we became even closer. Pop was such a great bloke, a proper family man. If you ever wanted to look up to someone and see them as an example to you, he was the man, and even though I can only remember him as an older gentleman, you wouldn't want to have got on the wrong side of him.

I remember a time when Richard had got into some form of trouble at school and Pop had come round to the house to speak to him. After barricading himself in the bedroom, Richard finally jumped out of the window when the door came flying in from the force of a size ten. Pop would spend hours with the pair of us, taking us to car museums and he would tell us stories of how he had helped design cars that we were looking at. It made me so proud to call him my Poppa.

After taking early retirement to spend more time with his family, fate dealt the family an evil hand. Mom and Dad sat us all down and broke the devastating news that Poppa had developed incurable cancer and had been given about six months to live. As you might imagine, everyone was utterly heartbroken and I remember just crying for hours. I really struggled to come to terms with the news until Pop rang me himself. He tried to get me to understand that it was just how life works out sometimes, and that he would fight to the end. He then said that maybe life would bless him with some more time to spend with his family.

Listening to him then, I finally understood what was really happening. Pop fought to the very end and surpassed the six months he was given by nearly a year, but eventually the cancer, as it normally does, spread to other vital organs and he deteriorated so quickly in his last couple of weeks that it became hard to even look at him. If you have ever witnessed someone succumb to cancer, you will know what I'm talking about. One day he was walking around the garden, the next he was lying dying in his bed, drugged up on morphine so he could die without being in agonising pain.

I will remember the last few days of his life forever. Richard and I had now pretty much moved in, just waiting for that day to come. Frank Sinatra, Poppa's favourite singer, was on the stereo and we just took it in turns to watch over him. Now I know people are going to think I'm crazy with my next sentence but here we go anyway. I had been watching over him one day and was just looking out of the window, talking to Dad, who was on the drive.

I felt something brush by me but thought nothing of it. I suddenly felt as if somebody was watching me and the temperature in the room changed instantly, plummeting. It dropped what felt like ten degrees and what was stranger was that it was July and baking hot. I felt shivers shooting up and down my back, and the hairs on my neck stood on end. It felt as if a strange presence had entered the room and I was absolutely shitting myself. I finally found courage from deep within to turn round, but I did it slowly.

As I spun one and hundred and eighty degrees, my eyes were aimed at the bottom half of the door on the other side of the room. My eyes started tracking a transparent figure that was standing there just looking in my direction. I gradually started to raise my arc of vision until I reached the face. To my shock, I recognised the ghostly shape as my late great grandmother, Poppa's Mom.

I have no idea how long it was, but we just stared at each other until the only thing I could think to do was say, "Hello." She gave no reaction but just started to evaporate into her surroundings and before I knew it, I was just staring at a blank wall. I couldn't really comprehend what had just materialised in front of me, and still to this day I get the same feeling I did then when recalling the event. After she had disappeared, I looked towards Pop and to my surprise, he was looking at me. This was the first time I had seen him awake for a while and I like to think that maybe he had seen her too. That made him more at ease with what was waiting for him.

A couple of days later he passed away, to the relief of us all. Even though we were obviously all saddened by his death, we knew he was no longer in any pain and I felt as if he was finally reunited with his Mom. After the doctor had been and my dad had washed him and given him a shave, we were allowed one at a time to go and sit with him and say our final goodbyes. I told him that I was going to miss him so much and I was happy to have had him as a Pop. Then I promised him that I would look after his toy car collection for him; a promise that I failed to keep, as my Dad and brother went behind everyone's back and sold them. Something, among other things, I will never forgive them for.

The funeral took place a week later and the place was filled to the rafters, a true sign of how many people he had touched over the years. I will remember how tightly my Grandma held my hand while the coffin was placed in the ground, a really moving event in my life. I don't think I ever really got over losing Pop, and the family seemed to just implode after his passing. It wasn't till I started typing this event that I really thought about how everything changed after that, and my emotions were taken back twenty years.

During this time, I had to really fight back the tears when reminiscing about these sad times. I also started to feel really guilty because it had been so long since I had thought of him and if it wasn't for this book I'm not sure when I would have. Sorry, Pop, still miss you like crazy and wish you could have been here for my wedding and the birth of Isabella. But who knows, maybe you were there in some form.

Chapter three – Toughening up

After leaving school and learning that I had utterly screwed up my GCSEs and maybe my life, I just started bumming around smoking weed every chance I got. I ended up signing on the dole, just so I had some weed money and a bunch of us would hang around Mark M.'s house smoking and playing video games into the early hours. Apart from having no real future prospects, and apart from getting stoned, these were amazing times. The laughs we had watching Lee hiccupping would amuse us all night, even though it must have pissed him off severely. We just stared at him, waiting for the next hiccup and then bursting into tears of laughter. Or when Dave and Lee and I would end up at my house and I would steal a bottle of my Mom's Hock from her wine stash after we'd drunk all our own. We would then end up singing all the golden oldies tunes until we passed out, or until Mom shouted at me to shut up. This went on for a couple of years and even though we had some great times, waiting around for our Giro to finally drop through the letter box was demoralising.

Life then started becoming more difficult. By now my brother's drug preference had changed and he was no longer just smoking weed. He'd started using class A drugs, such as heroin and crack cocaine. He was stealing more than ever to try and fund his uncontrollable habit and now every possession in the house that my Mom had struggled to buy had started to disappear. For me the weed was all I needed but as life started to throw curve balls, I started to experiment with other narcotics and with it all around me it wasn't too difficult to get hold of. I was never a fan of the heroin and from what I could see it doing to Richard, I decided I'd best stay clear of it.

But I did start to get a taste for the crack and would do it whenever I could. Richard would sometimes bring golf ball size pieces of crack home with him after doing a big car theft job and we would spend the whole night flying. I would forget how things were in reality and for that moment I felt free. But after finally running out of this devil's drug, the inevitable comedown would bring me crashing back to reality. I would then find myself searching around the floor, looking for bits of crack which turned out to be small stones or other foreign objects. After we'd run out of the reality-changing drug, Richard would then turn to his favourite and cheaper alternative drug, his good old friend heroin.

Like I said before, I would just try and put myself to sleep by hitting my favourite green herb. This continued for about six months until Richard was caught stealing cars by the police and ended up spending six months in prison. As he was my only source for the evil drugs, I was able to stop using them and I returned to my old ways.

The weed at the beginning made me feel happy and hid the mess I had made of my life. The problem was that the more I smoked, the more I needed it just to function and I started to become more and more depressed. I'd got to the point where sometimes I would contemplate ending it all. I felt lost and lonely without my favourite herb, but I knew if I wanted anything out of life I needed to turn my back on this future-sapping drug. I eventually summoned enough willpower and decided to quit both cigarettes and weed. It was a difficult struggle, but I battled through to safety and away from the marijuana.

I nearly forgot to put this story in, and it wasn't until I'd nearly completed this book that I remembered it. It's nothing amazing or anything like that, just something that I will always remember with a smile. One night, Marc had invited us around to his house for a bit of a party while his Mom and Dad had gone away on holiday. Mark M., who had borrowed his Dad's car, picked Dave and me up and drove us there. After an all-night drinking and drugs session, Mark drove us home and saying he was slightly intoxicated would be an understatement. Mark could always convince his Dad to lend him his car, even though he had no licence and no insurance, and this would be the night that the law would finally catch up with him. Or at least that's how it would look at first. We turned off the Coventry Road and headed towards Yardley Cemetery, when from behind us, blue flashing lights signalled for Mark to pull over. Mark's erratic driving had now got him into serious trouble, and as we all had a shedload of weed on us and I was carrying my Walther PPK look-alike air pistol on me, I had started to think this would be more than just a drink-drive incident. After Mark nearly hit a lamp post, mounting the kerb while trying to pull in, the passenger-side police officer got out of the car and headed for the driver's door. As he walked by, he gave me a quick up and down look before reaching out and opening the driver's door.

"Pass me the keys and come with me, please," the officer said in a thick Birmingham accent. Now as Mark had been drinking all night, he reeked of booze and pretty much fell from the Ford Escort and straight into the now annoyed officer's arms. He was quickly taken away and placed in the waiting police car. Dave and I sat there expecting the worst and at the very least, we thought we would be walking the rest of the journey home.

The pair of us were just sharing a conversation about how screwed Mark was and how we hoped that they didn't want to search us, when suddenly my door was pulled open and there stood an angry looking officer who started to demand information about Mark.

"So who's your friend?" As we had no idea what Mark had said to him we played dumb and told him to just ask him himself. He didn't take too kindly to our approach and started to threaten us with all sorts of bullshit charges from perverting the course of justice to lying to a police officer. Even though we both knew we would be done for if we were taken in on any charge, due to the clandestine objects we currently had in our possession, we were never going to grass on Mark, so we stuck to our guns and played hardball. Luckily, that night this officer was not in the mood to try and pin continued to interrogate Mark. After twenty minutes or so the driver's door opened and I started thinking, *Here we go, it's time for us to get walking.* But to our complete surprise and to our relief, Mark sat down and shut the door behind him.

"What the fuck are you doing? I thought you'd been nicked, mate," I said. Unbelievably, the dim-witted, or just 'couldn't be bothered to do the paper work' officers had let Mark go with just a producer, and they'd told him he would have to turn himself into a police station with all his relevant paperwork at a later date. Still, given that he could barely walk, never mind talk, we were in utter shock that he had been given the keys back and told to be on his way.

Mark turned the key and gently applied the accelerator, but with the police shadowing his every move he became nervous and at the next island he thought he was driving in Europe and went the wrong way around it right in front of the watching officers. Again, for some strange reason known only to them, they just drove off and left Mark to it. Even stranger, Mark never heard back from the police. It was as if the event had never taken place at all. I just think they were on their way back to the station after finishing their shift, and they just couldn't be arsed to fill in the paperwork, and they decided to let him off.

Dad, Richard and I have always had a strained relationship, always falling out with one another, and as we grew up the arguments would always turn violent. On one occasion Dad had turned up drunk at our house and started to act like a prick, swearing and being disgusting to my Mom. I was upstairs playing the computer when Richard came up and informed me that Dad was getting worse and that Mom wanted him gone. The only problem was that we both knew the only way he was leaving was either the police carrying him out, or on a stretcher under a paramedic's guide. Suddenly there were screams from downstairs and Mom shouted for us. With screams still echoing around the house, we reacted quickly and raced down the stairs and into the living room where Dad had started to attack Mom. This had now woken my two sisters, but as this had happened too many times before, they knew the drill. We always told them to hide upstairs and if possible, to try and contact the police.

The next fifteen minutes or so became an all-out battle to remove Dad from the house. Dad at this point had turned into a monster. He was like a wild animal. He was snarling and growling and like a dog with rabies, he had foam pouring from the corner of his mouth and dripping from his nicotine-stained teeth. To most, this would have been unnerving, but unfortunately, we had seen this before from previous incidents when he was drunk. The fight made its way to the hallway where Richard and I did all we could to fend off this demented creature. We wrestled him to the ground and I took hold of his arms behind his back and sort of held them there in a full-nelson lock. Richard, on the other hand, had now started to attack Dad with punches, kicks and knees, trying anything to beat him into unconsciousness. After probably about a minute I let go of Dad's arms, expecting him to collapse in a heap, but on the contrary, he stood up shouting and growling. He turned on me and took a step. I was in shock that he had taken such a beating, and he was still looking for revenge.

Then from nowhere a size six Duncan Fearnley cricket bat came crashing down on top of Dad's head. He turned around and stared in Richard's direction. Richard raised the bat again, but only for Dad to spin around quickly and set his sights on me once again. Now I was thinking that we had unearthed a real monster and what the hell were we going to have to do to him to get him out of the house. Suddenly he charged at me. Instinctively I turned and ran towards the front door.

As I made my way through the first of the doors and was about to open the second, there was a bang and he slammed the door behind me so hard it broke the glass in both doors all around me. Thinking he had locked me out of this raging battle, he turned his attention back to Richard. Like I said, when he slammed the door he had broken the glass, so I knocked any sharp pieces away and made my way back in and down the hallway. A cold breeze hit me in the face and I could see that the back door was now open, so I headed that way.

Not knowing what might greet me, I stayed cautious but my adrenalin drove me on. I needed to make sure Richard was okay. I reluctantly headed through the door and out into a little passageway that separated the house from the garden, where I found Richard standing over Dad, with a shovel in his shaking hands. Luckily for us he was just out cold and not dead, but we knew soon enough that he would come to, and then we could be back to square one. At this point I heard voices coming from the front door and it was two female police officers. I explained what was going on and hoped they didn't take my next comment the wrong way. I told them there was no way they could remove him.

Dad hates authority and especially women with it. They took my advice and radioed for some back-up. Luckily there was a riot team in the area, which turned up within a couple of minutes and headed down the hallway to remove our unwanted guest. Like I thought, he didn't go quietly. It took six burly police officers carrying him kicking and punching to the awaiting van, and he even managed to smash one of Mom's car windows in the process.

As we were growing up, Richard and I would always be fighting with each other, and one time I will always remember was when, for a treat, Poppa and Grandma had taken us away on holiday to Mottram Hall, a beautiful old country hotel where we could spend most of the day either in the swimming pool and the jacuzzi or down at the picturesque lake, fishing. One morning we were down at reception and as usual we started bickering with each other over something stupid, when one thing led to another and we started brawling. We ended up rolling around the floor and throwing each other over the back of the winged-back chairs and two hundred-year-old chesterfields. It got to the point where the hotel staff couldn't separate us and rang up to our room to get assistance. Poppa came down and gave us what for and dragged the pair of us back to the room and made us pack our bags. He then told us that the holiday was over and we would be going home that day.

These kinds of events happened weekly, but as Richard grew older and taller I would struggle to really defend myself against him. It wouldn't be till the night of France vs Paraguay in the 1998 world cup that I would finally be able to get the better of him in a fair fight. Before this night he pretty much had full control of the house and even though my Mom would give it her all, Richard would wait until she had her back turned and then he would attack. As I just couldn't beat him, I had to just stand there and watch.

I will never forget one time when Mom treated us all to a McDonalds, which we never really had. It turned out that the idiot at the drive-through had put the wrong burger in and it turned out that Richard's meal was missing. He went absolutely crazy at Mom as if she had done it on purpose, and he slapped her around the face, then threw the meal at her. I did try to defend her but was quickly knocked down by this bully boy. Back to the world cup night. It had started as a really good night. Richard, Faye, his girlfriend at the time and I were enjoying the football with a few reefers, while my Mom was at work. Mom would always demand that we should smoke outside or at the very least by the window, so my younger sisters wouldn't have to breathe in the toxic fumes.

That night Richard was just walking around upstairs with a spliff in hand, and he even smoked some while he was in my Mom's room. When she came home she understandably flipped her lid and gave the pair of us a good tongue lashing. I knew we had done wrong, so I took my bollocking gracefully. Richard, on the other hand, didn't take to being shouted at by his Mom in front of his girlfriend, so he confronted her. The pair argued until he slapped her around her face and then he tried to grab Mom by the throat.

For the first time in years I lost my temper, but instead of rushing straight over, I calmly placed my glasses on the side, and then I charged him. We ended up out in the hallway where I proceeded to grab him by the neck and drag him down the landing. As we reached the doorway to my sister's bedroom, I chucked him through the door, Richard crashing in a crumpled heap on the other side. Before the sneaky snake got the chance to retaliate, I jumped on him and pinned him to the ground.

"I have spent too many years watching you doing that. If you ever touch Mom again, I will kill you. Do you understand me?" I yelled. He didn't say a word. He just lay there with a confused look written across his face, trying his best to come to terms with what had just taken place. Maybe sensing the end of an era. I got to my feet and went back to my room, where I wanted to check on the state of Mom. Suddenly I had a feeling someone was behind me, like that sense you get when someone's watching you, but more threatening.

As I reached the doorway to my room I quickly jumped in, just in time to watch Richard flying by, trying one of his cowardly attacks. I took this opportunity to put him firmly in his place. So I grabbed hold of him and slammed him against the brick wall three or four times, leaving him battered and bruised on the floor. For the next couple of weeks he barely said two words to me. I think his ego took more of a beating than his body. After this you could definitely sense a change in the tide and he knew if he touched Mom again I would finish him off.

Even though he knew what would happen if he even shouted at Mom, never mind put his hands on her, we would still occasionally clash. One night after excessive drinking, we did just that, and this time things could easily have turned out a lot worse. The funny thing is that night I was more angry with Dad. I even tried to side with Richard, but because he was pissed and high on drugs, the knobhead turned on me.

Everyone had been drinking most of the night, when Dad and Richard started arguing about something stupid. Then, like an idiot, Dad picked up a piece of wood and smacked it over Richard's head. Richard at first, to his credit, didn't want to make a scene in front of Faye and her mate. So after regaining his bearings, he went up to the phone box to get some fresh air and rang the police to have Dad removed. Before there was any more bloodshed, I followed him up and tried to calm him down, but as we reached the house he started kicking the front door to get in. After a few kicks he eventually knocked one of the windows out. I spun Richard around to have it out with him, when from nowhere, he pulled a ten-inch kitchen knife from his trousers and started to threaten me with it. I took a couple of steps backwards, trying to come up with a plan to defuse the situation.

Then he turned around to try and go in the house. It was at this point that I took a chance and rushed him. The pair of us were now embraced in a life-threatening lock, shouting at one another to let go. After ten seconds or so we eventually crashed through the next-door neighbour's fence and smacked onto the concrete paving, where the knife flew from his hand. I pressed my shin against his throat until he stopped moving. Suddenly I heard shouting for me to stop and looked around to see one of my neighbours, who was a policeman, ordering me off him. Richard must have banged his head when he went through the fence as there was blood everywhere, and with the knife just lying there, God knows what the copper must have thought. Luckily, Richard took this moment when I was distracted and had it away on his toes.

Chapter four – New direction

September 11th, 2001 changed the world forever and also changed my life in a strange way. If the events of that day had never taken place, I probably would never had seen the war zones that I ended up visiting. I was working in a dead-end job at a place called b-wise, loading and unloading lorries. The money was okay and I didn't have many bills, just the twenty-five quid a week I gave my Mom for rent. I had a comfortable life, which I had never experienced before. I was able to go out and buy stuff that I wanted, like new TVs and PlayStations. Even though things were going well I always knew I wanted something better in life, to make a difference, maybe.

On that particular day it was the same mundane loading and unloading, when the managers came running out of the office and turned the radio on to the news. The whole warehouse listened in shock as the newsreader spoke of an utterly despicable act of terror that had been carried out on innocent people in America. I couldn't believe what I was hearing and wanted to get home as soon as possible to witness this with my own eyes. The day dragged until five and I raced home to see the events for myself.

My family were completely oblivious to the day's atrocities and they just thought there had been a small plane crash in New York. I switched the TV on and we all watched on in horror as the BBC's news reporters talked through the day's horrendous events. Something moved me that day. That left a considerable scar that I don't think ever truly healed, and it was probably the catalyst for me to take joining the Army seriously.

My best friend Dave had always shared the same dreams of joining the Army as me and when I informed him of my plans he jumped at the idea. Dave had come from the same sort of family upbringing as me. His Dad had left when he was young, leaving his Mom to raise four kids by herself without any money. Luckily for her kids, she flourished in trying circumstances and they made do with whatever they had. So it was true to say we were more like brothers than mates and understood each other completely. Even though we've had a few fisticuffs with each other over the years, we still remain great friends and we probably know each other better than anyone else.

We used to run every morning in the worst weather that nature could throw at us, or when nursing a vile hang over. On the runs I would share stories with him about women I had hooked up with on the previous night. I remember one tale stopping him dead in his tracks and his replying in disgust, "You dirty bastard." We would almost always have to stop for being bent doubled over in laughter.

Our training continued for about six months till we both plucked up the courage to go to the recruitment centre at the old Palisades in Birmingham. We both wanted to join the Parachute Regiment, not really looking at any other options, but just because we heard that they were the best. It always seemed that any time there was a conflict around the world and the Brits were involved, the Paras always seemed to be in the thick of the action, really mixing it up. They were always our first choice.

We took our BARB tests (tests that determined what regiments you were suitable for) and were told we had good scores. The Sergeant then told us we could find a role in a skilled unit and learn a trade. This in turn could have really set us up for future jobs outside the military, but we both declined because we wanted to be frontline soldiers. I had heard someone from the Army say once, "If you're not infantry you're not really in the Army." A stupid saying really, knowing what I know now, but back then we thought it was really macho. Infantry is just a little cog in a massive machine and without the rest it would just be useless. Our lives continued, balancing training and work while we waited for our selection dates. Then one day Dave rang to tell me that his Nan had passed away and that his head wasn't in the right place to continue with our Army dream. I told him that I understood completely and if he ever needed someone to talk to about it, that I would always be there for him. I then explained that I would be continuing without him, I had to. All my focus was now going into this and I didn't want to fail, because a lot of people were doubting me, and saying that I didn't have it in me. I will always remember my manager at the time saying that I could always have my old job back when things didn't work out.

I passed selection with grit and determination, but I changed my mind about the future regiment I would be joining. My choice was the Royal Regiment of Fusiliers after talking to some lads at the selection process. They told me about the incredible history of frontline operations spanning three centuries. I was chuffed to bits about passing and couldn't get the smile off my face the whole train journey home.

About two months before I started training I had arrived home from a hard day's work, completely unprepared for what was about to take place. I opened the front doors, and I was instantly greeted by a scared and worried looking Mom. I feared the worst and asked what was wrong.

"It's your father. He's been here all day, drinking. He's also been acting disgusting, trying to take his clothes off and talking in a sexual manner to me and the next-door neighbour," she explained. Mom had also asked him to leave, which he had flatly refused to do, saying that it was still his house, even though he hadn't paid a penny either for that or for the four of us. I knew this wasn't going to end well and from previous experience I envisaged a hard-fought battle to remove him. This time I would have to do this on my own, because Richard was currently detained. Dad was asleep on the sofa in the back living room, passed out from all the cheap cider he'd been drinking. I took a deep breath and gave him a shove.

"Dad, wake up. You need to go."

"Oh hello, JJJJonathon, hhhows things? IIIIIIm so ppproud of yyyou jjjoining the AAArmy," he drunkenly replied. I changed my approach.

"Get your shit and get the fuck out of here." Dad erupted from the sofa.

"Don't you ever to speak to me like that. I'm your Dad."

"Well, you've got a funny way of showing it. Mom wants you out, so get the fuck out," I demanded. The snarling mouth-foaming monster returned and staggered towards me.

"You're not too big to get taken down a peg or two. So let's go outside and settle this like men." I thought, *Perfect this is what I wanted from the start,* and I headed towards the front door.

"Stop, where are you going?" Dad asked angrily.

"Outside," I said and pointed towards the front door. "This way."

Dad mumbled as he pointed towards the French doors to the back garden.

Okay, this is not what I had in mind, but what the hell, we're in it now. Can't back out of this. So I went to follow him out when Mom came into the room and reminded me about the Army and how I needed to stay out of trouble. She then said that she had rung the police and she would try to stall him. I went upstairs and waited for the inevitable shouts, but it was my sisters who shouted for me to come. I looked around for a weapon. I searched for something that would sort out this situation once and for all. I grabbed the heavy end of my prized snooker cue and flew down the stairs like a man possessed, ready to cave Dad's skull in. To my shock, I was instead greeted by a police officer with a baton stick shouting in my direction to put the cue down, which I did. Dad was dragged from the house and bundled into the back of a police car and the ordeal was finally over. After the police had left, Mom told me that after I had gone upstairs he had attacked her. Liz, to her credit, had jumped on him and started punching him just before the police had arrived.

I have to say, though, that things with my Dad weren't always bad. When he wasn't drunk he was great to be around and we could spend hours talking about all sorts of crazy shit. With the help of a bit of green tobacco, the conversations would usually end up with a bit of a paranormal debate. Dad and I would always speak about this subject and even now when we see each other, it's usually our go-to topic.

One night he had come round for a bit of a smoking session, but before we rolled out our two sheeters, we wanted to grab some supplies from the nearby shop. Lee was also round at the time and we were waiting for him to finish in the bathroom before we left. I was standing by the door frame of my room, looking in and talking to my Dad, when suddenly he shouted, "What the fuck is that?" pointing towards where I was standing. I quickly spun around only to see what looked like a grey hunched-over figure scurrying down the long dark landing. When I say the next sentence I'm not exaggerating. I more or less leapt from my skin and ended up half way across the room in one bound. The feelings I had after seeing whatever the hell it was, have been imprinted in my mind ever since, and I will always get the same hairs standing on end when recalling it.

After we had sort of come to terms with what we had just witnessed, Dad said,

"Go and have a look and see if it's still there," to which I replied, "You're fucking crazy. I ain't going out there until I've got my head right and maybe after a change of underwear." We both approached the door with caution, and with a nervous outstretched right hand I switched the landing light on. With a flick of the switch, the light turned on for a second. Then, pop, the bulb exploded sending us retreating into the room. So I shouted for Lee to confirm where he was and that he wasn't messing about with us. He replied that he was in the bathroom and that he had no idea what we were talking about.

After Lee returned from his toilet break, the three of us reluctantly scaled the dark, creepy stairs down to the hallway and rushed out into the dark night sky. We took our time returning to the house, spending ten minutes sitting outside in the rain enjoying a few puffs of some herbal remedy. Maybe it was our eyes playing tricks on us. Who knows, but the fact we both saw the same thing at the same time begs the question about what we really saw that night.

I shared some great times with Dad. It's just a shame really, that he was also a complete knob sometimes, which has really cost us a good relationship. I remember when I was young and we would always go way down to Dorset to spend time at my aunt's house. One year, Dad said he would ride his Harley down with Richard on the back and the rest of us would go in the car. One thing about the Harley was that it had no rear suspension and Richard could only last to the first service station on the M42. Anyway, after arriving in Dorset, Dad wanted to head out on the bike to take in the beautiful surroundings and asked if either Richard or I would like to jump on the back.

With Richard still nursing a sore back end I jumped at the chance to spend some time with Dad. Like I said before, as a child I looked up to him so much and tried to spend as much time as possible with him. I climbed onto the back and held on tight, almost hugging the life out of him. With a quick twist of the throttle we were free, racing down the winding country lanes without a care in the world. To be honest, I was scared just to be on the back of this flame-spitting monster, but being alongside my Dad took a bit of the edge off it. Ten minutes passed and eventually I was able to open my eyes and started enjoying the breathtaking ride.

My fear had now turned into joy and I started to feel as if I was free from this world. Like a bird flying through the sky, with nothing holding him back. Dad started to apply the brakes and we pulled over at the side of the road to take in the scenery. I then noticed a giant naked man that was carved into a nearby hill. Dad told me it was called the Cerne Abbas Giant and he went on to explain about why it was there and stuff like that. It's funny what you remember as a kid. It only feels like yesterday that we were blasting down those country lanes, me gripping on to my Dad's muscular chest like my life depended on it.

Things between Richard and me haven't always been bad either. We've spent many times over the years getting on with each other and from time to time really enjoying each other's company. The hours we spent together playing computer games; me trying to beat him at Street Fighter, when he always seemed unbeatable with the character Ken. I will always remember a crazy night that I spent with him, and to be honest it's probably a story I shouldn't really share, but oh well, here goes. At the time he was living in a flat with one of his mates and had invited me over to spend the night. The plan was to go down to some of the local pubs and play a bit of pool and just get on it. On that particular night I was just hanging around with Mat and when Richard invited me over I asked Mat to join me, which he did. After arriving at the flat we helped ourselves to a few cans and started drinking a bottle of rum that Richard's flatmate had just brought back with him from the Caribbean. The stuff was proper rocket fuel, a couple of sips and I was feeling tipsy. We headed to a nearby pub and after the door staff gave us a quick look up and down, they allowed us entry. Bearing in mind I was only sixteen, I was well chuffed to be allowed in. The place was tiny, probably only six feet from the bar to the wall and it was absolutely crammed. To the point where it took about ten minutes to just dodge and weave your way to the toilet, without spilling some angry-looking thug's pint of Carling over his favourite going-out shirt.

After a few unsuccessful attempts to get to the front of the queue at the bar, we made our way upstairs. Here there was another bar, but much to our disappointment it was closed. We went in nonetheless and started to set up a game of pool. Then Richard's mate noticed that the serving hatch on the other side of the bar wasn't locked and he could reach in. So he did, and grabbed the only thing he could, which turned out to be a bottle of Malibu. Even though the stuff is rank, we guzzled it down regardless, just to top up the buzz that I'd started losing since I'd arrived at the bar. After finishing the bottle, my brother and his mate tried different ways of breaking into the bar to get to some of the good stuff. Finally, Richard's mate tried to pull the steel grating down which was protecting the bar from this bunch of thieves. The next thing I heard was his mate shouting for Richard to help him. The weight of the grate had taken him by complete surprise, almost dropping clean on his foot. After gaining access to the bar we took it in turns to help ourselves to whatever drinks we wanted. Suddenly the staircase that was just outside the room started to creak, as if someone was trying to sneak up on us. We quickly tried to return the bar to how it once was. The door to the room swung open and two upset looking bar owners rushed in trying to catch us in the act. Luckily as we had heard them coming, we just sat there looking as if nothing had happened, but only paying attention to the game of pool we were involved in. After being told that we were not supposed to be in there and with us claiming innocence, we were led down the stairs and back into the main bar. We then found a table to congregate around and Richard went and ordered a round. He returned with a tray of drinks, and we started to enjoy the pulsating beat of the music.

The place was really jumping now, and with zero space between everyone, it was only a matter of time before someone got upset by some drunken idiot banging into them. After the third occasion of someone banging into him it was Richard's mate that snapped first. He angrily turned around, then grabbed the nearby offender by his denim jacket and pushed him into a nasty looking bunch of women. This was all the fuel the fire needed and with this, the whole place erupted like a pissed-off volcano. Chairs and tables were sent flying in all directions and we had to start to take cover as one smashed into the lights that were just above our heads. Now the boyfriends whose girlfriends had just had their drinks knocked over them from an angry push, sought retribution. As the revenge-seeking mob headed my way I smashed two bottles of hooch to use as a makeshift weapon, and I started swinging them in the direction of the nearest guy. He was an absolute mountain of a man, but luckily for me, the very thought of a jagged bottle heading in his direction soon put him out of the fight. His mates soon decided it wasn't worth it either and returned to their girlfriends.

Now everyone was fighting, and the place was completely out of control, which led to the door-staff pinpointing us as the troublemakers. Suddenly someone's bear-like grasp gripped hold of me and dragged me over a couple of tables and out into the hallway. I was then manhandled to my feet and chucked through the doors straight onto the cold wet stone floor. I stumbled back to my feet and tried to mount a final attack on the door staff for touching me. This in turn was met with stiff resistance and after a quick scuffle and a few badly aimed punches, I found myself recovering on the pavement, lying in a huge puddle. As I regained my feet, I headed back towards the double wooden doors and tried to force my way back in to continue the battle, but with no success, and finally having to give up and take a seat on a nearby kerb.

After a couple of minutes Matt came flying out in the same superman flight path as the one I had taken earlier, and he was fated to land in the same bloody puddle as me. As Matt started to get to his feet the same double doors swung open and out came Richard and his mate. Unlike us, they left with more elegance and grace. Up on their own two feet with only the hand of the door-staff placed firmly on their backs, cautiously guiding them from the war zone and out into the wet night sky. After drunkenly staggering back to the flat I thought the excitement of the evening had finished and was ready to turn in for the night. Richard though, had other plans. In his drunken state he suggested that to make the rest of the night fun he would go and set fire to someone's shitty old car. I think at first this was only said in jest, but egged on by us all, he headed down to the car park and carried out his early threat. With the three of us watching safely from the seventh-floor balcony, he scurried between the rows of parked cars before finally stopping next to his red metal victim. He broke into the passenger side's back door and cut a massive rip in the back of the seat. He stuffed a load of newspaper in there and lit it. Returning to the flat, we looked on as the flames slowly starting to grow with intensity, finally taking full control of the inside of the car. The flames were now licking the inside of the windows. Then, pop, finally bursting their way out in search of fresh oxygen, until the car was completely engulfed in menacing red-hot flames. It had now got to a point where even the nearby cars started to come under attack from this air-thirsty merciless monster. Bang! The sound of the petrol tank exploding made us shit ourselves and we ducked down behind the wall, trying to avoid any flying objects.

The inferno raged out of control for a further ten minutes, before the flashing lights and ear-bursting noise of the inbound fire engine got our full attention. After the fire was finally tackled and extinguished, the crew left the area and returned to base. But Richard now had other ideas. He pressured his friend into going to do a car himself and after about ten minutes of been egged on, he finally crumbled and disappeared into the darkness to conduct another dastardly mission. This time the petrol tank must have been nearly full. The explosion rocked two cars parked next to it and now the uncontrollable fire started to engulf those two. The fire raged on until the same fire crew returned and doused our laughter with foam. After the fire engine left, Richard left it thirty minutes before returning to the car park, and with no cars now safe, picked out a brand new BMW as his final target of this memorable evening. When the fire engine returned for the final time it was this time accompanied by two police cars. After the flames were put out, the police officers started searching the nearby area for the arsonist. We watched on through gaps in the curtains, trying our best to keep the sound of us chuckling like a pack of hyenas out of earshot.

This is an incident I wish had never taken place, but when we were young and drunk, we found it extremely funny. But as I have had this happen to *me* since, I now know the feelings our actions would have caused. Maybe that was my payback for my role in the childish and dangerous prank.

Richard as a teen was always a kind of idol to me and I would watch on in awe as he built himself a name in the local community. All the local troublemakers knew him and didn't say shit to me, but better than that, all the local girls thought he was God's gift and as I was his younger brother I got a bit of attention myself. Anyway, he would sometimes turn up at my school in a brand new BMW or Mercedes Benz that he had recently stolen, and he would give me a lift home. He'd show off his rally driving skills that he had honed over the past five or so years in police chases. I remember a time that lives with me until this day. It was once when he stole Mom's Renault Savannah (sorry, Mom) and even though it was like a boat on wheels, it was a proper beast. We were just driving around the local area, chilling in the beautiful sunshine with the sound of Tupac Shakur pumping from the door speakers.

Not far from where we lived there is a place called Sarehole Mill, which has many wooded areas, with the River Cole running through them. Between two of these areas there is a road that cuts between them, leading to a ford. This road is like a rally stage. Twisting asphalt leads you down a slight hill. Trees line the sides of the roads and with one error you would definitely be heading to the scene of an accident. As soon as Richard took a right turn off Wake Green Road, I knew what he had in mind, so I made sure my seatbelt was tightly fastened. He straightened up the blue beast and floored it, the nose of the car lifting like a plane during take-off. We raced down the tight road, whistling past parked cars, the sun blinding us every now and then as it broke through the branches of the three-hundred-year-old oak trees.

Before you reach the ford there is a tight, right-left-right chicane and Richard barrelled down the hill towards it. As we approached the sequence of corners, the Savannah flatly refused to do what he had asked of it. In a loud burst of tyre screech and understeer, we mounted the kerb and headed straight up the driveway of some elderly couple, knocking plantpots and gnomes over in the process. After getting his bearings, he slammed it in reverse. Then in a cloud of smoke and more wheel spin, we flew back off the angry old-age pensioners drive, and back out onto the road, narrowly missing knocking over the grey-haired postman, before heading towards the ford at light speed. We blasted through the shallow river, absolutely soaking three female pedestrians with pushchairs who were walking across the bridge. We looked back in the rear view, laughing our heads off, and then we returned Mom's car before she realised it was missing. But it was a hot day, so she had probably not even moved from her sun lounger.

Chapter five – A new life

New Year's Eve 2002, and we had been invited to a party at Claire's house. Claire was a woman I had been seeing on and off for the past few months. The parties she used to have at her house were epic, lasting all night and finally finishing at six in the morning when all the alcohol had been polished off.

This was going to be a joint celebration: the actual New Year party and my going away party, something I knew would be difficult for Mom, and which it turned out to be. She told me that she loved me so much and that I had to make a promise to her. She wanted me to promise to her that whenever possible, I would make sure that the Americans were in front and not behind me as they were notorious for friendly fire, something that I ended up having first-hand experience of when stationed overseas in Afghanistan. That's a story I will divulge in greater detail later. It was a perfect night, apart from a few tears, none on my part, I hasten to add (Jonathon doesn't cry). With alcohol around and deep emotions in the air, it was only inevitable that there were a few tears.

I started my training on Monday 5th January 2003 at ITC Catterick in North Yorkshire. I remember just before I left home speaking to my Mom and her telling me to look after myself. She also said that she loved me very much and that she was very proud. I wanted to tell her that I was having second thoughts about joining, but I knew deep down that I couldn't. Even though I was thinking this, I didn't have another choice really but to get on that train, because I didn't want to let anyone down. I met up with a few other recruits at New Street station in Birmingham, and we continued the nerve wracking journey north. As the train neared Darlington station, the bravado had cleared to leave a thick layer of uneasiness in the air.

We were welcomed from the platform by a screaming and scary-looking corporal who yelled in our direction to get on board one of the coaches that was waiting for us. At this point now, I was looking for an escape route back to the welcoming sanctuary of Hall Green. After reluctantly getting onboard, we travelled for twenty minutes or so to arrive at Vimy Barracks. We were taken into a large hall, where the rest of the recruits were just milling around making small-talk. 'Where are you from?' and 'What football team do you support?' were the most popular questions. A bellowing voice shook everyone into a deathly silence and we were told to take a seat in the adjacent room. The same intimidating voice informed us to wait quietly for the company commanding officer, Major B. to brief us.

We finished the briefing and left with more questions than answers. We were ordered outside and left in Sgt B.'s command, a fiery redhead from Newcastle with an explosive temper. We were taken to the accommodation block and given a bed space in a four-man room and left to unpack. Cpl R., who would be my section commander, came into the room and introduced himself. He told us to be outside the block in ten minutes to collect our kit from the stores. We were marched to the stores, where we waited for about two hours until everyone had been issued with everything they would need for the next six months. If we made it that far. The rest of the evening was taken up with nervous chat with my new roommates, and trying to get my head around the day's whirlwind events. I'd gone from just being a civilian that morning to now, on the road to maybe becoming a soldier, something I had always dreamed about.

The next six-week block of training was a constant routine of waking up early and cleaning the accommodation. Every morning we were escorted to the cookhouse as a company and then we were rushed through our breakfast. We learned quickly in training to eat fast, taking another mouthful before swallowing the last. This would be followed by a beasting PT session, where we quickly learned that it was a bad idea to piss off the PT staff, because it would always mean getting reacquainted with your sausage and egg. We would then spend the rest of the day in class, learning the theory side of the SA80, the standard issue Army rifle. How to take it apart, clean it, and all the names of the different parts.

Classes about rules and regs would follow thick and fast. Then there were the night classes that were about as boring as watching paint dry, and we found that we would spend more time fighting off sleep than learning about human rights. These six weeks were a whirlwind of beastings and classes, where we didn't know if we were coming or going, and many nights I would lie awake thinking about quitting and going home. The thought of how happy my Mom would be, seeing me pass out of training was the only thing keeping me going at the time. Having her in the back of mind kept me motivated and determined for this not to beat me.

The platoon had a long weekend coming up at the end of week six, but with a big obstacle standing in our way. It was the first tactical exercise, where we would spend three nights out in the woods and put to the test all our fieldcraft skills which we had learned in the past six weeks. We would also have to prove to the training team that we had earned our regimental berets. Up until this point we had been wearing crow caps, a terrible camouflage baseball cap. These caps showed everyone else based there that we were still new recruits. If we didn't pass our upcoming tests, then we could be sent back to the start of training and miss out on the long weekend.

This would have been heartbreaking to say the least. Luckily, I passed my tests and earned the great privilege to wear the Fusiliers' cap, badge and hackle, which was a great honour. We were dismissed from the square and I rushed back to the block to change into my civvies. After getting changed, I headed to the waiting coaches to take us to Darlington station and then onto the train back to Birmingham. I had a great weekend with my family and friends and it was especially good seeing my mates. I couldn't wait to tell them about all the crazy stuff that I had been experiencing. The feelings I had on Sunday morning when I had to head back to Catterick were sickening, but off I went regardless, to the next phase.

I returned to Catterick to start the next phase of training, weeks seven to twelve, at the end of which we would be given two weeks' leave, but there was going to be a massive shock in store for us. Cpl J., who had replaced Cpl R. as our section commander, had now turned up. A mountain of a man, who stood at six-foot-four and built like chiselled stone. A soldier who would roam around the block looking for unfortunate victims to unleash an evil beating on, and trust me, if he caught hold of you it spelled trouble. What was worse was that the maniac was in the next room to me and he didn't have to travel far to fulfil his psychotic needs. Fortunately for me, I was rarely attacked, and we built a strange rapport with one another. He would spend most evenings in my bed space watching TV while I would prepare my kit for the following day's events.

I recall one event that showed his crazy train of thought. The platoon was taking part in its APWT (Annual Personal Weapons Training). This is where each soldier would have to prove they were an accomplished shooter. I was stationed in lane ten and Cpl J. was standing behind me, observing four lanes that he was in control of. Suddenly, he picked up a huge piece of timber that was being used to identify each lane, and then proceeded to smack me over my head while I was in the middle of a shot. I was left in agonising pain, my head spinning and ears ringing. Then astonishingly, he spoke in a thick rugged accent.

"What the fuck are you doing? You going to shoot those targets? What? Are you blind?"

I was in complete disbelief as I turned to him and explained that I couldn't see any of the targets after he had smashed me over the head with one of the range markers, to which he replied, "Oh yeah, don't worry, I'll pass you," and he did.

Another time he showed his crazy side was when I had come back from the cookhouse and had taken an apple with me. He was standing in the hallway when I returned and straightaway he started questioning me about my whereabouts. I told him that I had been for lunch and was returning for my notebook. He suddenly turned aggressive, grabbed me by the throat and started to demand why I had stolen an apple from the cookhouse.

"I didn't steal it. I just didn't have enough time to eat it and I'm going to have it later." Apparently, this wasn't the answer he wanted to hear, so he lifted me to the ceiling. He then squeezed my throat in his bear-like hands until I nearly lost consciousness. That was when he discarded me like an unwanted fish and with a loud thud I crashed down on the cold concrete floor. I got my breath back and hurried to my uneasy feet. He then stood there laughing and said that he was only joking about the apple and wouldn't report me. I thought to myself, *He won't report me!!! Is he on fucking drugs? I should report him*!!!

I remember a time when we were all on parade outside the block and the snow was beating down on us. One of those really nice, cold winter days you only get up north. Somebody then stupidly threw a snowball in his direction, hitting him flush on the head. He went absolutely crazy and started shouting and screaming in our direction. After thirty seconds of foul and abusive language, he started to walk angrily in the direction of the company. Then he spoke calmly.

"Okay, then. Who's the brave man then?"

Obviously, the guilty party didn't have the balls to own up, so the company just stood there in silence, expecting the inevitable.

"Come on then, who was it? You were brave enough to throw it, but not brave enough to admit it."

Then someone from the back of the company nervously shouted out.

"You only think you're hard because you have rank."

This set him off and he took off his rank slide and beret and discarded them on the ground. He headed directly towards the company, arms outstretched to the sides.

"Come on, then. One at a time, you fucking wasters."

The company dispersed in all directions, like a herd of antelope being charged down by a lion. A few unfortunate people got a right slapping, but as it usually turns out, the guilty got away scot-free.

To be really honest, despite his crazy antics, I never hated him. He was, in fact, a great soldier and you would definitely want him by your side in battle. Fortunately for the rest of the lads he had unmercifully petrified through his reign of terror, he slipped on some ice outside the armoury one cold, dark morning and broke his ankle. He was replaced by Cpl C., who was from my future battalion. He was bit of a joker. Always getting in trouble with the higher ranks and would sometimes ring up women he was seeing when we were on exercise. He would then get them to talk dirty down the phone so we could hear, while they were completely oblivious to the fact that they had a bunch of randy recruits as an audience.

One night I was just relaxing in my room when Cpl L. burst through the door and told everyone to stand by their beds as there was a surprise room inspection from Sgt B.

Fuck, here we go, I thought, *this is going to be a very long night.*

I was always prepared for this, but still, you knew that if he found even the smallest of things you would spend the rest of the night paying for it. The usual sentence was extra kit inspections, and maybe some other form of soul destroying punishment. Sgt B. came flying into the room, the door crashing off the wall behind it.

As I expected, he was in a foul mood and started to rip into Arnold in the first bed space. I could see items of his locker being tossed unceremoniously out of the nearest window. Maybe it was just because his kit was in a shit state, or at least that was what I hoped.

My early thoughts were quickly dashed, as Sgt B. emptied the contents of the other two lads' lockers out of the window. He moved into mine and proceeded to scrutinise my kit, even though I knew it was in good order. Out of the corner of my eye, I could see items of my neatly ironed kit flying out of the window and after thirty seconds he left the room without saying a word. I think everyone started to realise that we were really in for it. After the rest of the block had received the same treatment we were summoned outside and felt the wrath of Sgt B. He went absolutely berserk, screaming and shouting, saying we were the worst bunch of sperm-waste recruits he had ever come across. He went on to say that he was going to make everybody quit that night. Our next order was to retrieve our kit that now been blown all around the camp and take our whole bed space, including our Army locker and bed, to the parade square. Then there would another inspection at ten o'clock.

This was now starting to turn into the night from hell and with no end in sight. I started moving my room to the inspection area, hoping that this would be the end of things, but I knew deep down that it was probably only the start. It was nearly half ten when Sgt B. finally turned up and it was evident his mood hadn't changed for the better. People's kit was flying here, there and everywhere and now he was like a tornado whirling through people's bed spaces. We were told that there would be another room inspection at twelve o'clock back in the accommodation, and we didn't hold any high hopes that this would be the last.

I carried my kit back to my room and started the long arduous process of ironing and placing kit back in its appropriate spaces. Sgt B. entered the room and this time he displayed a different demeanour. Even though no one's kit took a flight from the nearest window, he started issuing out show parades and mine was at one o'clock at the guard room. The worst thing was that mine was to be dressed in full NBC suits, which those who know can be utterly horrendous, especially when you're accompanied by a member of the PT staff. I and ten others made the journey to the guard room where Sgt B. was waiting, and after a quick look-over, he sent us away with a flea in our ears. He then told us to be back there in twenty minutes in PT kit. This continued for the next couple of hours until the group of us heading to and from the guardroom had been inspected in different states of dress. Thankfully, Sgt B. finally stopped his reign of suffering at just after half three.

I think it must have taken most of the week for the platoon to recover from the inspection debacle and every time I got a glimpse of Sgt B. I would scamper the other way and out of sight. One thing for sure, we now knew he meant business and everyone started to switch on. From that day forward, I always kept my locker in perfect condition, just in case he paid another surprise visit.

The rest of this phase passed by quickly, and I was really starting to enjoy myself. Now I had the feeling that I'd made the right choice, even though every now and again my morale would come crashing down to earth after being on the wrong side of a soul-destroying beasting. We had a small parade at the end of week twelve to show how much our drill had improved. We passed this and were sent on leave for two weeks, which felt amazing.

Chapter six – Being broken down

Returning from leave is always difficult, even when you love the Army. It was a struggle but reluctantly, I dragged my out-of-shape ass back to Catterick. I had definitely burnt the candle at both ends this leave. Too much junk food and alcohol and I was sure to pay for that later. Before we'd gone on leave the training staff had been scaring us with stories of bayonet training. This had also been backed up by recruits that were six weeks in front of us, who I'd got talking to while queuing to collect my laundry. At the time I thought that maybe they were exaggerating just to shit us up, but it was soon apparent that they had been completely truthful.

I was rudely dragged from my bed at stupid o'clock in the morning and told to be outside the block in fifteen minutes. We were all warned not to be late as there would be severe consequences. Inevitably, someone was, and they picked the worst possible day to piss the recruitment team off.

We were marched at high speed to the armoury to collect weapons and bayonets and then marched swiftly on to a grassed area just behind the laundry block. The area usually had a small stream running through it, but as the weather had been horrendous for the past three days, it was like a raging river, with thick mud banks either side. We stopped short and we made sure we were in three ranks. The drill was: when your rank was called forward to move, you were to drop on your stomach and crawl at a good speed down the muddy bank into the water and out the other side. While you were crawling, you would be then getting an absolute bollocking for no apparent reason, but just because they could.

This went on for about an hour or so, crawling from one side to the other, while all the time trying to keep the barrel of our weapon out of the mud and water, for fear of extra punishments. If we did get caught ignoring those warnings, our punishment was to be dragged from the water and put in a small pen. Then we were forced to do knees to chest and other ingenious exercises, the end result being to try and make us throw up the water we'd ended up drinking when crawling through that gut-wrenching swell. Then a loud voice that I recognised as Sgt B. screamed at us to halt and for everyone to form up in three ranks. Whispers around the platoon thought we had finished the torture, but I had a feeling that the worst was yet to come. As usual, unfortunately, I was right.

We were marched back through the water and over a small hill, where we were greeted by a scene of small pens about ten feet by twenty, and about ten lanes each with a dummy suspended by a rope to a wooden platform. We were separated into groups of ten and my group was told to form up behind the relevant lane, while the rest of the platoon were herded into the pens like sheep. Sgt B. then shouted, "This can be as easy or as hard as you want." Usually that means you're getting beasted hard no matter what you do. He continued, "If you work hard and give me a hundred percent, it will be over shortly. If not, then stand by." The group that I was with had been told to fix bayonets, which I nervously did. Cpl L. got our attention and showed us what he expected of us when charging the dummy. He stormed down the lane screaming and shouting, "En garde."

Then he started to thrust his bayonet deep into the target, and returned the weapon to the starting position, which was to be held across our chest with the bayonet pointing towards the sky, just to the side of our left shoulder. It was now my turn and I tried my best to replicate the poise and controlled aggression of Cpl L. I reached the target and attacked, which was met by Cpl L. yelling in my direction to up the anger levels. This was a difficult task to achieve as I don't lose my temper often, and it takes a hell of lot for me to do so.

While my group was charging the defenceless targets, the others were being put into stress positions. Then they were made to scream and shout at the top of their lungs, to try and get their aggression levels pumped up. After I'd finished on the lanes, the group I was with was then moved into one of those pens and started the screaming and shouting exercises. Now the people around me were being sick, due to the physical and mental torture we were under. This continued for the next few hours until our sickening ordeal was brought to a long and overdue end. We formed up back into three ranks and headed in the direction of the block, but with everyone still on edge.

Now with every word that left Sgt B.'s mouth we expected to be taken somewhere else and continue the torture. Thankfully it never happened and with the words, "Platoon halt," we stopped outside the block. We were all covered from head to toe in mud and shit. Some lads even had the trails of sick on their T-shirts, evidence of the pure and twisted evil that had taken place that day. We sat outside the block and started to clean weapons, while everyone tried to come down and relax from the day's life-changing events. You never know how much your body can really take, until it's pushed to its very limits.

During this phase we also started to learn more about NBC (Nuclear, Biological and Chemical Warfare). Up until this point it had been mostly classroom work, apart from the occasional beasting session in full NBC suits, including respirators, and let me tell you one thing now. It's a horrible experience to be sick in one of those things. Today was the first time we were going to put everything we had learned into practice, so we reluctantly headed to the gas chamber to conduct this part of our training. We were told by Sgt T. what to expect, and everyone started to practise removing and placing back the canister on their respirator, until we had it down to a fine art. At times like this everyone wanted to go last and avoid being the first victim. The thinking was that the training team would get bored torturing people in the chamber and when your turn came around, they would just get you in and out.

The first victim came flying through the door choking on the CS gas that they had been forced to breathe in. They gasped for fresh air as snot and all sorts of fluids started leaking uncontrollably from their nose and mouth, as if someone had turned a tap on in their nasal passage. The rest of the platoon looked on in horror as the waterworks continued. Now everyone probably started wishing that they had gone in first, as they would have been unaware of the outcome. Now my mind was in overdrive, trying to predict how the evil gas would affect me. After about fifteen minutes the first group had finally recovered from their experience, but by then, there was a steady stream of new casualties staggering about with trails of snot and tears dripping from the red-raw eyes and noses.

"Next," Cpl L. shouted in my direction. I slowly headed towards the chamber with four others. We stopped at the entrance and were ordered to put on our gas masks. Seconds later we finally made our way through the red steel door which then slammed shut behind us, and into a cloud of unmerciful white gas waiting to strike as soon as our naked faces appeared.

Sgt T. had just got a fresh batch of gas going and proceeded to take his mask off and show off that it had no effect on him. He then started to sniff it directly from the source, like some kind of crazy drug addict. Cpl R., who was in there with us, got my attention.

"Right then, this is the drill," he said, "You will take a deep breath. Remove your canister, put it into your bag, and replace it with a new one."

"Okay, Corporal," I mumbled back. I took a deep breath of protected air, and I started to untwist the canister. I then removed it and placed it in my bag. At the same time, I fetched my new one and started to connect it to the mask. When practising this without any consequences it's an easy task. The problem was now trying to line up the canister in the gloomy confines of the chamber, and it started to become difficult. I forgot that you needed to twist the canister to a slight angle before the two would grip together, and now I was starting to run out of breath. Thankfully, just before I was forced to take a breath of gas-filled air, the canister clipped in. Then I twisted it tightly. I got the thumbs-up and we moved on to the next drill. Now we were told to remove the mask completely and that we would be asked a series of questions.

"Take your mask off," Cpl R. demanded. I removed it and waited for the eye-watering gas to attack.

"Name and number," Cpl R. barked.

"I am 25162266 recruit Appelbe-Wootton," choking my response back.

"I can't hear you."

"I am 25162266 recruit Appelbe-Wootton," I shouted.

"That's a posh name, recruit. You royalty or something?" he sarcastically asked.

"No Corporal, not at all," I shouted back, like the very notion had upset me.

Now the gas had started to take hold, my eyes were streaming and I had a burning sensation in the back of my throat, which was starting to become excruciating. It was like an angry swarm of fire ants had infested my throat, and they were stinging me at will.

"What football team do you support?" he asked.

"Aston Villa, Corporal," I painfully replied.

"How many brothers and sisters?"

"One brother, two sisters, Corporal," I started to think that I would never get out of this hell, when mercifully the steel door creaked open. We were then led like prisoners from our ghastly custodian and into the beautiful North Yorkshire fresh air.

"The secret now is not to rub your face, just try and pour water over it so it washes straight off," Sgt T. explained. "The more you rub, the worse it gets. Just let it dissipate naturally," he continued.

I thought to myself that there was nothing natural about that, but then gradually the pain turned into an uncomfortable feeling, then slowly disappeared, leaving me with a nose full of snot. Another great day of training completed and something else to ring home about.

This phase of training continued at a speedy rate and as the weeks went by I started to feel more and more like a soldier. The platoon had started to get its act together and the beastings started to become less frequent. The thing was that you could never really get complacent, as one was never too far away. After week eighteen we had our final long weekend leave before we were due to pass out, so I made the familiar four-hour-long train journey south back to Hall Green.

Chapter seven – Becoming a man

I returned to my second home in Catterick with the thought that I only had six weeks left before I was due to pass out on the parade square in front of my family, but I knew that there would be some very difficult times ahead. We had two exercises left. One was Tac Ex three, which was a dig-in exercise, and the last would be Final Ex, a week-long course in Otterburn on the Scottish border, which I think everyone dreaded. The company would also have to pass the final CFT, an eight-mile weighted march across the back area at Catterick. The people who know this march will agree that it's an utterly horrendous area, with huge climbs and steep descents over gravel roads, where loose rocks wait patiently for misplaced steps and will turn your ankle in an instant. Then that could be your course over with. This had happened to a fellow fusilier, Tim B. He had damaged his shins during a march and had to wait six months for them to heal before finding himself in my platoon. At the end of it all, we would have our final passing-out parade, which we were told would involve a week of drill hell, but as I always liked drill, I wasn't too concerned. Anyway, it would be the last week before having two weeks' summer leave and then going on to my battalion.

We were now being pushed to our absolute limits on every PT session, the staff trying to find weird and wonderful ways of breaking us. Luckily, as the course went on, my body had built up a resilience to this, and could now withstand extreme punishment. Tac Ex three was now firmly in my thoughts and I had started to envisage what the training team had in store for us. The general consensus of the lads that I had spoken to who had already passed Final Ex, said that this was the more difficult exercise.

On the morning of the exercise in question, we paraded outside the block for a full kit inspection. We were formed up in a hollow square facing in, while the platoon sergeant called a piece of kit. You would then in turn hold it up and show that you were in possession of it. If not, you were made to do a hundred press-ups before going to collect it from your room. After the inspection was over the platoon was marched to the parade square and loaded into the waiting coaches. We were then driven the sixty or so miles to where the exercise would commence. The journey took the best part of two hours, but this gave me a chance to grab some very valuable sleep.

As we approached camp, the inevitable rain had started to fall, getting heavier as we came to a standstill, as was always the way. This is where the saying 'It's not training when it's not raining' comes from, I guess. We were ordered from the coach and told to locate our bergens and webbing from the storage bins underneath the coach. We were sent to an area where our weapons were being stored. Waiting for us was also the 94mm LAW (the Army anti-tank weapon), which was used as a kind of torture device for some unfortunate to carry, usually the most gobby. The purpose of this exercise was for the platoon to work as a team to build three trench systems deep enough for us to stand in and be able to use as protection against attack.

After collecting weapons and any additional kit, which included everyone's favourite rations, we were told to form up in our sections, and were given our blank ammunition for the exercise. Then we had to load up all our magazines and were told that we would be moving off shortly. When the call was made, I struggled to my feet, and formed up. My back was already trying to give up from the extreme weight of my bergen and I had only just started. We moved off in single file just as the rain intensified. I kept the distance between me and the guy in front to the required distance and just started to take in the local surroundings. I could see rolls of thick, black, angry looking clouds in the distance and started to come to terms with the fact it was going to be one of those exercises. We patrolled for a further hour until we reached a large grassed area where I could see evidence of previous trench digging. My section came to a halt behind Cpl C., and I took this moment to get my breath. We were then briefed that we would dig throughout the night until the trenches were to the required standard.

The next thirty hours were spent constructing our muddy living quarters and it was a nightmare. We would spend hours digging one part, only to find it would collapse with us in there, and with the rain pouring in, we were constantly in about six inches of water. After what seemed like a lifetime we had completed our mission, and after putting down my spade, I collapsed on the ground with exhaustion. Then they told us that we needed to go and help the other section to complete their trench. Where they had been digging, the ground was less forgiving, and their trench was still only half-way complete. We now took it in turns, one section digging and the other resting. After we had finally finished the second trench I didn't even know what day it was. The last God knows how many hours had been a blur of mud and rain, and just trying to grab a wink of sleep whenever I could.

The platoon was then marched to another site where there were pre-dug trenches. These had been built for safety reasons and had their sides reinforced. So all that time digging and we weren't even going to spend a second defending them. The pre-built trenches were where we would spend the next twenty-four hours, defending against an attack, with it quite likely being an NBC attack of some kind. The first ten hours was spent in a routine of staging on, making sure weapons and kit were clean, and just personal admin, like getting something to eat. I went for the theory of eating cold rations just in case we were attacked half-way through cooking them. But cold sausage and beans was a bad idea. It took me about five years to eat beans again.

Then predictably, we started to come under attack from an unknown enemy, from a wood-line two hundred metres to our front. Then my section commander briefed us to stay in and defend the trenches. He told us to put on our gas masks and NBC suits, as they thought the enemy was about to launch a chemical weapons bombardment. We did this in pairs (the buddy buddy system), one man covering the other getting his kit, then vice versa. The enemy had now vanished like ghosts and we spent the ten hours living in masks and suits. We had to show that we could eat and drink while wearing this stifling attire. Suddenly the words GAS, GAS, GAS echoed around the trenches, and we were suddenly under a substantial enemy attack. I could see a white mist making its way through the dark trench, looking for any unmasked victims it could find. I knew straightaway it was the return of my old friend, CS gas.

A heavy machine gun opened up on us from the front and the enemy started to advance from all sides, and we were now starting to take heavy fire. I got a tap on my shoulder from Cpl C. He told me that we were going to withdraw from the trench and escape the area, and to pass it on. As soon as we got the call we dragged ourselves from the gas-infested trench and fell in on the platoon commander. He said that now we had a gruelling two-hour extraction from the area and as the threat levels were still high, we would have to complete the march in full NBC kit. The march was more like a run and people started to drop like flies, only to be yelled at and dragged to their feet by the nearest guy. My feet felt like blocks of concrete and I was breathing like an asthmatic chain smoker. It's hard to recall what I was going through as I was on auto pilot by then, my body just gripping on to survival and hoping I could get to the end of this in one piece.

At times like this you just keep going. There is something inside you that just doesn't let you quit and with every recruit that I ran past, I felt more and more invincible. I suddenly came crashing to a halt straight into the back of someone. It turned out to be Sgt R. and I expected an absolute rollicking for nearly cleaning him up. I must have caught him in a good mood as he just looked at me and said, "Who's that?"

"Appelbe-Wootton, Sergeant."

"Okay, sit down there and take off your respirator." I collapsed on my bergen, my body shaking uncontrollably. I then took a big intake of oxygen and tried to catch my breath. This had been one of the worst experiences of my life and I hoped this was the end of it, praying there wasn't a sting in the tail.

"END EX," Sgt R. shouted. Everyone looked around in relief, just glad that this horrendous ordeal was finally over. Bedford trucks turned up and I gingerly climbed in one and found a seat. More and more people clambered in and soon there were more people than seats. Some almost sat on my lap, but I didn't care. I was just glad I had made it through this. We returned to Catterick and spent the next few hours cleaning weapons, and then back to the block to start the arduous task of cleaning our kit.

The next couple of weeks were spent preparing for the CFT and the final exercise. So unluckily for us, the physical exercises were turned up a notch. I could finally see the end to this difficult and personality-changing journey and was really looking forward to becoming a fusilier.

The morning of the CFT came round quickly and we were told to form up on the parade square to get our kit weighed before the start. We formed a queue and I waited nervously, hoping my kit was at the right weight. I was next to be weighed. I hung my kit on the scales and it weighed in bang on the forty-five-pound minimum weight. I wasn't worried at all about this task, as weighted marches had become one of my strongest activities. My mind had a way of just taking the boredom and monotony of just walking and the occasional run, so I was very optimistic that I would complete this in the two-hour time limit. The only thing that could scupper me would be an ill-timed injury.

The time came for us to start, and the PT staff got everyone formed up into three ranks.

"Prepare to march, quick march," shouted the PT staff. We moved off at a steady speed and doing so, I started to prepare my mind for the two hours that followed. I could always find ways of numbing the boredom, by counting each step until I reached a thousand then starting all over again. A strange thing, I know, but it worked with me. With every stride of my long legs I got a little bit closer to passing, just completely focused. In my mind I was counting the steps and there was no way I wasn't going to pass. There were a few difficult climbs throughout, but the company finally reached the finishing line at one hour and fifty two minutes. Strangely, only three guys failed, when usually a whole gaggle of lads did. Luckily for them they got another chance to retake and pass later on that week.

Now only one giant hurdle remained on the horizon. Final Ex. This was what the last five and half months had come down to. I knew it was going to be difficult, but I had been through so much I couldn't let this beat me. This was going to be a week of pure hell and with no let-up. It would include all aspects of field craft, river crossings, huge attacks followed lastly by a full-company night attack, when live ammunition was going be used by for the first time. I had mixed feelings about that, but I knew at the same time it would be a fantastic experience. All wings of the military coming together and working as a team to suppress multiple targets.

We travelled the two hours to Otterburn camp by coach, so I took this time to try and grab a couple of hours' kip. Knowing that we were about to be pushed to our absolute limits of what a human body can deal with, any sleep was better than none. To those who have never been to this place, its scenery is absolutely amazing. Picturesque you might say, but don't let this place fool you for one minute. She can be an evil mistress. No matter what time of year you go there, it always seems to be damp and cold. The hills are steep and rugged and when wet, extremely treacherous. The worst thing, and I mean the absolute worst thing about this place, is the midges, a kind of biting fly that drives you insane. There is no escape from them in the summer, they just feast on your blood like a deranged pack of vampires sucking you dry. There have been times on exercise that I have just wanted to quit and escape their torture. They've even managed to get inside the ear piece of my radio and attack from there.

A bump in the road woke me and I wiped the drool from side of my face, from where I had been dribbling in my sleep. God knows what I had been dreaming about, maybe a Big Mac meal or something. I reluctantly headed off the coach and collected my kit, which had foolishly been dumped in a puddle by some idiot. Cpl C. shouted, "Four section on me," so I raced over and sat on my wet bergen and formed up in one line. Blank ammunition, additional kit and rations were handed out and somehow, I ended up with the LAW.

"Thanks," I said sarcastically to Cpl C., to which he replied, "Any time." Then he said, "You have it now for the first day and then we'll pass it around." The platoon moved off, with our section bringing up the rear, me as last guy.

We patrolled for about five hours in the pouring rain. My boots now felt as wet as the raging river that we had been tracking for the past two hours. We stopped every now and again for the platoon commander to do a map check and for him to rendezvous with Sgt R. to make sure we were heading in the right direction. Officers with maps, never trust them. Eventually we came to a wooded area and the platoon halted. I hit the deck and took cover behind my bergen and kept an eye out for a fictional enemy, who at this point had stayed well hidden. After what seemed like an eternity and with my head and neck now aching from the constant strain of staring down the SUSAT scope of my rifle (The Sight Unit Small Arms, Trilux is a 4× telescopic sight, with tritium-powered illumination used at dusk or dawn, mounted on a variety of rifles and to be used by all infantrymen), the word was passed down the line for us to prepare to move. I checked my pouches and staggered to my feet. I wrestled my bergen to my back and moved off, following the rest of the platoon into a small clearing in the wood line.

We were then spread out into a square formation, with one of each of the four sections taking up a side of the square facing out, with the HQ in the middle. Now we would wait it out to see if the enemy had been tracking us and if they would mount an attack.

Thirty minutes or so went by and the word coming down the line was for us to start to prepare our shell scrapes. This was a small bunker dug into the ground about two feet deep and big enough to house two infantry men with all their kit and sufficient room to sleep in. The buddy buddy system works well for this now. With one person digging, the other will get some food and a brew on. Right then, now to establish the rules of the harbour area This is a safe area where we rest, hidden away from the local enemy.

- Weapons should be to reach at all times.
- If not in your shell scrape, then helmets must be worn.
- Reduced noise and no torches after night fall.
- If you break any of the above, stand by and be prepared to crawl on your stomach around the track plan. (A track that has been cleared of any big sticks or stones, and where a string line is set up at hip height, so you can find your way round to the stag position, without tripping over mysterious objects at night.)

The stag list was written, and everyone knew their time of duty. Mine was two till four in the morning, so I made myself comfortable in my sleeping bag and fell asleep. But I found myself waking up periodically when hearing people crashing through the trees, looking for the next person to go on stag, and I kept hoping it wasn't me. Thankfully, a quick look at my watch reassured me that I had another two hours left before I received the dreaded news. Suddenly I heard a branch snap close by, which was followed by the whispered voice of Tim B.

"Johno, is that you?" At times like this you just want to stay as still as possible, hoping he thinks he has the wrong person and moves on in search of his relief. As I'm not a complete bastard, I replied, though.

"Yes, unfortunately it is."

"Your stag, mate." I shoved Jimmy and we both started to pack away our sleeping bags and any kit that was lying around. When we leave our shell scrape to go on stag, we have to leave everything ready to go just in case we get bugged out. (This is when the harbour area is attacked, and you have to leave in a hurry.) It's a horrible order to hear at two o'clock in the morning when it's pissing down, something everyone dreads to hear.

We headed down the track plan to the stag position and were briefed by the off-coming guys about the arcs. (This is where you have a left and right of arc which is usually a tree that is easily visible, and which is your area to watch out over). Now it was a battle against one of the biggest enemies you will face when on stag: sleep. You're on one hand trying to stay vigilant and look out for any enemy, and on the other, your mind and body are trying to convince you that you need to close your eyes. It's funny when you are in this state, because you start to convince yourself that you can see people moving in front of you. The more you stare, the worse it gets, until you finally realise that it's a slim tree swaying in the cool night breeze.

We battled through to the end without anything happening and then Jimmy went and woke the next two guys for stag. After returning to our sleeping bags, I grabbed a bit of shut-eye until we were woken for first parade. Then we took turns to clean our weapons, washed and shaved, usually with cold water, then finally we got some food down us. The rest of this day was taken up with patrolling lessons and stag duties, while also trying to avoid getting beasted around the track plan for any slight misdemeanour. On the third day in glorious Otterburn we were briefed on an ambush that was going to take place that night. We were briefed that a small enemy convoy of vehicles carrying weapons was moving through a specific area, and we were to hit them. We would then extract from the area under the cover of fire support and back to our current location. The thing was with this, you knew it wasn't real, so it was hard to get yourself up for it. But believe me, when it *is* real, you have no trouble. It just sort of happens naturally.

We moved off on foot just after nightfall and reached the location about an hour later. The road that the convoy was apparently going to use was situated at the bottom of a wooded hill. The platoon was separated into four sections. There was the main group, a left cut-off party, a right cut-off party, then behind the main group there was the HQ party, along with some spare guys and a couple acting as runners. The platoon commander was situated with the main group and he would be the first to fire. Then everyone else would follow his lead and put some rounds down. The wait was agonising, just waiting there hoping the made-up enemy would turn up soon. As we were lying downhill, the pain in my neck at times had become unbearable. I had to keep trying to rest my head on my arm, doing whatever I could to relieve some of the pain, but at the same time trying to avoid it looking as if I had fallen asleep.

Like clockwork the rain had started to fall and before long it was if I was lying in a swamp. My whole body now started to shudder as the damp had made its way through my skin and straight to the bone. All I wanted to do was stand up and shake my body back into order, but I couldn't. So I had to just lie there and ride it out.

The first group of soldiers appeared through the mist from behind a tall oak tree, moving from right to left. They were soon followed by the vehicle that was carrying the weapons and then behind that trundled another group of soldiers. Suddenly a loud burst of automatic gunfire broke the silence, and everyone started to rain down ammunition on the surprised enemy. After all the enemy were down, the right cut-off group, which I was part of, now acted as a search team and went down to check the bodies for any information that we could use against them. We retrieved any intelligence and the call was made that we needed to leave the area in a hurry.

I moved off at high speed, but as I had spent the last four hours lying on the cold wet ground, my legs were reluctant to move at the desired speed. It was now twenty minutes since we had withdrawn from the ambush sight, and finally the platoon started to slow down to a quick walk, then ultimately a normal patrol speed. We stopped in a small clearing and moved into all-round defence to see if we'd been followed. After about thirty minutes, the platoon continued on its way back to the harbour area and I prepared for a quick power nap before I was due on stag. The platoon was told not to bother getting our ponchos out (a squared piece of canvas that you pin out to make a shelter) and to just sleep in our shell scrapes, as there was a high probability we would get attacked in the night.

I had just nodded off when a burst of gunfire woke everyone from their uncomfortable slumber and those dreaded words rang out.

"We're being bugged out. Get your kit on and meet in the rendezvous area."

I threw my bergen on my back and made my way to the RV. The platoon now sped off, while a small rear party exchanged bullets with the enemy until we had lost them. We took refuge in another small wooded area and waited out the rest of the night.

The exercise was now coming to an end and with only one final objective standing in our way. The mission was to head off in search of the enemy's camp and attack them. We started the patrol at three o'clock in the afternoon and headed north towards a large hilly area. The first obstacle that we tackled was a decent-sized river, which we had to somehow cross. Even though it was late June, the water was bloody freezing and at its deepest point it was up to my chest. The river's current was trying to force me further downstream where it opened up into a raging torrent. One slip now on a loose rock would send me shooting downstream to an almost certain death. Finally, the river released us from its powerful grip and we continued the journey to eventually come face to face with our elusive enemy.

Then suddenly we came under attack from a machine gun position on a hill just to the west of us. My section started to return fire while three section moved around to the left-hand side of the enemy, and used a small stream as cover. They then crawled leopard-style towards the enemy, throwing a grenade in and storming the bunker, killing the enemy. These attacks continued for the next two hours until the area was declared clear and we moved off to an overnight spot where we regrouped. We were briefed on our final mission, which would be to completely destroy the enemy.

The op started at three o'clock in the morning, when all good Army missions start. We moved off using the cover of darkness and headed to our designated positions. We now waited for the heavy machine guns to fire us into battle. We spent the next hour just sitting around in a stream, trying to keep the feeling in our feet and the morale in our heads. The sound that we had all been waiting for erupted from a nearby hill and the words GO, GO, GO crackled over the radio. Now each section took it in turns to suppress and attack the enemy at multiple locations. As soon as we cleared one bunker, another would open up on us and we would then have to take that one out. This seemed never-ending until finally the words. "End Ex" were shouted over the radio, and that was it, the end of the exercise, finishing at just before six.

After being debriefed by the company commander, Major B., and then by Sergeant Major M., we were rounded up into Bedford trucks. We were driven the forty-five-minute journey back to camp, during which pretty much everyone had succumbed to their broken bodies and had drifted off to sleep. Once back at camp we finally got warm and scoffed down a very filling breakfast, and we spent the next few hours cleaning weapons. The coaches arrived and took us back to Catterick.

The final days of training were now spent practising drill for my passing-out parade. My Mom, Nan and Auntie Liz were due to make the long journey north to witness me finally becoming a fully-fledged soldier, and I was so chuffed to have made it this far. Training had been the hardest and most rewarding time of my life, with many challenges along the way. Some physical, but more mentally. Even though it had nearly broken me many times, I knew I could do anything now, such was the confidence that had been installed in me.

The morning of the parade had arrived, and I couldn't wait to finally see my Mom and show her that I had made it. The company was marched on to the square and halted in front of the growing crowd.

"Left turn," CSM shouted. In one fluid movement the company turned to face our audience. We were then ordered into open dress and waited to be inspected by a Brigadier General and some other higher-ranking officers. As they started to march across the square I could see the Brigadier's sword glistening as the sun broke its way through a wall of thick cloud. They moved down the line, stopping every couple of soldiers, and started to ask questions about training. Then from nowhere a wasp landed on my face and just stayed there. I didn't dare move, my body stood rigid, as pride and confidence flowed through my veins. As the inspection party approached me I hoped they would cruise straight by, but at the last second the Brigadier stopped.

"Hello. Name and Number?" he politely demanded.

"I am 25162266 Fusilier Appelbe-Wootton, Sir" I said proudly

"Did you enjoy training, Fusilier?"

"I did sir, very much." While the questions continued, the wasp had not moved a muscle. It was like he was on parade with me. Luckily as the Brigadier moved on, CSM M. turned to me and said, "Well done for not moving," and with that, he flicked my new friend off my face.

After proudly marching around the square, looking as bold as brass, while the band played some catchy tunes, I started trying to locate my Mom amongst the excited crowd, finally catching sight of her wiping away a few tears from her mascara-stained cheeks. We then fell out for one last time and I had now completed my six months' training. What a moment in my life! I knew so many people had doubted that I could ever get to this point, but here I was. We marched to the NAFFI where my family members were waiting, and I located them through the bustling crowd. Mom looked like she had been crying again with happiness and I was so happy to see her. Knowing she was so proud of me really moved me, even though I probably didn't show it. Deep down I felt like a million dollars and felt like going to a room somewhere and shedding a few of those happy tears.

After an hour I went back to the block for the last time and collected my kit. I loaded it into the back of Mom's car. As Mom drove out through the main gate, I thought to myself that I would never set eyes on this place again. It had been more than just a home to me over those past six months. This was a place where my whole life had been turned around and I will always be grateful to it for that. I now had just over one week's leave before I joined up with my battalion and took the next step on this roller coaster of an adventure.

Chapter eight – Learning the hard way

The next stage of my Army experience was going to be at a camp in North Luffenham near Rutland Water; a place called St George's Barracks. I met up with Tim B. and we travelled by train to Oakham. The train arrived at ten-thirty in the morning and we jumped in a taxi and made the short journey to our new home. The taxi pulled in and the driver said, "Here, you guys, sounds like someone's getting a right bollocking in there."

We nervously approached the front gate and flashed our identification. We were told to go to the guardroom and await further instructions. Suddenly a tall well-dressed soldier came calmly walking from the guardroom and in a loud cockney accent started yelling in the direction of four soldiers who were lined up near the battalion flags. His voice blasted through my body, almost making me drop my TV that I had brought with me. Unluckily, he then turned his attention to the pair of us and with a blast of his machine gun-like mouth, started interrogating us.

"What the fuck are you fucking looking at, you fucking retards?"

We just stood there like a pair of idiots in shock, completely overwhelmed by this verbal attack.

"You pair fucking deaf, you fucking mongrels?" He now started moving towards us, screaming and shouting in a frequency that I couldn't even understand.

"Listen, you fuckheads, don't make me repeat myself. Do you understand?"

I was now just trying to remember what the first thing he asked me had been, and I started mumbling all sorts.

"What's wrong with you? Do you have a speech impediment or something?"

"No, Sir, I ju…"

"Sir," he reloaded and hit me again, "Fucking Sir? I fucking work for a living. You address me as Sergeant or staff. Do you fucking understand me, knobhead?" he demanded.

"Yes Sergeant," I replied.

"Right then, I'll let you off this time as you're new, and lucky for you I've got people to deal with. So get out of my fucking sight and don't let me catch you monging it again. Because if I do, stand by."

I couldn't believe what had just happened and turned to Tim and said. "Fucking hell, mate, first day and we've already pissed the Provo Sergeant off. What the hell are we in for here?"

That night we ventured over to the NAFFI and found a quiet seat in the corner. Our plan was just to have a couple of cold ones and to check the quality of the food out. Then after that we'd just head back to our rooms and get an early night, hopefully not pissing anybody else off in the process. I returned to the bar for a refill when a voice from the other side of the room called out, "Hey Red Ass, mine's a Carling." He then turned to his mates and asked them what they were drinking. He turned and called me again, "Red ass, that's three Carlings." I looked at Tim and he just nodded his head. What choice did I have? I had only been here ten hours and didn't know who these guys were. After my early dressing-down I wasn't in the mood to piss anybody else off. The guy said thanks and took the three thirst-quenching drinks back to his appreciative friends.

We finished our drinks and headed for the exit, when the same strict voice yelled over, "Red ass, where you going?" I thought *For fuck's sake, I know I'm new, but I'm not having the piss taken out of me,* so I turned around in scorn.

"Don't worry, mate. Only wanted to buy you one back, come over here and sit down." Apprehensively we took them up on their offer and sat down around their table. They introduced themselves.

"I'm Sgt B. but you can call me Pete, and this is Mick and Jed, corporals who work with me."

I was so used to addressing people with rank, it took till at least five pints to stop it. With the drinks flowing nicely I started to forget about where I was and soon ended up back in Mick's room with a few tins to continue the night. Then Mick suggested that we should play this drinking game called *pass the punch*, which I stupidly agreed to.

"The rules are: we all stand in a circle and the highest-ranking person flicks the coin. Heads, you punch to the left, tails, you punch to the right, with your weakest hand to the body," explained Mick. Pete flicked tails and the game began. The first punch sent Jed staggering backwards and collapsing onto Mick's bed.

There are going to be some sore bodies tomorrow, I thought.

Now it came down to me and Tim lined one up. Bang! Right under the ribs, which knocked the wind out of me.

"Fuck, Tim, your Mom hits me harder than that when I'm in bed with her," I joked. Everyone burst into laughter, including Tim, and the crazy game continued in that fashion.

A bottle of vodka then materialised from somewhere and soon we were struggling to even see, never mind hit anybody. It moved from weak hand to your strongest, until someone drunkenly suggested head shots were now available. It was now one-punch roulette, and we were hoping the coin never landed in our direction. We also knew someone might still be capable of landing a clean shot. The game finally ended when Pete was sent sprawling unconscious to the ground, and after checking his condition, I staggered to my room and passed out in a drunken mess.

The following morning the unearthly beeping sound of my alarm brought me around. Luckily, I'd remembered to set it the night before, otherwise God only knows what time I would have woken up. I grabbed a quick shower and a shave and headed unstably to the cook house. Tim was already there and looked as bad as I felt.

"Fucking hell, mate, that was a bad idea last night. A really bad idea. My ribs are fucking killing me."

"Your ribs?" I exclaimed, "Look at my eye! I told you to aim for the top of my head, you wanker."

We burst out laughing, but this just enraged my hangover, which soon then made my full breakfast completely inedible. We marched back to the block just as an angry looking Provo Cpl was conducting a block inspection, and I knew then that the day was about to get a hell of lot worse. The company was ordered outside and marched to the guardroom. Unluckily, I could see my friend from yesterday, Provo Sgt F., eagerly waiting for his next victims, arms folded and with a huge cheesy grin written all over his boat race.

It was a red-hot day and the smell of last night's alcohol was now leaching from my pores and the sweat that had started to drip down my forehead was stinging my eyes now. We were left standing to attention for an hour and I could see people in the front ranks starting to wilt in the intense heat. I was really starting to struggle to even stand up, my body swaying from side to side, but deep down I knew the punishment that was coming would break us. Two PT staff turned up and now I knew we were really in for it. The company was marched to the old airfield and beasted almost until breaking point. We were forced to do all sorts of stress positions; running with weights, carrying people and just generally getting hammered into the ground. It even got to a point where I almost felt like quitting. This is something that happens a lot in the Army and it wasn't the first or the last time. It's one thing doing this sober, but quite another when nursing a devastating hangover.

There were moments when I just wanted to drop down dead, but my body wouldn't allow it and I survived to the very end. This continued for an hour or so and then eventually we were marched back to the guardroom where Sgt F. was waiting. He picked out twelve people, in which Tim and I were included, and we were told to parade back there at six o'clock for a show parade, when we would be given a list of jobs that needed doing before we could leave.

The selected twelve marched back to the guardroom, and after a quick inspection we were given our jobs, which included cleaning the guardroom inside and out, even removing spider webs from up lampposts. This was proper army bullshit. Eventually, after two further inspections, we were released from this agonising torture and allowed to return to the block. Then Tim and I went back over to the NAFFI, where all this punishment had started, to grab a bite to eat. Mick called us over and asked if we wanted to join him for a few drinks, which we politely declined. The last thing I needed was a repeat of the last twenty-four-hours, a real eye-opening start to battalion life.

I started to get used to the battalion way of things, even though there were only about fifty guys stationed here. The rest had been deployed to Northern Ireland on a six-month tour. After their posting finished, they would return and then the whole battalion would take up its residential posting at Palace barracks.

One night I was in the NAFFI having a couple of drinks with Tim, when a few lads that I had got talking to the previous night came in. One of the lads, Woody, came over and we got chatting. He was a bit younger than me, but we had the same sense of humour and we really clicked. After a few drinks he said that they were all going to Grantham to continue the night and did I fancy it. I wasn't that keen to start with, but with a little persuasion they soon twisted my arm.

We were drawn into a small bar by the catchy beat that was drifting down the street, and we congregated around a fruit machine. We all tried our luck to win a few more beer tokens and much to everyone's anger, I dropped forty quid out of it. I could see a group of women gathering around the pool table and juke box at the other end of the bar, and I caught the enchanting stare of a very attractive brunette. I played it cool, just firing a small smile back in her direction while heading to the toilet. As I left the little boys' room and returned to my cold Stella, an outstretched hand reached out and gently held my arm.

"You not going to come over and say hi then?" She spoke in a seductive American accent.

"Yeah, course I was. But I thought you were with those guys and I didn't want to cause a scene," I replied.

"Oh, don't worry about them. I'm not interested in any of those guys," she playfully replied. I thought, *Bonus! Been here half an hour and already pulled a cracker. This is going to be one those great nights.* Was I in for a shock!

We spent the next hour just chatting. I told her how I'd just recently passed my training, and that I was about to be posted to Northern Ireland. She then told me that she was here doing a degree in psychotherapy and that she'd moved here from Boston a year ago. She'd agreed to go and meet a couple of friends and said we could catch up later in the Hog's Head for a few drinks. As she didn't have her phone, we planned to rendezvous by the front door at about twelve. Finally, we shared a quick kiss goodbye, before we went our separate ways. As we walked down the High Street looking for the Hog's Head, the lads had started to take the piss out of me, saying that I was all loved up and they could hear wedding bells and that sort of rubbish. I responded with, "Fuck off, man, I don't fall for birds, it's the other way around." A bit of bullshit really, but I didn't want to lose face. Even though I'd only just met her, I did feel like there was a small spark between us, and yes, maybe something could have materialised out of our chance meeting.

We got to the pub and straightaway, aftershocks were being ordered. The night was starting to really heat up, great music, great crowd and in about half an hour's time maybe a great bird. What else could you wish for? I had such a great feeling about this night and just hoped nothing was going to go wrong. The lads had stationed themselves at the side of the dance floor, where we had a great view of the dancing women. I was absolutely flying, looking forward to meeting up with my American chick, and I must have let my guard down for a second, just daydreaming about what could be happening later that night.

Out of the corner of my eye I witnessed Woody crashing face first on to the dance floor. I took a step to try and locate his attacker, and: Bang! The room went white. It must have only been for a few seconds, but it felt like ages. I thought I must have been knocked out, but after a few worrying seconds I soon realised I was still standing up. Bang! A second impact, and I was now in pure survival mode. I tried everything to get back my equilibrium, but everything failed. My vision was now gone, and I knew I couldn't afford to take another blow to my unprotected head. I only had one real choice and it was to take a knee and cover up. By now I could only feel what was going on around me with my other senses and could feel my attacker above me, ready to strike once more. Bang! Bang! Bang! Three more shots rained down. I could feel a presence above me but was in no fit state to fight back. Unfortunately, all I could do was just ride out the storm and hope I would be rescued soon, by one of my mates or one of the door staff. I felt helpless in this desperate state, just trying to recover, but because of the alcohol and my injuries I just couldn't get to my feet.

As I crouched there in my defensive state I was thinking how this had never happened to me before, and how I had taken some big punches in the past. This time it just felt different, and I instantly thought that maybe somebody had bottled me. Eventually the commotion around me just evaporated and finally my legs decided they were ready to work. As I struggled to my feet a bouncer helped steady me and shouted for someone to bring a towel. It was a strange feeling. I was almost blind, with only a small tube-like passage of vision, which I can only describe as like looking down a Smarties container, but with really bad blurred vision. I started to feel a warm sensation running down my face, so I cupped my hands to see what was dripping. I could see that my hands were red, and blood was pouring from multiple wounds. I remember a woman asking if I was okay, and I just replied, "Do I look like I'm okay?" By this time, I'd started to try and use the brilliant white towel to stop the bleeding, but I didn't know where to cover first. I pressed it onto my face to try and stem the flowing river of blood, but within a second it was completely saturated.

I wanted to leave the bar under my own steam. I pushed a helping bouncer aside and stumbled outside, where I bumped into the lads I'd come with. Woody had now come to, and he was being helped into the back of Nick's car. I'd started to recover and come round, but I was still struggling with my vision. One of my eyes was firmly shut and the other about half-way closed. It felt like something was strange in my mouth and after feeling around with my bloodied fingers I realised I was missing a few teeth. This angered me more and I wanted immediate revenge. I could see a group of lads standing on the other side of the road and one of them kept looking over and laughing.

I knew this bastard was my attacker and I thought, *I don't care what happens next. I'm going to fuck him up.*

There was a Budweiser bottle lying by me, so I reached over and took in my shaking hand. I broke the end to leave a nice sharp edge, perfect for my planned attack. My plan in my head was to go up to him and stick it straight in his throat and watch this fucker bleed out, like he had with me. That's how angry I had become. I was still a bit unsteady on my feet as I made my move towards my prey. This is what revenge felt like. Just as I moved into range, a big burly bouncer rapped his bear-like arms around me and dragged me off. He then said that he'd just saved me from making a huge mistake and to leave it to the police.

I was bundled into the back of Nick's car and we raced away from the bloody scene before the police arrived and started asking too many questions. With Nick probably over the limit, it was wisest to make a quick getaway and head back to base. Talk in the car on the way back to camp was quite jovial, when we started knocking Woody about being dropped by one punch. Soon the booze in my system had started to wear off and I now had an extreme pain radiating from my left eye. We arrived back at camp and were taken straight to the guardroom. Up until this point I hadn't really seen what was left of my mangled face, but when I saw the guard commander looking at me in horror, I imagined it couldn't be too clever. We were told to sit down on an old torn-up sofa, one that looked like it was only good for an old shaggy dog to lie on, and then the duty medic was called. I remember joking with Woody about never going out with him again. He had a large scab on the right side of his mouth, probably about two inches long. Then when he laughed it opened right up, like his mouth had doubled in size. The medic now started to hand out field dressings and it was at this point it became apparent that we probably needed hospital treatment.

The pair of us were taken to Peterborough hospital under the care of duty Sgt B., and seen immediately. I remember only very little of nurses stitching my face, head and ear back together. But I do remember at one stage having to be held down by Sgt B., after having a needle stuck through my ear. Apparently after they had stitched my face back together they tried to start work on my ear, but I was having none of it. I jumped from the bed and tried to attack the helping nurse. I was completely out of my mind and have no recollection of this ever happening. I found out the next day when I bumped into Sgt B.

I woke the following morning in a hospital bed and it felt like I had been hit by a train. I could barely see two feet in front of me and really wanted to look at what was left of my face. Woody was in the bed opposite me and had eighty stitches keeping his cheek from becoming his mouth again. We shared a brief conversation, before I staggered in the direction of the nearest toilet to get a close look at what that fucker from the previous night had done. I had to pretty much press my face up to the cold mirror, just so I could examine the damage and what I saw wasn't good. I couldn't even see the bridge of my nose. It had been swallowed up by the swelling around my eyes. My left eye was completely closed and the other one wasn't much better. My ear had been stitched back together and I had a few big bruises and lumps on the top of my head. I returned to my bed feeling a bit sorry for myself and just sat there waiting for the nurses to come round.

I kept thinking about what the Company Sergeant Major was going to say and if I was in any trouble. I knew that we hadn't been in any out-of-bounds places. Or so I thought, but still, I couldn't help thinking I was going to get a roasting. This was all I needed. I'd only been in my battalion five minutes and already had a name for myself, granted for only getting my head kicked in, but still people still knew who I was after that. The doctor came round and gave me a full examination, but he struggled to get my left eye to open. He then informed me that I needed to go for a CAT scan, and after that I would need to see an eye specialist as the eye looked in a very bad way.

I sat around waiting for a few hours until I was called for my appointment. I went for the scan first and the doctor was quite amazed that I hadn't any fractures. She said I must have a very hard skull and also reassured me that there was no other damage and that I had been very lucky. Then they sent me to the eye specialist, where the news wasn't so good. It looked as if I had a detached retina that would hopefully fix itself, but I would need further appointments to see if my eye would return to where it had been previously.

I was given the all-clear to return to camp, but I had to come back in ten days to check on my eye's recovery. I'd received a text message saying someone from my battalion was on his way to collect me, and now I started to think about what I was going to say to my CSM. Was he going to grill me, or would he believe my story? I would get an answer to my fears shortly. A minibus turned into the hospital entrance and I recognised the driver as a corporal from the military transport department. I jumped on board, where he took one look at me and jokingly said. "Good night?" I cracked a smile and took a seat. As we took the nervous journey back to camp, he reassured me that the CSM wasn't mad, he just wanted to know if I was okay. He mentioned that one of the other lads that I had been with the night before had told the guard commander that the attacker had used a knuckleduster. I was in shock and it was the first I knew about that, even though I'd thought something wasn't right the second I'd been struck.

The minibus was waved through the main gates and I was quickly taken to the company office where the CSM was waiting for me. I reluctantly marched into his office and halted in front of him, nearly falling over as my legs were still not a hundred percent.

"Sit down. How are you feeling? I must admit you look fucking awful," he commented.

"I'm okay, sir, just a bit unsteady. But hopefully I'll make a full recovery." I went on to tell him about what had happened and that I needed to return to the hospital in ten days for further checks. He had questions for me, of course.

"Right, now I need to ask you one more question and I want you to be completely honest with me. Do you understand?"

"Yes, Sir." I started to shit myself, because I thought that I'd fucked up somehow.

"Were you really in Grantham last night or in Stamford? I ask because I've heard rumours that you were in Stamford."

I had known from my very first day that Stamford was out of bounds after six o'clock from previous trouble. It had transpired that a group of soldiers from my unit had put some local lad in a coma. Now the CSM thought I was there, and they had taken some sort of revenge. I told him again that I was telling the truth about where the event had taken place, and that I knew the consequences of lying to him. He said that he believed me, and he would speak to me on Monday morning when I returned to duty. He then surprisingly also told me that he had called my Mom and had filled her in on what had happened. He had told her that it was probably a good idea that she came and collected me, instead of me travelling back home on the train. He justified this by saying that he didn't want people seeing serving soldiers battered and bruised and making the battalion look bad.

I could tell as soon as I saw Mom that she was holding back the tears and I just climbed into the car without really saying anything. She spun the car around and headed towards the main gates before turning right and making our way back to Birmingham. On the journey I fell asleep and when we finally arrived home, Mom told me that she had stopped at a set of traffic lights, where she witnessed a passenger in the car next to us staring over and pointing at my mangled face.

I was told to rest up and was given medication to help with the healing. By now, my eye now was acting very peculiarly. I would turn my head and it was as if my eye took a few seconds to catch up with the head movement. This was a very difficult time for me, and with my appointment with the eye specialist coming up soon, I hoped all would be okay. If it wasn't, I faced the real possibility that my Army days could be over before they'd really had a chance to blossom.

I returned to camp on the Monday morning and went for my meeting with the CSM. He told me that my story about my whereabouts had checked out and the police wanted me to go and make a statement. Before I left his office, he reminded me of my loyalty to the battalion. He informed me that as there had been so much bad press about the battalion in the recent past, and even though I hadn't done anything wrong, I should think about how this could be perceived. He went on to say that he had every confidence in me that I would do the right thing and that I should just think of this as a learning curve. With the words of the CSM still ringing in my ears, I found my lift and headed to the police station. After I arrived I said that I couldn't really remember the night in question and wouldn't be able to identify the group of lads. I went on to say that I didn't really want to take it any further and that I just wanted to move on and forget the whole incident had ever happened.

After completing a short rehab, my eye luckily returned to normal, but that couldn't be said for my confidence. That took months and I was always wary of people around me when I had a few drinks in me. It had been the first time I had been in a fight and not been able to fight back, or even defend myself properly.

It's funny how things changed for me after the knuckleduster incident and probably in a good way. I was well known around the battalion as the guy who went out on the piss and got my head smashed in. Even people I hadn't ever met before would come up to me and ask about what had happened that night.

Even though this was a difficult time for me, I started to feel part of something really special, like I had become part of a family. One night especially springs to mind. I was in the NAFFI when I was approached by a few lads just returned from Northern Ireland. Somehow, they had heard what had happened to me, and they said we should go back to Grantham. They said that there was a load of lads who wanted to search for my attackers and give them a right hiding. Teach them not to mess with the Fusiliers. Even though I declined, I still thought, *Wow! This is what the Army is all about. They don't even know me from Adam, but still they want to go out of their way for me and put themselves in harm's way*. Maybe this was the learning curve that the CSM was trying to get through to me.

Chapter nine – Fitting in

A few weeks passed, and it was now my turn to finally get a taste of Northern Ireland. I was about to be flown over the Irish Sea to start my two-year posting. This was something I was very happy about, to finally put all the shit of that fateful night behind me and start the next challenging chapter of my military career.

After arriving in N.I. we were all bundled into the back of seven and a half-tonne trucks and driven the long journey to Palace Barracks. We stopped at a set of traffic lights and, hearing the local lingo bursting through the thin aluminium walls for the very first time, I remember thinking that the local people had no idea that there were thirty or so soldiers huddled up together in the pitch black in the back of this stinky old lorry. We arrived about ninety minutes later, not really knowing where the hell we were. The shutter at the back of the lorry started to creak and crack, and with a loud bang it was suddenly forced open. As the beautiful sunlight burst its way through, it burnt my retinas as I struggled to pick out moving shadows. I hoped it was welcoming soldiers and not balaclava-clad IRA thugs greeting us with barrels of AK47s pointing directly at us.

I was still part of HQ Company and waiting to be assigned a company, and I still had one more element of training to get ticked off. So for the next week I was sent with a number of lads to Ballykinler to complete my N.I. training. This is where you spend a week learning what is expected of you while you're serving here. They showed us videos and pictures of what can happen if you let your guard down, one such video still so vivid in my mind. It was of two corporals who, while conducting operations in Belfast, accidentally drove into a funeral procession and were quickly identified as British soldiers. They were dragged from their car in broad daylight, taken to nearby wasteland, beaten, tortured and then finally executed. Even though this event had taken place in

1988, I was now under no illusions that this was still a very dangerous place. One mistake could easily cost you your life.

I completed my Northern Ireland training and returned to Palace Barracks, where I was finally told what company I was going to. I had to report to B company lines on the Monday morning when I would be told what platoon I was going to be part of. I was a bit nervous and apprehensive about joining a new company. Until this point I had mainly only been around people who had joined with me, or just after. I had not really spent any time with lads who had served on operations, and I didn't know what kind of reception I would receive when I got there. The weekend raced by without incident and before I knew it, I was making that dreaded walk over to my new company. I reported to Lance Corporal P., who was the duty corporal at the time, and was ordered to wait outside the block until called. My nerves hadn't settled, and this was only made worse by the dirty looks I kept receiving from passers-by. It was like every hateful look was saying that I wasn't wanted in their company, even though they didn't even know me yet. Finally, somebody called me.

"You the new guy?"

"Yes, Corporal," I replied.

"Right, then, follow me." He led me into the block and up the stairs towards a blue door. The room I was headed for was room 104 and I was shown to a bed space.

It was at this point I realized he was not a corporal at all, but just a fusilier, like myself. The sod hadn't even had the common courtesy to correct me. I started to unpack my belongings and took in my new surroundings. It's always a nervous time when you first turn up somewhere new. You don't know what to expect, and you end up believing what anybody says. I had been assigned to six platoon, but I would have to wait a while until I got to meet them. Most of the guys, including the platoon commander and platoon sergeant, were at a shooting competition and weren't due back till later in the week. Luckily, one of the lads that I had been bunked up with for the past few weeks had also come over with me from HQ Company, so we spent our time with each other.

Damien H., or H as I would call him, is a great lad. We sort of got introduced to each other in North Luffenham, but never really hit it off. He had joined after me, about six weeks later. At first, I thought he was a bit of a dick, but the more I started to hang around with him the more he kind of grew on me. When I came over to Ireland we shared a room and he was the first guy I went out to Belfast with on the piss. He's the kind of bloke that when you were on the piss and if there was any trouble, you knew he'd got your back. With him by my side I never felt in any real danger and we had some really crazy nights, some things that could never go into a book.

Once we went into Belfast on a night out, just the two of us. To start with, he was on his best behaviour, but before long he started necking shots and I began to envisage how the rest of the evening would turn out. He drunkenly talked me into going to a bar that I knew was out of bounds, but he assured me that he had been there many times and had never had any trouble. I only really went with him to make sure he stayed out of trouble and for some reason he seemed to listen to me when he was being a drama. We took a black cab to the bar, another big no-no as we were only supposed to use cleared taxi firms. He said that he had always used them and had never experienced anything out of the ordinary.

We pulled up outside the bar and I could tell from the clientele that was hanging around the establishment that this wasn't the kind of place where off-duty soldiers should be enjoying a night out. Just before we got out of the cab, I again made my concerns apparent. But this time I knew if I didn't go with him, he would go in alone and the mood he was in, there would definitely be trouble. The bouncers gave us an intense look up and down, it was like they were trying to sniff out trouble. After thirty seconds or so, one of them turned to me and asked if we were soldiers, and they said that it would be a very bad idea to come in if we were. I said we weren't and that we worked for a gas company and we were contracted to a job at the docks for the next six months. Whether he believed me or not, we were allowed to enter and headed straight to the bar, where H ordered a couple of pints.

The bar was rocking and full of fit Irish birds and I could now see the attraction of this place. Still, in the back of my mind I knew we shouldn't be in there. If any of the hooligan locals got wind that our cover story was bullshit we could be right in the thick of things, and maybe we would be lucky to escape this place in the same state as we entered. After only ten minutes of being in there we were approached by two beautiful busty blondes, who with a thick Belfast accent asked us if we were soldiers. I repeated my cover story and offered to buy the pair a drink, which they accepted. The two of them were draped all over us and it felt as if the heating in the club had been cranked up to the max. The smell of brain-washing perfume and vodka Red Bulls started to play on my emotions and I could feel myself falling for my mysterious blonde. Luckily, common sense decided to make an appearance and I started to have random thoughts from stories I had heard about how the IRA used beautiful women as honey traps.

After finally getting my senses back, I was now trying to play it cool and not blow my story. I did nearly slip up when one of the women asked me about how long I had been here, which I nearly answered with, "I was deployed here about three months back," but stopped myself just before deployed and continued with, "My company asked for volunteers to do a three to six-month contract and I've been here about six weeks." The problem with this lie is that you never know who you're talking to and they could turn out to also work for a gas company and rumble you.

It happened once when I'd had got talking to some women in a local bar and they asked what I was doing in Belfast. I told them I was a football scout working for Birmingham City (thought it would be more believable than saying from Aston Villa) and was over here for the weekend, looking at a few of the local teams, which included Glentoran. At this point, the lady who I had been getting friendly with started telling me about her brother, who played for Glentoran, who was in fact their star striker. She then went on to say that he was here with her and proceeded to go and fetch him. She returned and introduced us, and I couldn't believe my luck.

I was now deep into this lie, but I thought, *Fuck it*, and began laying it on thick. He started getting excited by the prospect of maybe joining a high-level team (if you can class Blues as that) and went off to the bar to buy me a drink. By this time, I was thinking I could be on for a right winner tonight, free drinks and a half decent bird. As the night continued, my new best friend started to annoy me and eventually I had to make a quick getaway after saying I was going to the toilet.

A few hours later, hailing a taxi, my new best friend re-appeared and started chewing my ear off again. The final straw came when I got in the taxi and he got in too. He started saying that I could really help his career and all that sort of rubbish. I eventually had to threaten him with violence to get him out of my taxi, and I took this as a lesson learned about how deep one should dig themselves. Looking back now, I think he was just a bit of an idiot, and maybe not a footballer at all.

Back to my situation in the out-of-bounds bar; we had now ended up on the dance floor with our not-too-shy lady friends, and with the DJ pumping out some great classic RnB tunes, I started to feel more comfortable. As I looked through my blurred vision at the dancing crowd I could see H just standing there, just staring at two big trees propping up the bar. I started to fear the worst and tried to get his attention. Finally, he caught my worried stare and smiled in a way I had seen many times before and since this night.

It was about now that he ripped his shirt from his muscular back and starting to kiss his patriotic English tattoo on his bulging right biceps. I tried to get to him before anyone got hurt, and I made my move towards him. I started to drag people out of my way in a desperate rush, almost sending an unfortunate kissing pair flying onto a nearby table.

I was too late. During my scramble to get hold of H, he had confidently made his way to the bar and set about cutting down those two trees. I looked on in utter shock as he grabbed the pair each by their shirt collars and slammed their heads together. When I eventually reached him, both were out cold and bloody on the grimy bar floor. Unbelievably, H was standing at the bar, calmly ordering two more Stellas. Now bouncers and some of the unconscious guys' friends starting frantically moving towards us, and with all my strength I had to pretty much drag H from the bar and into a nearby taxi, while he was still trying to guzzle down his fresh Stella. The angry looking group quickly headed our way, while I was arguing with the taxi driver to just drive before he got his car smashed up by the revenge-seeking bloodthirsty mob. As the first guy neared the door and reached out to grab the locked handle, I started to expect the worst, but thankfully the taxi driver finally came to his senses and put his foot to the floor and in a cloud of tyre smoke, we escaped the area with our lives and got away to safety.

"What the fuck, H? Are you fucking crazy?" I shouted, at which he just started laughing.

"We got out of there, didn't we? You worry too much, mate." Unbelievable!

It wasn't just when I was with H that things turned nasty. There seemed to be a lot of lads in my battalion who just couldn't grasp the gravity of where we were, and they would go out at night there with the same mentality they had when they were on leave.

Where the worst that's probably going to happen is that you get a bit of a beating, or you get arrested by the local constabulary.

It was the end of a drink-fuelled evening and I'd been out with a few lads, just a normal Friday night, really. I was leaving one of the local clubs, when I started to hear raised voices coming from a bar down the street. I looked over intensely and noticed a few lads that I recognised scuffling with some of the locals. I raced over and quickly took stock of the situation. Now, most of the drama had died down and then one of my mates from six platoon, Sean M., came walking towards me while at the same time telling the other lads to shut up and calm down. I took a look around and noticed it was a bunch of younger lads that had only just turned up at the battalion. Sean then told me that they'd been mouthing off to some locals, who in turn had attacked them before being separated by some door staff and sent on their way.

Suddenly a group of lads, probably ten in total, turned the corner and headed our way. Michael, another lad Joinsey, and I started trying to round up the youngsters to throw them into the back of nearby taxis. Then another youngster started gobbing off about being in the Army, so I quickly grabbed hold of him and shut him up with a few well-aimed slaps. The angry looking group had now got within striking distance as we bundled the last few stragglers into the safety of the waiting taxi. The feisty group now encircled Michael and me, and they were screaming and shouting in that Belfast accent that we were about to get fucked up and that lads from the Shankill estate were on their way to finish us off. We stood back to back and held on to each other's shirts. I said to Michael, "Whatever happens now, don't let go."

By this time, a few brave lads had started to move forward to engage us, but they were met with stiff resistance. I threw punches with my one free hand and sent powerful kicks to their bodies or bollocks; wherever they landed was good for me. One of our attackers tried to sneak his way to the side of us, but he was met with a front kick to the chest which sent him crashing to the concrete. The situation started to grow more dire as the crowd started to grow in numbers, and their aggression had been upped by fresh members. I started to fear the worst and knew we needed to flee the area as soon as possible.

A black car with tinted blacked-out windows came flying round the corner and mounted the pavement, sending the angry crowd fleeing in all directions. The rear passenger-side window started to slowly come down and the first thing that entered my mind was that it was a fucking drive-by. I looked around for any cover but to no avail, and I just waited for the inevitable weapon to become visible.

"Get in now," the welcome voice of Claude shouted in our direction. So we both frantically clambered through the open back window as he hit the accelerator, and with my legs still hanging out, we headed back to camp.

The rest of my platoon returned from the shooting team and I was called into the office to meet my Platoon Sergeant and Platoon Commander. Sergeant J. introduced himself and laid out his guidelines of what he expected from me to fit in to his platoon. I was then introduced to Second Lieutenant O'H., who reiterated Sgt J.'s rules, and said that only the best was expected of me to fit in.

I was glad to have finally met most of my new platoon, but there was one person I hadn't. Everywhere I went people, kept asking me if I'd met Lance Corporal S. yet. I kept thinking to myself, *Fuck, who is this guy everyone keeps going on about? He must be some crazy bastard.* Well, it wouldn't be long before I got the chance to meet him. It was a Friday night and it was six platoon's time to take over the guard duty. I checked the company detail and could see Cpl S. was the guard second in charge and so I thought, *Here we go. Time to meet this elusive beast that everyone keeps going on about.*

Cpl N. marched us to the guard room and we were given our tasks. I was first on CCTV and received a full handover/takeover from the off-going fusilier. I hadn't been on long when someone stuck their head into the CCTV room and asked if I wanted a brew. I could see one stripe on his rank slide, so I replied with, "Yes, please, Corporal." I had no idea who he was, but I thought there was no way it could be Cpl S., because from all the stories I had heard, I couldn't imagine him making me a brew. He returned with my drink and placed it on the side next to me.

"Thank you, Corporal," I replied.

"Don't worry about the Corporal bit. You can call me Chris. Chris S…" I was in shock. How could this be the guy everyone was telling me about? One of the kindest, most well-spoken people you would ever have the privilege of meeting, a proper gent. Don't get me wrong, he looked like he could do you some right serious damage if you ever got on the wrong side of him. Or if you were unfortunately picked on the opposite side when playing rugby, which I witnessed a few times in battalion rugby matches.

I will always remember a time when we were on a practice riot in Ballykinler. It had been a hell of a day. A real war with the Green Jackets, as they had been playing enemy for us! Chris was my shield team commander and we had been in the midst of a really good old battle. The shield teams had been out in front of the vehicles and then withdrawn back, when we noticed Chris wasn't with us. I started to try and locate our commander, when I caught sight of him with no shield, no stick, just beating the hell out of people with his bare hands. Not that we needed to, as he was dealing with the situation quite nicely, but we decided to rush out to save the crowd from further beatings.

The practice riots here were unbelievably crazy, maybe even worse than the real deal. The morning after one, we could barely get ourselves out of bed. The day would usually start with just some run of the mill briefings about how the course would be split up into different elements. This was where we rotated between different types of training; baton gun training; defensive driving if we were one of the drivers; how to put ourselves out in case of a petrol-bombing attack; and then we would take part in what they called the gauntlet. We would have to start at one end of the street, dressed in full public order uniform with shield and stick. We would then have to battle our way past people who in turn were wearing protective suits, and they would do whatever they wanted to do to take us down. Finally, we would be left with no stick and no shield, just our hands and our wits to survive the last attack. After everyone had gone through this cycle, we would stop for food before we put everything we had learned into place in the evening's main event.

This would entail how riot conditions change, starting from just a bit of verbal aggression from the crowd, all the way up to a full-scale battle where it's pretty much fighting for survival. We had taken part in the first two phases and apart from a bit of argie bargie, it had passed without any serious trouble. It was now time for the main event. At Ballykinler there were two large steel gates at the opening of the village, and with us on one side and the rioters on the other, it was all set up for a gladiator-type battle. The gates were slowly opened, and we just charged towards them, screaming and shouting like some kind of thirteenth century angry Scottish clan attacking their English invaders. To the credit of the rowdy enemy, they didn't take a backwards step, but instead charged towards us in the same manner as we were doing, and with a massive crash of shield on angry protesters, we hit.

It was now a full-on fight with both sides taking casualties, and sometimes we had to really think hard to remember that it was only a practice riot. After pushing the angry mob back towards the main junction where the road forked into two, they made good their escape to go and re-group. My section was now sent to clear the back alleys and gardens of the pretend Irish village. As the rest of the mob was concentrating its efforts elsewhere, we had a wild time just catching up with stray protesters and giving them a good old-fashioned kicking; only returning the favour from when we had played enemy for them, I hasten to add.

We noticed two guys heading down a side street, so we gave chase. As I rounded a corner, my world went white. My head banging on the pavement and a soldier's size tens rushing by my head brought me back to reality. I just lay there on the concrete, trying to take stock of what had just happened. At first, I thought something was wrong with my vision, but it turned out that my visor had been completely smashed by whatever had violently hit me. I found out afterwards that the enemy had tied boxing gloves filled with sand onto broom handles and as I had rounded the corner, some good-for-nothing scrote had cleaned me out with one brutal swing of his makeshift weapon.

After fixing a new visor to my helmet I headed straight back into the fight, seeking immediate retribution. I now didn't care if I found the culprit or not. The only thing I knew was the next scumbag rioter I came across was going to get it big time. I met back up with my section and chased a group of lads into an open area. Then we engaged with them in a battle to the end, but more and more rioters joined the fight until we were completely outnumbered and surrounded. We formed a defensive position, so our backs were up against a brick wall, and we started to fend off the countless waves of pissed-off attackers. It seemed that however hard we hit them, they just kept coming back for more. It was if they enjoyed the violence just as much as us.

Finally, our defensive line was breached, and it had now become a fist fight. A giant member of the enemy grabbed me and started slamming me up against a wall, while another cowardly reprobate starting to attack my mid-section with dirty body punches. I now knew I would have to fight fire with fire and started fighting back. The cowardly body-puncher was dispatched quickly enough with a well-timed right hook, which just left me to dispose of the jolly green giant that was manhandling me. In this situation you have two choices, throat or bollocks. As this was a practice riot which had obviously got out of control, I chose the guy's manhood and attacked there. Three or four punches to his unprotected crown jewels later chopped down this big tree and he fell to the ground in an agonised heap, holding his now battered nether regions, to go along with his bruised ego.

The battle raged long into the night until we finally got control of the situation. I think it was the realisation of the training team that people were starting to get seriously injured that really brought proceedings to an end. After the riot had ended we were just hanging around the Land Rovers, talking about different battles that we had each been involved with. Suddenly this giant black guy came walking over and started to demand the identity of the fucker who had punched him in the nuts. I didn't fancy another fight with this six-foot plus monster and as I'd just spent nearly six hours fighting, I decided it would better for both parties to keep my mouth shut. I also think the fact he looked even sodding bigger now I had calmed down also influenced my way of thinking.

I thought I had seen the last of Otterburn now I was in N.I., but much to my horror, the company commander had picked this despicable place for us to conduct a week's exercise. After hearing the news, my body shuddered at the very thought.

After the ferry journey to England we jumped onto coaches and made the long trek north towards our cold and wet destination. The whole way up you could tell no one on board, apart from probably the senior ranks, was looking forward to a week- long exercise. This was always a good chance for them to punish us, I suppose.

The company was there twenty minutes and we were straight out on the back area. Then we tabbed across harsh and hostile ground and with the rain falling heavy enough for me to drown in, it was business as usual. 'If it's not raining, it's not training' came into my thoughts again. Anyway, we spent the next few days doing the usual bullshit exercise stuff, river crossings, day and night patrols, being bugged out of our harbour area at stupid o'clock. All the good stuff like that. The things that made you glad you'd picked the infantry that day in the recruitment centre.

One night the platoon was told they needed to move to a different harbour area, which was up on a nearby mountain, probably only two hours on foot; or so we were told, although that estimation turned out to be wildly inaccurate. We headed off as normal in single file, leaving the usual five or so paces between one another, but straightaway I noticed how much the weather conditions had changed. The wind was now whistling in from the north and cutting through the hundred-year-old pine trees and hitting us straight in the face, almost taking my breath away. It got to a point where I needed to tuck my chin into the collar of my combat jacket just to try and get a little bit of respite. After breaking cover from amongst the trees, we headed out onto some fields where the underfoot conditions were acting mischievously, trying to slip me up with every step. It was now a massive challenge just to stay upright and as it was pitch black, I had to rely on all my senses to make sure I did.

The local farmer, who this land this belonged to, had only gone and dug great big holes, about five-foot square with some of them at least six feet deep. Now we all faced the reality of falling straight into them without any warning. Due to the fact we were conducting a full tactical exercise, all torches were completely forbidden and the only thing standing between us becoming piss wet through and stuck in one of these sinister holes was sheer luck.

I remember just following the man in front, trying like crazy to walk in his footsteps, matching him perfectly stride for stride, watching his cat's eyes flickering in the dark, when suddenly he just disappeared out of view and straight into one of those soul-destroying holes. As we were carrying kit upwards of one hundred and fifty pounds, we were in no condition to drag ourselves to safety and we relied entirely on the nearest lads to come and rescue us. People found themselves being dragged unceremoniously out of those farmer's traps, by whatever part of their body or kit the others could get hold of. After helping someone from an unwanted soaking, I started to follow, once again picking every step with an element of caution. Again, I watched on as someone disappeared. It was as if the ground just opened up and swallowed them whole. After rescuing Codhead for the second time in as many minutes, I continued my journey through this minefield of black watery holes.

I could now distinguish between water and the ground, from how the water was a slightly darker colour than the ground. Well that's what I thought anyway. I tracked the edge of another pool which took me towards a barbed wire fence and thought to myself, *There is no way there will be one here.* Then I took a step. Unfortunately for me I was very wrong, and I headed straight towards a black abyss of muddy water and shit. Luckily, though, just as I was about to fall straight in head first, I grabbed the last row of barbed wire with my right hand before I became another victim in the farmer's sick game. Regrettably I was still in need of assistance, as I still had my left leg completely submerged and with the weight of my bergen trying to drag me under, I was now just stuck, with my legs sort of in the splits position while still gripping to the fence with one hand. I waited for someone to come and rescue me and finally got dragged to my freezing feet by my Platoon Sergeant.

Finally, the Platoon Commanders saw sense and gave us permission to use flashlights to stop anyone seriously hurting themselves or even worse. Finally, after about an hour we made our way through the minefield of mud and water, and we clambered over a barbed wire fence, eventually escaping the field's evil grasp.

Now we were out in the open the wind was more of an evil adversary than before and without any trees providing cover, I felt like it was trying to cut me in half. The rain that had been stinging my face had now turned to snow. At first, I didn't even notice it was snowing. It was only when I looked down at my weapon I could see it settling on the top of the hand guard.

As the snow intensified, we headed up a nearby mountain to try and locate a place to stay the night. We spent the next three hours roaming around trying to locate our designated harbour area, but it seemed every area the boss took us to, all the trees had been chopped down. God knows what map he was trying to read, but it got to a point where he was relieved from map-reading duties by the Platoon Sergeant, much to his disgust. It was now a battle between life and death, with every failed attempt to locate our sleeping accommodation another person went 'man down'. The weather conditions were absolutely appalling, because by now, we were trying to make our way through three-foot snow drifts.

The Platoon Sergeant began to recognise that people were really starting to struggle, and he tried in vain to contact nearby units to mount a rescue of some form. Disappointingly, he was told that there was no way a chopper could be called in, and any vehicles would be incapable of navigating the steep and dangerous terrain. The only way out of this dire situation was on foot, and with the other units not having a clue where we were, it would be only blind luck that would get us out of this situation without someone succumbing to the worst that nature could throw at us.

Each step took maximum effort and I had now come to terms with the thought that I might not make it off this mountain. This was one of only a few times in my life that I mentally prepared myself for death. We were to finally take refuge from the conditions at the next wood line, only to then be informed that it had been cut down. I just fell backwards into a huge snow drift and that was it. I was ready to go. My body had taken all it could, and

I felt at peace, just ready to fall asleep and leave this evil situation behind me. Suddenly a voice in my mind shouted at me to get my ass up and stop being weak. So I did. After struggling to my feet, I noticed someone else slumped in the beautiful white snow, who had also thrown in the towel. I headed his way and dragged him back up, telling him it wasn't far, and to just hang on in there.

In the end, after what seemed like a lifetime, we finally reached our original destination shortly after three. They told us to set up our ponchos and get some shut-eye. After locating a suitable area, I set up my living quarters and tried everything to get some warmth into my broken and bruised body. Even though I was knackered, I thought a nice hot brew would do the trick, so I reached into my webbing to retrieve my water bottle. With my hands shaking uncontrollably, I struggled to undo the cap on my bottle, and after five failed attempts I finally prised the lid open and tilted the bottle towards my shaking mess tin. Strangely, no water poured out, even though the bottle was full. Feeling confused, I turned the bottle around, so I could inspect the problem and with one of my shaking fingers, reached in to find to my horror a solid block of ice. I was devastated, absolutely gutted. I just sat there in disbelief, thinking *What next?* My morale was hanging on by a small thread and I was dying for a sip of PG Tips. I honestly would have killed for it, if I had been capable of locating some. After my failed attempt at making a cup of the hot stuff, I gave up and made myself ready for bed. I leant forward to undo my laces and remove my boots, but my near frost-bitten fingers were again met with an icy barrier. My laces had frozen solid and would not budge. No matter how much I tried and begged, they were frozen solid. I felt like just bursting into tears. Finally, at near breaking point, I managed just to wriggle enough space to release my feet from their frozen prison and with the last ounce of strength I had, I zipped up my sleeping bag and fell asleep.

After what seemed like only a minute, I was rudely woken up by Colour Sergeant C. to carry out a morning attack on a nearby fake enemy. This felt like a massive kick in the bollocks after the previous night's hardships and it turned out I had only been asleep for just over an hour. You really have to love the Army sometimes. Bastards!

Chapter ten – Close calls

The NAFFI in Northern Ireland was quality. Friday and Saturday nights were buzzing. Before Colonel W. took over the battalion, all the local birds were allowed into camp, so you didn't even have to go into Belfast to pull. As long as you didn't mind the fact she had probably been with a few of your mates.

I remember a night I had been over at the NAFFI and to be honest, I'd had a bit of a bad night when it came to the ladies. I didn't pull anything, well, apart from maybe a muscle with some dodgy dance moves. I retreated to my room and got into my bed, sparked up a fag and started watching the end of *Match of the Day*. Suddenly the room door swung open and in walked some young brunette bird looking for some other guy. I told her that he wasn't in this block and I hadn't a clue where his room was.

"How about if I just spend the night here in your bed, then?" She just came out with it. Apart from *Match of the Day*, I didn't have any other plans, so I took her up on her offer.

The following morning, I woke to the realisation that I still had my brunette companion snoring in my left ear. After a quick morning repeat of the previous night, I now had the difficult task of walking her to the guardroom and getting her booked out of camp, or as many people call it, 'the walk of shame'. We made our way downstairs without being spotted, and as I got to the fire exit I opened it and said. "Let's go this way." Once she cleared the path for the door to close, I slammed it shut and told her to walk straight up the hill, and then I ran back upstairs to my room and locked the door behind me. Something I'm not too proud of now, but back then I was a different person. A bit of an ass-hole when it came to women, I unfortunately have to admit.

One night after leaving the NAFFI I headed back to the block a little the worse for wear. You know, when you end up taking one step forward and then two steps sideways. It was one of those kinds of nights. As I walked down the side of the block, I passed by one of the downstairs laundry room windows, and I noticed that the light was on. At first, I couldn't quite grasp what I was seeing, but soon realised that one of the lads that I knew well was trying to hang himself. I quickly rushed in and started to try and pull him down. Luckily, I had come in just in time and he hadn't quite got to that point of jumping. He started to argue with me, saying that he wanted to end it all and I should just leave and let him finish the job. I told him there was no way I would allow that to happen and to stop acting like he had nothing to give.

It was at this point that he climbed back on to the chair and slipped his makeshift noose around his pale white neck. I quickly reached out and aggressively grabbed him before he got a chance to kick the chair away. I unravelled his makeshift noose, which turned out to be two old Nokia phone chargers tied together. After I got him down from the chair he started to try and attack me like some kind of deranged monster. At first, I just tried to calm him with words, but after he tried to pin me up against the door and he grabbed me by my throat, I snapped. I took hold of him and pushed him up against the counter and told him to back off. He rushed me again, but this time before he could lay a finger on me I smacked him. After he hit the deck I held him then, and I shouted for the Company Duty Corporal to assist me. While I waited for help to arrive, I started to try and reason with him, but he was so emotional it was difficult to get any sense from him. He just kept mumbling something about how his girlfriend had cheated on him. Finally, Wes turned up and between the pair of us we managed to calm him down.

The upsetting thing about this shocking ordeal was that this would turn out not to be an isolated incident and just a sign of things to come for this young fusilier. The last thing I heard about him, he was living on the streets next to New Street Station in Birmingham, a very tragic case for one of the country's heroes, but something that is unfortunately echoed across the whole of Great

Britain. The government just doesn't do enough for us servicemen and women.

We had been sent on exercise to the northern coast of Northern Ireland, not far from Coleraine, and apart from it being bloody freezing, it was a nice little exercise, mostly because it was just practising vehicle patrols. Which is always a good thing; well, I always thought so anyway. We had reached the final day and the platoon was conducting drills which included checking culverts at the side of roads for anything suspicious. Nothing hard, really!

I was sitting in the rear of two vehicles and after the first had moved off, the driver in ours, who was really the commander of the Land Rover, prepared to move off. He had earlier asked the driver if he could get behind the wheel, even though he didn't hold a full licence to operate it. Anyway, Nicky attempted to pull away, but the Snatch stalled. It then took a further three attempts to get it started; very temperamental vehicles, especially when cold. After it finally burst into life, Nicky floored the accelerator to catch the other vehicle, which was now just a dot in the picturesque landscape. We raced at high speed down the steep country lanes, trying to catch up with the other vehicle, which had now, unbeknown to us, had its own mechanical issues and had just stopped in the middle of the road.

To be honest, Nicky was going at a stupid speed and completely ignoring the icy and snowy road conditions, and it wasn't till someone shouted for him to slow down that he finally realised that the Land Rover in front wasn't moving. He slammed the brakes on, but to no effect. We had hit a patch of black ice and there was no way in a month of Sundays that this three-tonne beast was ever going to stop in time. I will never forget the sound of locked-up brakes and screeching wheels as we headed to an almost certain serious accident. Everything was now in slow motion as the stranded vehicle in front became bigger and bigger, and I braced myself for the impending impact.

As we got within ten metres or so, two guys completely unaware of the deadly situation that was unfolding behind them, started climbing from the rear of the stranded Snatch. If it hadn't been for the lighting quick reactions of Scotty, who dragged them back inside and slammed the door shut, we would definitely have been dealing with a fatal accident that cold winter's day.

At the last possible second, Nicky tried to swerve and avoid the Snatch, but with steep banks on both sides and not really enough room to squeeze by, we ploughed straight into the back of the other vehicle, leaving both completely destroyed. I had been holding so hard it felt as if I had broken my arm, but as I looked around the mangled cab, I could tell I had come off the best out of everyone else. Blood was splattered up the riot shields that were slotted down the back of the seats, after Mike had smashed his head up against the metal Electronic countermeasure device during the impact. Climbing from what was left of the Snatch, I walked around to the impact sight and it was utter carnage. I could barely recognise the front of the Snatch. The news of the accident spread, and the area was soon overrun with senior platoon staff and first aiders, all trying to assist with the incident.

The twelve of us were carted off to Coleraine hospital, where everybody was checked out in priority order. The one person who *had* appeared to have made it out of the accident unscathed was next seen on a spinal board. It later turned out that H had broken his back. After being given the all-clear, with just a bit of bruising to my arm, I was reunited with the rest of the crash victims and taken back to Palace Barracks where a full investigation was carried out. A lot of us maintained that we had been asleep at the time, when apparently the two in the front had switched seats, and when everyone had come round from the crash, the pair of them were already out giving first aid. But Nicky was eventually dragged in front of the company sergeant major to explain his actions. Luckily for him, he was allowed to keep his rank, he just ended up with a shedload of extra duties for his troubles.

Chapter eleven – Hot and cold

I will never forget my first full-scale riot. Yes, I had been involved in little skirmishes before, but nothing like this one. This day changed my whole perspective on how I perceived Northern Ireland, and I started to understand more about the troubles that had plagued this country for so many years.

On the morning of the twelfth of July 2004, we were ordered to be up early-doors. Four-thirty to be precise, and in Army terms this can sometimes be seen as a bit of a lie-in. We collected our weapons from the armoury and headed for an early appointment with the cookhouse for a bit of breakfast. First parade was at five fifteen, when we would prepare the Land Rovers for the day's tasks. This would always turn into a bit of a laugh, watching a team of soldiers trying to fit all our equipment into the back of the Snatch and arguing about where we would all sit, each of us trying to get one of the two back seats, so we could have the back door slightly ajar to enjoy the beautiful fresh air rushing in when we were on the move. The back of the Snatch could be an unbearable place most of the time, especially in the summer with the temperatures creeping their way up into the mid-thirties. This situation was only made worse with all our kit on, which included our fireproof undergarments that also doubled up as long johns in the winter months. Good old British Army coming up with effective cost-cutting ideas.

The convoy bumped over the speed bumps at the camp entrance and headed off in single file. My Land Rover was second from the front, commanded by Sgt J., who I admired and tried to base my Army career on, but ultimately failed. He was a fantastic soldier who led by example and who I would follow into any battle regardless of any fear I might be harbouring. A great soldier and a man that I still now have the greatest respect for.

We headed north towards a small barracks in North Belfast called Girdwood, a place that I had staged on many occasions. The front sanger (guard tower) looked out onto a large housing estate which was separated by a peace wall, with protestants to the left and catholics to the right, and depending on how brave we felt, it determined which way we would drive or walk when leaving the camp for daily patrols. We stayed there for about half an hour, waiting for further orders from the police. This lull gave us all time to think about what could be waiting for us when we were finally deployed. This was always a difficult time because there was no adrenalin to keep us from feeling nervous and we hoped our training would kick in when it really mattered.

Finally, we got the all-clear over the radio to move off, and now there was no more time to think about the what ifs. My platoon was tasked to meet up with a police unit and to head to Lisburn Rd where there had been reports of clashes between rival protesters. I was now in no doubt about the task in hand and envisaged trouble ahead, and I also thought that this was going to be an important day in my Army career. Something I couldn't wait to tell my mates back home about.

We rendezvoused with the police unit and travelled a short distance to the location of the clashes, annoyingly, only to find the area quiet and without trouble, which was a big surprise and disappointment to most of us. We parked up and dismounted. We then intelligently positioned the vehicles in such a way that meant no one could approach us from behind and that there was only about two feet between each one. The thing about the Army and stuff like this is you can sit around for hours on end waiting for something to happen and most of the time nothing does. This day certainly had that feel to start with, but the real danger of this is you start to become complacent. Thankfully, as always, Sgt J. would remind us to the contrary. There were a few drunk stragglers that passed by who threw a few obscenities at us, but most were repelled by the threat of force being used against them.

As the day dragged on in the baking heat, we grew more and more frustrated by the lack of action. Then suddenly a report came over the radio which brought us all to attention. The radio operator said that a large group, maybe two to three hundred people, were heading in our direction. This mob had already been hostile to another unit, so we knew they would want to try and mix things up with us, which we were quite happy to reciprocate.

The group arrived in dribs and drabs, but they were easily pushed back by the stern word. Soon the mob grew into vastly more than the two to three hundred that were estimated earlier, much closer to a thousand or maybe even more. It was now apparent that we would be right in the thick of it if they decided to take us on, and it didn't take long for the first bottle of piss to hit me flush on the visor. The furious mob had now turned violent and was trying to breach our cordon, but it was met with controlled aggression.

The way we had positioned the Land Rovers meant we had created a wedge shape between every other one. So now alcohol-fuelled rioters had become trapped from the crowd behind them and couldn't escape from baton strikes. Now rocks and the random golf balls being struck with tennis rackets whistled by like bullets, and I ended up taking a direct hit to my unprotected delicate area by a well-aimed or lucky-shot protester. I didn't want to show that it had hurt, so I found protection behind a Land Rover to make good my recovery.

After shaking off my injury, I returned to the cordon just in time for the petrol bombing to commence. About four to five petrol bombs were aimed in my direction, but without successfully igniting themselves, until the sixth engulfed me and another soldier in a blaze of fire. The smell of burning materials kicked us into action and we followed our training procedures to put ourselves out. This was to hit the deck and roll to try and suffocate the flames. I then waited for the fire guy to save us from the intense heat.

Finally- the fire was put out and I dragged myself to my feet and continued the fight.

Earlier in the day, Sgt J. had designated me the baton gunner and I was now being called forward by him to take out one of the main petrol bombers.

"AP, see that guy, blue jeans red top?"

"Yes, Sergeant," I replied.

"Next time he pops up in the open, take him out."

"With pleasure, Sergeant." I took cover just behind the righthand side of one of the Land Rovers so only my right side was visible, and I started to track my target. I was still taking the random rocks and golf balls, but I was determined to take this guy out. My opportunity came when he appeared from behind a blue Ford Escort. So I took aim, took a deep breath and steadied myself. I then placed my index finger on the steel trigger and went to fire. Suddenly, out of nowhere, a young boy ran into shot, so I aborted my mission. I couldn't risk hitting him instead of my target and luckily for that good-for-nothing villain, another clear shot never materialised.

The crowd started to thin out as more police presence had moved into the area. Now most of the crowd to our front were just milling around, enjoying the last of the day's sunshine, with a can of their favourite tickle in one hand, and puffing on their hand-made Golden Virginia roll-ups, which I must say I preferred the smell of burning petrol to.

After nearly fourteen hours of duty the call was made for our platoon to mount up and head back to Palace Barracks where we could finally get a well-earned rest. But then from the radio a voice that I recognised as Lt O. ordered the convoy to stop and he said the words that you never wanted to hear: that someone was missing from another unit. We sat there for an agonising ten minutes, hoping they could locate the missing soldier. When the radio rustled into life once more and informed everyone that he had been located fit and well, we finally moved off and arrived back at camp twenty minutes later to the great relief of everyone. After handing in my weapon and grabbing something to eat, I sent a text message to my Mom to reassure her that I was okay, just in case she caught any of this the following morning on the BBC news.

While we were based at Palace Barracks in Northern Ireland, all the companies were moving through a monthly cycle. A month on guard, a month on two hours' notice to move, and following that, a month on eight hours' notice to move. Then finally either a month at Girdwood or at New Barnsley police station. Apart from being on two hours' notice to move, this was a good cycle. The two hours' NTM was rotten, because we couldn't leave camp unless we were only going to the Tesco down the road, and we definitely couldn't have a drink. Well, to start with, we were allowed two drinks, but you know soldiers can't be trusted. One leads to two, two leads to four and so on before someone was up on orders the following day after they smashed the block up. Remember that, H? So that rule was banned very quickly.

My company was coming to the end of one of these dreaded months and we were only a couple of hours away from taking over the eight-hour cycle. Talk around the company was rife of what people had planned for the evening. Everyone was talking about what was going to be their first beverage when they finally finished and as this was a Friday, I imagined there was going to be some sore heads the following morning.

Whispers had started to swirl round the company that a major police operation had taken place at an old farm just outside Belfast and that one of the battalion's companies would be tasked to support the police. We hoped that it wouldn't be us, as we had only a couple of hours to push before A company was due to relieve us. So we hoped it would be them who would take over the task. I was sitting in my room just chatting to some of the lads about how drunk we were going to get that night, then from downstairs an angry sounding voice echoed around the block for everyone to get on parade. At this point I started to get the feeling that there would be no boozing tonight and as I got outside and formed up, I could tell that everyone was thinking the same as me.

Company Sergeant Major P. breezed through the company headquarters door and addressed his company.

"I have some good news and I have some bad news," he roared. "The bad news is you're not coming off two hours' NTM tonight. The good news is no one's going to have a hangover in the morning." He went on to explain that there had indeed been a massive operation carried out by the police and that the company might still be called upon to assist. He continued that HQ Company wanted to keep two companies ready to move, just in case something happened, and as we were already prepared to deploy, it would be us first to go out on the ground.

Sgt I. called everyone from six platoon to his office and explained in further detail what was unfolding and what our next step was. We would go to the armoury to collect weapons and then return and leave them in the office, where there would then be a stag system put in place for the platoon to take turns watching them. At the same time, everyone else went to the cookhouse or the NAFFI for their evening meal. After that we would return to the block and await further orders. We were called back on parade an hour later and informed that everyone one was to go to the ops room for a briefing. It quickly came apparent that we were in fact going to be deployed and were briefed on the location of the farm and the surrounding areas. The operations officer then explained that the farm had been harbouring a locally known terrorist group. He went on to say that when they had been arrested, the police had searched the property and found a huge weapons cache, along with a load of cash and drugs. Our mission was to head to the site and secure the nearby area until first light. So then the police could continue their search in daylight, as it was feared that the ghastly mob had boobytrapped the basement and some of the small outbuildings around the farm. This sounded like a good task and most of the lads seemed chuffed to be involved, but there were a few who were pretty pissed off and just wanted to go and sink a few ales in the bar.

At half seven the call was made to load into the Land Rovers and make the thirty-minute journey to the terrorists' hideaway. We would then rendezvous with the police and be given our orders for the night. It was already well down below freezing on this late November night and the back of the Snatch felt more like a freezer. I reached into my day sack and retrieved my softy (a thermal jacket, which felt like wearing a sleeping bag.) I put it on under my combat jacket and settled back down, just listening to the occasional chatter on the airwaves. Lance Cpl McN. (Mac) was the vehicle commander and we started our usual banter about who had been with the worst women. I promptly reminded him about the night I caught him with some bird outside BomBastics, a nightclub in Belfast. I remember staggering out of the front door and looking down the street and to my surprise, only finding Mac hugging some biggish woman. I can only say it looked like he had his arms wrapped around a telephone box, with only his hands and the side of his face visible. We both burst out laughing as we recalled the evening in question, but only after Mac had tried turning it on to me, saying that I was indeed the telephone box cuddler.

The temperature soon started to plummet even more, and news over the radio depressed us further. We were told that we would be staying here for the night, with the police arriving at eight the following morning to conclude their searches. It was now nearly ten and it was our vehicle's time to start our stag. Two people would stay inside and monitor the radio, while the other two would patrol the area around the farm, and then switch over after an hour. Mac and I patrolled first and that left Evo and Steve with the radio.

We disembarked the Snatch and I followed Mac, leaving five paces between each other. It was pitch black and the ground was unpleasant. Both of us struggled to see hidden ankle-breaking objects on the ground. We continued the patrol and met up with another two soldiers who were coming from the opposite direction. We quickly exchanged a few words about the current situation, the terrible weather and asked if either pair had seen anything suspicious.

We approached one of the small outbuildings that had been cordoned off, ready to be searched the following morning by a specialist police team, when suddenly I heard what sounded like people whispering nearby. I caught Mac up and told him what I'd heard. We took a knee and tried to gather information from our surroundings. At times like this I would try and take in everything, as much as possible, but we needed to be aware how sometimes the sound of the wind could play tricks with us. I tilted my head slightly, so my right ear was pointed towards where I thought the conversion had materialised from, but now all I could detect was the breeze and the sound of the M1 motorway humming in the distance.

We returned to the Land Rover and passed the experience over to Evo and Steve. Mac then got on the radio and briefed everyone to keep vigilant. The next hour dragged with only the sound of chattering teeth keeping us amused. This cold was evil and with no sleeping bags, it was going to be a long and uncomfortable night. Mercifully, the clocked slowly made its way to ten and our stag duty finished. I tried to get myself comfortable on the Snatch floor, but the grooves and the badly positioned steel bolts kept me awake. I found myself rolling from one side to the other, trying to find a position more comfortable than the last, and with the temperatures falling even further, there was now a new battle to contend with.

I finally fell asleep, but I found myself constantly drifting in and out of weird dreams and shivering uncontrollably. I kept coming around and finding myself in that weird place, where you're not sure if you're awake or not. It was at one of those moments when I thought I heard the voice of Sgt S. crackle through the radio. He thought he had seen movement from nearby and wanted to know if any patrols were in that location. I gave Mac and the other two a shove and we listened intently to the radio. I started to feel my adrenalin rise and could feel the tension beginning to fill the Snatch. Suddenly Sgt S. shouted that there was an unknown assailant in close proximity to the main farm building and for everyone to move in and block their exit. He briefed everyone to approach with caution, because one of the guys looked to be carrying a long-barrelled weapon.

I made ready my SA80, leapt from the Snatch and moved off at high speed, trying not to trip over clandestine rocks or any other objects that might have been hidden. As I approached the main farm building a flash of torchlight hit a reflected stripe on someone's chavy tracksuit bottoms. Three other guys and I headed in the direction of the sighting and got a glimpse of two silhouettes clambering over a rickety old fence, which nearly collapsed under the strain of the fleeing miscreants.

I was now in a foot-chase racing through the pitch black, trying to locate our elusive pray. We headed down a steep bank, but I lost my footing trying to slow down at the bottom. The night was as black as coal, and crashing into a barbed wire fence was a very unwelcome and painful surprise. After unpeeling myself from my capture, I continued the hunt for the hidden and crafty enemy. But by now I had lost sight of the intruders and I slowed down to get a better perspective of the area. Suddenly, from behind a natural rise in the land, what sounded like a motorbike engine burst into life about fifty feet from me. I watched on in shock as a quad bike raced off across this uncaring terrain, trying to escape capture.

Foolishly I continued the pursuit, trying to hop fences in the pitch black and cut them off, but to no avail. I finally had to give up the pursuit after stacking it, trying to leap a small fence in one bound. After a short moment and a few deep breaths, I clambered to my feet, and headed back to the vehicles. I gingerly climbed into the back of the Land Rover, nursing my injuries that had been wickedly inflicted by the barbed wire fence, just in time to hear over the radio that the scoundrels on the quad had been arrested trying to escape the area.

The rest of the morning was uneventful, with the police finally arriving at seven fifty to finish off the search. Then thankfully we were relieved twenty minutes later by A company. We headed back to Palace Barracks and straight to the armoury to hand weapons in. The company was finally placed on eight hours' NTM at two o'clock to the great relief of the lads, and we all finally got that beer we had craved. Well, to be honest, it was a lot more than one.

Chapter twelve – Same mistake

A couple of weeks later I headed back to Birmingham for a long weekend, and after a grafting few weeks at work, I was glad to be home. I'd arranged to go out on the Thursday night with a group of friends, and my sister Liz had asked if she could join us. We ended up on Broad Street and after sampling a few of the bars, we made ourselves comfortable in Flares, where from previous experience I knew that anything could happen. I've had some fantastic nights in there.

We hadn't been in there long when I noticed a beautiful blonde girl looking in my direction. She gave me a cracking smile when our eyes finally met. Usually I would make the first move, but I was rocked onto my heels when I saw her heading my way.

"Hi, sexy, my name's Kelly, been trying to get your attention since you came in," she said, with her glossy red-hot lips pressed firmly up against my ear. This sent hot shivers racing down my neck.

"Nice to meet you, I'm Jonathon," I replied. For the next five minutes we chatted about where we were from and what we did. Unbelievably, it turned out she was from Brighton, but lived in Bangor in Northern Ireland. She told me she worked in a hair salon and was only here on a works do.

She was a real joker, a proper laugh and we spent the rest of the evening in each other's company. I will always remember Liz saying how she was like the female version of me. At the end of the night we exchanged numbers and after giving her a kiss good night, we went our separate ways.

Before I knew it, my leave had come to an end and I was back in Ireland, gutted, with the joys and fun times of leave a distant memory. As usual I was pretty pissed off to be back at work, but I'd arranged to meet up with Kelly in Bangor, which gave me something to look forward to. After getting H to promise he would be on his best behaviour, I agreed he could come with me, a decision I would later regret, but more of that in a bit. She text me to say she would be in a club later that night at about eleven, but for the life of me I cannot recall the name now.

After arriving at the rendezvous, I waited with H at the bar for Kelly to arrive, so I took this time to familiarise myself with the layout of the club, just in case H decided to break his early promise. As usual it wasn't long before he decided that he had taken exception to a few lads sitting at a table near the window, after apparently one of them had looked over in his direction. So instead of watching for my date to arrive, I was now trying to stop H beating the shit out of some unfortunates sitting at the other side of the club.

Luckily, I caught a glimpse of her arrival and after calming H down, I went over to meet her.

"So you're here then. I thought you were going to stand me up for some reason," she said.

"Why would you think that?" I replied.

"You know what you Army guys are like, a different woman in every town. Thought maybe I was just a one-night thing," she explained. Again, her hot red lips, this time mixed with her tantalising perfume, started to get me all hot and bothered.

Now one thing about Kelly I must explain is that the woman could drink, and when I say drink, I mean like a fish. Apart from a few crazy Russian women I met in Cyprus, I had never met anyone like her when it came down to the booze.

Back to the night in question. We headed back to the bar and ordered a few drinks. I should have realised right then that things were going to head south when she ordered a round of absinthe. My earlier worries about how the night would eventually play out were starting to become front and centre in my drunken mind when she also ordered H one of these night-changing drinks. He washed four or five of these down like he was swigging water, and he headed for the dance floor to find his next prey.

"That was a bad idea," I said.

"What was?" she replied.

"Him drinking those. Things are probably going to turn ugly for someone," I explained.

After reluctantly necking those unwanted shots I was feeling absolutely trashed. I just wanted to throw in the towel there and then. She was like a machine, though. She just kept knocking them back like they had zero effect on her, and then to make it worse, she just kept ordering more and saying, "Let's get fucked up tonight." At this point all I could think was that I already was, and please stop. Now you have to imagine the predicament I was in. I knew I couldn't drink any more, but I didn't want to lose face. I'll have to admit that I was being out-drunk, and for people who really know me this was a very rare event indeed.

Luckily, I still retained a shred of my inebriated senses to come up with a dastardly plan. So I started pouring my shots of absinthe into the pint of lager of the unaware victim who was standing next to me. Every time he and Kelly were looking the other way I pretended to neck mine, only to sneakily dispose of it in his drink. Suddenly I heard a commotion from the other side of the club and spun around just in time to witness a table full of drinks flying through the air, headed towards the dance floor. Before I even saw H, I knew he was responsible for the flying wall of glass. This had his signature written all over it.

I told Kelly I would be right back, and I headed towards a growing, concerned crowd. I started wrestling and trying to reason with H to calm down and trying to get him out of there before the police turned up. After finally getting him out, I signalled a passing taxi to pull over, and I shoved him in. I was now in a bit of a bad spot. I really liked Kelly and didn't want to just take off without saying anything, but I just knew I couldn't leave him alone in this kind of mood. So I rang her to explain what had happened and that I needed to take him back to camp and hoped she understood. She was brilliant and told me that we could meet up the following night and finish what we'd started.

The next night I travelled back to Bangor to indeed finish what I had started and spent the night at her place, and the following morning she dropped me back at camp. This would become a regular event until one night after she had consumed nearly a whole bottle of absinthe and I experienced a horror drive back to Hollywood while she was pissed out of her mind. She pretty much spent half the journey mounted up on the paving. After this I started using a local taxi firm and apart from the occasional threat from taxi drivers about being a member of the British Army, it was a lot safer than a ride in the death car.

Now I wouldn't say that I loved Kelly by any stretch of the imagination, but I did grow really fond of her. We had a lot of things in common, but somehow, like I usually did, I found a way of screwing it up and never really got a chance to say how sorry I was for the way I treated her. Well, maybe once, if I had acted quicker, I might have been able to have had that chance, but when I saw her I was in complete shock. This chance meeting happened about a year or so after leaving the Army. I was working with Mat at the time, collecting recycling around Birmingham. I had pulled on to New Street and was stuck in traffic, when from nowhere I noticed this blonde woman staring in my direction with a look of anger glistening in her eyes.

At first, I mistook her stares for those of just some random weirdo, but the more I looked at her, the more I started to recognise her as Kelly. I was stunned to see her just standing there in the most random of places, and all I wanted to do was go and say sorry for any pain I might have caused her. I pulled the van over at the next available parking space and ran towards the area where I had moments before just seen her. Unfortunately for my karma, she was gone, long gone. Maybe after seeing me it had brought back the bad feelings she might have still carried towards me. Who knows? But I never got the chance to apologise.

Chapter thirteen – Welcome to Brecon

I was just starting to get used to my new platoon when I was tasked to join up with the bomb squad for a three-month tasking to take over as their infantry escort. At first, I hated the idea of this and wanted nothing more than to go back to beloved six platoon. I met up with the ATO guys (Ammunition Technical Officer) and was shown to my room. I dropped my stuff off and headed for a briefing with the team. They told me all about my role, which involved setting up cordons, providing cover when out on the ground, and then sometimes I would be tasked to deploy the robot and get it ready for the boss to take over. I had a few mishaps along the way with that, but more on that later.

I was then told that because I was now working with them, I was on permanent ten minutes' notice to move. So my kit had to be always ready and there would be no drinking whatsoever, which for me at that time in my life was a great disappointment. I loved nothing more than a big piss-up. After the briefing I headed back to my room to unpack my personal belongings, and I started to think how much of a shit duty this was going to be. I got myself comfortable on my bed, but then there was a knock at the door and the boss entered and told me that we had a job to go to. So I had to get ready and head for the vehicle.

At the time there was a lot of building work going on in the camp to improve some of the facilities. While they'd been digging trenches for pinning the foundations of the gym, the unlucky builders had unearthed some old mortars that had failed to detonate from attacks years previously. We headed for the gym and I couldn't help but think that this was just a practice drill all for my benefit. So to my shock and surprise on arriving thirty seconds later, I could tell from the anxious looks on the builder's face that it was no such thing, and I would have to conduct myself professionally in front of the battalion HQ's watching eyes. They had just turned up to see what all the fuss was about!

I nervously set up a cordon around the mortars and then headed into the nearby buildings and started to remove people who were unaware of the event unravelling outside, just in case one of those little fellows decided it had waited long enough to detonate. The boss bravely and safely removed them, and we took them down to the range and destroyed the little demons. Even though this event was over quickly, I really enjoyed myself, and started to think that this wasn't going to be a bad posting after all, and I couldn't wait to get out on the ground properly.

I wouldn't have to wait long to test out my new skills. There had been a spell of incendiary devices being placed at shopping centres around Belfast over the past few months and we had now been deployed to a nearby British Home Stores. We raced down the twisting and wet roads and then turned left into the main retail park. After we found the doomed store, we screeched to a halt just short of the main building. I had a quick look around to take in my new surroundings, and then I jumped out and made contact with the local police. I jumped straight into my new role and started setting up the cordon. It's funny how human beings can sometimes be completely oblivious to what's going on around them. I had to shout at a few unaware shoppers who were still trying to go about their mundane daily duties, and they were not best impressed by my loud and angry English language aimed in their direction. I reminded them that there was an actual device nearby and if it went bang, they were near enough to be caught up in it. This finally got their attention and they reluctantly scurried off to the safety of their vehicles.

I returned to the vehicle and started to reverse the robot down the unsteady ramps, while the boss took a look at what he was dealing with. I heard the radio burst into life and it was the boss. He said all he needed was his helmet and jacket. I hurriedly ran down to him past the on-looking BBC News Northern Ireland crew and through the main double doors, and I met him in the ladies' aisle. From where I was standing, I could see the device just sitting there in a dirty old black holdall. The boss bravely walked down towards this evil contraption and casually snipped the wires. He then picked the bag up and returned to the waiting vehicle. I watched on in awe, my body pumping full of adrenaline, but for him it was just like a normal event. Something he had obviously done a thousand times.

One day we were practising our drills and one of those was how quickly we could remove the robot from the truck and set up a cordon. I plugged the robot into the controller and slowly started to reverse it down the ramp, when suddenly it malfunctioned, turned left, mounting the side of the truck and violently tipped out in my direction.

I watched on in horror as this nearly two hundred thousand-pound specialist bit of kit came hurtling towards me. In a panic, I dropped the controller and quickly got out of the way of the incoming insurance payout. Not only did the robot crash down in the middle of the parade square, it also landed clean on top of the earlier dropped twenty-five-thousand-pound controller. Not a good day, but luckily my boss eventually saw the funny side of it. The only price I paid was that I became the butt of the jokes for the next few weeks.

Like I said before, now I was posted to the bomb squad I was on permanent ten minutes' notice to move and there was a strict rule on no drinking. One night the unit was invited to a party at another camp and the boss said we could have one drink, make some small-talk and then we would return to camp. After we got to the party, the boss met up with some old pals, and as it usually does, the one drink led to another. It wasn't long before it was apparent that the one-drink rule had been chucked out of the window.

The drinks continued to flow until it was soon two in the morning and disappointingly, the party had started to come to an end. We were all a bit the worse for wear as we made our way back to Palace Barracks. The driver of my vehicle was completely out of his mind. Drunk as a skunk. I held on for dear life the whole way back. For those who know a bit about kerb-bashing at two in the morning, they'd agree that it always livens things up. Thankfully we arrived back at camp in one piece, but that probably couldn't be said for the truck's poor wheels.

We all headed for the sanctuary of our welcoming beds. I staggered to mine and collapsed in a drunken heap on top, not even bothering to undress or get under the covers. I was woken by what I thought was my phone going off and tried repeatedly to switch it off. After ten or so failed attempts to silence this annoying alarm, I realised that it wasn't my phone after all, but in fact the noise was coming from next door, the boss's room. I could hear the boss staggering around and thought the worst. We were about to be crashed out to a job. The inevitable bang at my door followed and I rushed to my feet and headed towards the waiting trucks.

The horror journey was a twenty-minute, blue light nerve-wracking drive to God knows where. I was in a terrible state, trying not to watch as the driver rushed through red lights and rain, narrowly avoiding a taxi, the driver of which had carelessly pulled out in front of us. We came to stop where a police cordon had already been set up. I was so drunk I almost fell from the vehicle while trying to make contact with the female police officer. She asked if I was okay, and I was trying to act sober, replying that I'd caught my boot when climbing out. I hurried to the rear and started to prep the robot for its duties, taking care that I didn't have a repeat of the training incident. This time it played ball and I reversed it down the ramps and then fitted it with a different arm with a new camera.

While I was drunkenly carrying out my tasks the boss walked up and took a closer look at the device.

"If I wasn't still feeling the effects of so many double scotches, I would just cut the wires and be done with it," he said. But luckily, on this occasion it was time for the robot to take care of it. The metal mechanical life-saver trundled down the cold wet road into the early morning mist and disappeared behind a tall brick wall towards its mission. We all watched on, tracking its progress through a small four-inch camera screen from the back of the vehicle.

Bang! A huge explosion broke the crisp, dark silence and we all waited with baited breath to see if the robot had survived its ordeal. The device had triggered a second nearby bomb, which had badly damaged our metal friend. We recovered what was left of him and packed the rest of our kit away. Throughout the event my drunken, hung-over state had retreated slightly, but was now back with a vengeance and I wished I was back at camp in a nice warm bed. Instead I now stood at a freezing wet cordon, desperately hoping this would be over shortly. Two hours went by before the area was finally declared safe and I was reunited with my comfy warm bed.

The time had come for me to return to my platoon, which at the time I was not best pleased about. I had come to really enjoy working in this new role, when every day was different from the one before, but in the back of my mind I always knew this was only for three months. So, reluctantly, I headed back to B company after saying my goodbyes. The next few months passed without any serious incidents, just the normal day-to-day work, and I was back to enjoying my hangovers every Saturday and Sunday morning.

One Monday morning I was called into Sgt J.'s office thinking I was in there for a bollocking. Surprisingly I was told that my name had been put down for the next Junior Non-Commission

Officers' course to get my Lance Corporal. I was chuffed to bits and couldn't wait to tell my roommates and family back home the good news. While I was happy, I knew deep down I would have to be at the top of my game to survive the six-week training course in the Brecon Beacons, getting hammered all over by the cam-cream-wearing monsters.

Brecon, for those who don't know, is hell on earth and in the winter the beautiful looking surroundings can easily kill you. The place has claimed many victims over the years. It's like it's an entity, similar to a wild animal searching for its next prey. It will stalk you until it finds a weakness, then, bang! You're a man down, or worse, you're dead. That's how bad the place can be.

I remember a time when I was there, and our platoon was out on a map-reading exercise at night. I was the rear guy in my section, and all I could see of the man in front through the pitch blackness was the two cat's eyes (reflected strips) stuck to the back of his helmet. So my only reference of which direction we were travelling in was him. I noticed he had stopped and I thought we must be doing a map check. So I walked in and took a knee behind him and said, "Last man in." Then I noticed that we were by ourselves and there was no sign of the rest of the section.

"What the fuck's going on, Dave? Where are the rest of the lads?" I asked.

"Not sure. I thought I was following someone, but it turned out to be a tree," Dave replied.

"A tree? A fucking tree? Trees don't walk, mate. You've been smoking something?" I demanded. We had no option, but to stay where we were. I hoped the rest of the section would realise soon that they were two men down and come back and locate us. Unfortunately for us the beacons had something else in store for us.

People always say that Brecon has its own weather system and that night it showed its ferocious white teeth. When we'd arrived, the weather hadn't been too threatening. Don't get me wrong. It was cold and there was a light covering of glistening white snow on the uneven ground, but now we were right out in the open without a shred of cover in sight. It decided it was going to attack us. Now the wind was blasting us like machine-gun fire, only letting up every now and again, like it was reloading itself ready for another attack. This was followed by a mixture of rain and sleet, and this attacked like a swarm of angry wasps stinging our faces at every opportunity.

We huddled together, clutching onto survival as the Brecon Beacons hit us with everything it had, until our bodies were shaking uncontrollably, and we weren't far from throwing the towel in. We knew that the only chance we had was to go and seek cover, but this would limit our chances of being found if we moved too far from the section's last known location. We headed towards a group of trees and eventually found some very welcome protection amongst the spiky branches. They were now our only source of defence against the life-threatening wild weather. Now we had to keep our eyes and ears peeled for any signs of the rescue party.

Two hours or so went by with no let-up from the multiple-weapon enemy. Just as we thought the rain had stopped, the Beacons sent a fresh wave of angry wasps to attack our naked faces. So we tried to pull our combat jackets up as far as we could to limit the pain. Eventually I saw flashlights in the distance, so we started flashing ours in their direction, finally getting someone's attention. The lights moved towards our location and we were able to finally seek safety from this drastic and dire situation. The rescuers checked us over, and determined we were okay. We followed our friends back to the old farm buildings where we were staying. After a change of clothes and a hot brew we were both back to normal, but with a lot more respect for this dangerous environment.

Before my course headed to Wales we took part in a pre-selection cadre in camp, where we spent a week having our fitness levels checked to see if we were up to scratch. In other words, we were beasted to breaking point to worm out the weak ones. You know it's bad when you're made to sweat in a swimming pool from the pure evil fitness exercises the unpropitious PT staff had concocted.

I knew from the very start that this was going to be one of the worst courses for a long time and that it would be more like survival of the fittest. All the training staff were just pure animals who loved the Army and loved the fact they could beast people even more. One of the staff, Corporal Phil H., had a particularly bad reputation as a strict taskmaster. Especially when he had camouflage cream on his face, then you knew you were really in for it. On the final day of pre-selection, we were informed whose section we were all in and who my section commander was going to be. I looked down the list in search of my name and hoped I could avoid the cam-cream-wearing monster. To my absolute horror, my eyes found the aforementioned Cpl H. and he was indeed my section commander. I nearly quit there and then, knowing his reputation.

The course was ordered to muster on the parade square at twelve hundred hours on Sunday, ready for the coach to take us to Belfast ferry port and on over to Birkenhead, and then south to Wales to start the six weeks of thrashings.

I headed back to the block and spent an hour just sorting out all my kit ready for Sunday, before meeting up with a few of my mates in the NAFFI for a final piss-up. I spent the whole of the Saturday just recovering from the previous night's debacle, finally crawling from my pit in the early afternoon and heading straight to the NAFFI for a much-needed sausage and egg bap times two. I spent the rest of the day just chilling, watching the football and eating crap while the clock quickly ticked down towards Sunday at twelve.

I arrived on the parade square to find everyone, including the training staff, in very good moods, laughing and joking with everyone. Even Cpl H. was joining in with all the banter. Deep down I knew this was only the calm before the storm, and what a storm it was going to be. I jumped on the coach and found myself a seat next to the window, and we took the short journey to the ferry port. We made our way through passport control and headed onto the ferry. The lads excitedly dispersed all over like mice, with everyone heading in different directions looking for something to do for the next eight hours. When we got to Birkenhead, we made the long nervous drive south towards one of our infantry soldier's most feared destinations.

We arrived in Brecon and were shown to our run-down accommodation. We were told to be outside in an hour's time with all our kit ready for an inspection. I prepared my kit and headed outside and formed up. After a short discussion we were marched down to a big open area and were ordered to form up in a hollow square. The course staff then told us that if we were missing an item of kit, we would be sent around the camp on a run of punishment. I was quietly confident of avoiding any extra physical training, as I had every item on the list; or so I thought.

The Sergeant started to read out the list and I watched on as, one by one, members of the course were sent round the camp on their penalty runs. I even chuckled to myself on a few occasions, until my turn came for me to show Cpl H. my arc markers. I retrieved them from my webbing and held them up high, so he could see them clearly. He approached me and violently grabbed them from out of my sky-pointing right hand.

"What the fuck are these?" he asked.

"Arc markers, Corporal," I replied. I watched on in shock as he then proceeded to throw them over the perimeter fence. Then to my utter disbelief, he sent me on my punishment run, which I couldn't understand, as I had the aforementioned item.

I returned from my run, only just breaking a sweat and stood behind my kit, waiting for the next item to be called out. Cpl H. then returned to my location.

"Arc markers?" he asked again. I looked at him in a confused state and before I could think of anything intelligent to say, I was sent on my way back around the camp for another run. I again returned to my kit and this time he was waiting there for me.

"Arc markers?" he asked again. I started to think, *What the fuck is he going on about? Has he got some personal vendetta against me?*

This time I replied that I had already shown him my markers and he had thrown them over the perimeter fence. This foolish outburst angered him even more and he made me do one hundred knees-to-chest reps for backchatting him. This traumatic event nearly killed me and after barely recovering from this ordeal, I was then sent on another lap of the camp. I'd started to get a vision of things to come and wished I'd stayed in NI. As I approached my kit I could see him standing there, arms folded with a massive grin splattered all over his green and brown face, waiting for me to return.

As I knew what was going to happen, I didn't even stop, just continued running past him and onto another gruelling lap. Three laps later he finally showed mercy and shouted for me to stand behind my kit. He then told me he'd only acted like that because I'd laughed earlier about people who had been sent on their runs, and he wanted to punish me for acting like a cock. 'Pot' and 'kettle' sprang to mind at this point, but I didn't think adding that to the conversation would help our already strained relationship. After being given permission to go and collect my arc markers, I returned to the block and lay on my bed. I started thinking that this course was going to be hell, if what had taken place on the first day was anything to go by.

The following morning we'd been told to be ready for seven and that we were going on an eight-mile booted run with forty five pounds' worth of kit, plus helmet and weapon. The platoon was transported by Bedford trucks and driven thirty minutes to the start point. As we drove further and further into this God forsaken place, the terrain started to get steeper and steeper. The ground had become that extreme that even the trucks began to struggle, sometimes even getting stuck.

As I looked out of the back of the truck I could see a figure slowly appearing from the thick mist that was hugging the moist ground. The mysterious apparition finally came into view and then I recognised the ghastly figure as Company Sergeant Major T, who strangely was also known as Spider. CSM T. was a fitness fanatic who loved nothing more than spending his free weekends running all over this place just for fun! He had taken part in marathons and had even walked across the Sahara dessert. So I was under no illusion that the morning's eight-miler wasn't going to break some of us, but I just hoped it wasn't going to be me. You know you're in for a bad deal when the guy in charge of the fitness of this course overtakes the Bedfords that are carrying the troops about to join the PT class.

We arrived at the start position and CSM Taylor addressed the course.

"Listen, everyone. Today is going to be a nice easy march just to see where everyone's fitness levels are." I knew this was a load of bollocks when we were ordered to put on our helmets, as this never happened on a normal eight-miler. We were about to get beasted to within an inch of our lives. Usually eight-milers are a mixture of long spells of quick marching followed by short burst of running, but when he shouted in his London accent for everyone to prepare to double, we all knew this was no ordinary march.

The first two miles were run at lightning speed up a step ascent, along narrow winding roads. The ground conditions under foot were horrendous. Everyone was slipping and stumbling over loose rocks that littered the steep rocky roads. As soon as I started I knew something wasn't right in my legs. I had this burning feeling that kept shooting up and down my shins, but I just kept going, trying my best to block out the pain. I think it must have been because my body was aching all over, but after about four miles I had completely forgotten about my shin issue and was now on autopilot just trying to survive to the end, and hopefully complete this devastating run in the allotted time of two hours.

With about a mile to go, the agonising burning sensation returned to my shins with a vengeance and now each reluctant step punished me more than the last. I was hooked into an all-out battle with my body and mind. On one hand, my body wanted to break down and give up, and on the other hand my mind would not allow this to happen. I had never given up on a run or a march up to this point and I wasn't about to start now.

With gritted teeth and every ounce of determination in my crumbling body, I reached the finishing line in a staggering time of one hour and thirty one minutes. This was the fastest I had ever been around an eight-miler and the fact that this was pretty much uphill the whole way was even more mind-blowing. Even though I'd completed this task I knew I might have picked up a bad injury on the first day, and that might haunt me for the duration of this soul-destroying course.

The next few days were taken up with fitness in the morning and lessons in the afternoon. Thankfully the pain in my shins had disappeared and was no longer concerning me. The Monday of the following week was going to be another big test of fitness, as it was going to be the first of the many two-mile booted runs with kit and weapons. These always seemed to be killers and with the added effect of the Brecon Beacons conditions added into the mix, it would push everyone to new limits.

The dreaded Monday arrived, and I was ready to face this two-miler head-on without any fear. My kit was weighed, and I was then formed up in three ranks with the rest of the platoon. Company Sergeant Major T. appeared again and informed us that we had fourteen minutes to complete the course. Bear in mind this usually had a twenty-minute cut-off time. The platoon gasped with shock when we heard those ridiculous timings, and what followed shortly completely took my breath away.

"Whoever fails this run will go again straightaway and you will only have thirteen minutes and so on." I thought, *Fucking hell, if you don't pass it the first time with fourteen minutes, what's the chance of passing it with less?*

The platoon set off and within a minute the dreaded shin pain returned, and it was now I knew I was in big trouble. The pace was fanatical and the pain beyond belief as I struggled to keep up with the fastest group. My legs were unwilling to move any quicker and now the PT staff who were setting the pace started slowly moving out of sight. I knew I wasn't going to complete this task in the allotted time, but I just couldn't move any faster.

Everything now seemed to be going against me. One of my laces now unravelled itself and was trying to trip me up at every step. I had to stop and fix this annoying problem immediately, before it sent me tumbling towards the unforgiving and bloodthirsty ground. I was soon getting shouted at for addressing my laces and told if I stopped again I would fail the run. I now had to make up so much time just for it to be respectable, so I really started to push it, but with each ill-placed footstep the agonising pain reverberated up my shins. Suddenly I could see the finish line and shouts of encouragement from the other lads who had already passed was music to my ears. I had about two hundred metres left and ran it like an Olympic athlete on the home stretch. In a time of fourteen minutes and forty five seconds I gladly passed the finishing line. I was then segregated from the people who had passed and waited for the rest of the failures to join me.

I kept thinking if I hadn't stopped to take care of my lace I would be now enjoying the feeling of being a winner. Instead I had that sinking feeling, knowing I had put everything into that two-miler, but I would take no reward. Well, unless you call repeating the run a reward. After five minutes everyone was in and we all now got a right bollocking for failing this task. We were sent on our way for the second time and like I predicted, no one could get anywhere near the magical thirteen minutes. So as we were promised, we were sent out again and this time the cut-off was twelve minutes.

This was crazy. I was now on my fifth and sixth mile and my body was breaking down step by step. There was no way I could complete this in the time given and I couldn't see any escape from this unbeatable misery. Predictably, no one passed this punishment and for our troubles the survivors were made to crawl back the two miles to camp. The only relief now was that I wasn't putting any pressure on my shins, but I couldn't say the same for my knees and elbows. They were now taking the full brunt of the course staff's evil and sadistic torture. I returned to camp in absolute agony and now knew I faced an uphill battle to be fit and ready for the following week's activities in the field.

The following week started with the platoon deployed out deep into the hills and valleys of a very wet and windy Brecon. We were again taken by Bedford to an old barn where we would spend the next five days practising drills. These included map reading, day and night patrols and learning how to take control of a section. I had obviously learnt map reading skills before, but it was never one of my strong subjects. Thankfully, the way Cpl H. explained things made it very easy to understand. Even though he could be extremely evil when he wanted to be, he was also a great soldier.

He had a way of explaining things which seemed to just stick in your mind. It's funny because about two years later when we were both serving in Afghanistan together, I reminded him about how evil he was on this course, at which he just laughed. It was then I really started to see another side him and would have followed him into any battle, no matter what.

One night we had just returned to the barn from a long day's patrolling and found that our evening meal for the night was going to be range stew. This was a mixture of all sorts thrown together in a big container, something that I had no interest in ever eating. The staff had concocted a brilliant but sickening idea to have a race to see which section could eat theirs first and whichever section won wouldn't get beasted up and down a nearby hill.

Unfortunately for us there were three containers and three sections. So between eight of us we would have to try and consume this faster than the others. As you can probably imagine, with the evil training team we had, this was a dastardly trick and all three sections got beasted, regardless of who won. Now imagine everyone with a stomach full of this nasty food that was just waiting to make a quick escape at a moment's notice. Not only was I being sick myself, I was trying to avoid crawling through piles of the stuff that had been deposited along this hilly route. This continued for about thirty minutes until the evil staff had finally laughed as much as they could and released us from our misery.

Before we could return to camp we would have to complete another two-miler and this time I felt quietly confident I could finish in the fourteen minutes that we were allowed. Everything started well, and I was easily keeping up with the staff this time, when from nowhere my nemesis returned. This time there was no escaping it, the burning pain was unreal this time and I needed to slow the pace, or I wouldn't complete this run at all. I could see people in front starting to struggle and pull over, injured, to the side of the narrow rocky path. I remember running past one of the lads from my company who was the company physical trainer. I started to think if he was failing, then what chance did I have?

Eventually I succumbed to my injury, thinking maybe if I stopped now I could save myself further injury and stay on the course. I was reluctantly bundled into the back of the waiting ambulance and I sat down next to Cards, the injured physical trainer. I was sent to the medical centre and after a quick examination was told by the doctor that I had stress fractures in both shins. He then said that I probably should have come to him when I first had the pain and unfortunately this was the end of the road and I was off the course. At first, I was absolutely gutted, because I thought this was my time to get promoted and if I'd just tried to finish the run, maybe I could have just battled through the rest of the course. There were four of us who had been injured and we were told that we might have to stay here for the duration and play enemy. This was heartbreaking, knowing that we could end up watching everyone else pass the course, while we sat on the sidelines, injured. Thankfully we were booked onto a ferry the following day and were told to go and pack our stuff and be ready for six the following morning. We would be driven back to Liverpool and then we'd board the ferry back to a wet and windy Belfast.

We returned to Ireland and as my company was in Girdwood, I was taken straight there to join up with them. I felt like a right failure and was summoned straight to Sgt J.'s office to explain the situation. I expected a bit of a bollocking as I thought I'd let him down, but that wasn't the case.

"Don't worry about it. Things like this happen. When you're back in one piece, I'll let you have another crack at it. For now, look forward to your upcoming two weeks' leave, and when you return to Belfast we'll have another chat about things."

Chapter fourteen – Shipshape

My leave started in the usual way. My friends would always be sitting outside my house, waiting for me to return home. We would then get straight on it, grab a load of beers and spend the night playing on the computer, me teaching them lessons on football and wrestling.

On the Saturday night we were out on a piss-up in Solihull, when I suggested we go to a strip club I knew called Sensations. From the outside the place looked a bit of a dump, and you would probably drive clean by without noticing it was even there if it wasn't for the pink and yellow neon lights inviting you in. I'd been there many times and the nights were usually incredible. Apart from the obvious temptation of beautiful half-dressed mysterious women all with a story to tell, it was a really good place to chill out and have a few drinks. After we arrived I was pretty much pounced on by a pack of incredibly sexy ladies that performed at the establishment. So I spent the next hour or so relieving my leather wallet of my well-earned crisp twenty pound notes for lap dances from most of the women in there.

A fresh bunch of guys got the attention of the girls and we were left to ourselves, just laughing and joking about how good the night had been so far. I then noticed a very hot looking brunette dressed in a very seductive white dress, making her way to my table. She sat down next to me and crossed her silky, smooth legs, in that way women do to make sure they have your full attention.

"Hi, I'm Morgan," she said.

"Jonathon. Nice to meet you."

"So you fancy a dance then?" she went on playfully then, "I've seen you've had one with everyone else in here, and I'm feeling left out,"

I went along with her and followed her to a private room. I took a seat on the black leather sofa, as the unmistakable beat of one of my favourite tunes kicked in. She moved like a goddess. Her deliciously well sculpted hot body was wrapped around me like some form of exotic snake. I just couldn't keep my eyes off her, it was like I was mesmerised by her every skilful move. The smell of her intoxicating perfume seemed to have me locked into some form of a spell, and she knew it. She could have had me eating out of the palm of her hand. I was in trouble. Big Trouble. Her flawless body glistened, as the well positioned lights illuminated her silhouette, which made her look like the woman of my dreams. Michael Jackson's *Dirty Diana* finished, and she escorted me back to my table. I caught the unbelievable gaze from her beautiful brown eyes as she flirtatiously climbed over my lap to sit down. Her red-hot lips brushed the side of my face, almost making me shiver, as she finally sat down next to me.

We started talking about the Army, and it was then she confessed to me that she'd always had a thing for soldiers. At first, I just thought it was her way of getting me to spend my hard-earned cash on her all night, but I soon realised that she wasn't after my money. She came and went for the rest of the night, going to dance for some of her regular clients. She told me that she really liked me and that she didn't want to take my money because she thought it was weird.

The night was drawing to an end and by this time I was feeling the effects of the second bottle of Bollinger champagne that I'd drunk while I'd been there. I signalled to Morgan that I was leaving. She stopped what she was doing and hurried over, and she slipped a rolled-up piece of tissue in my hand.

"What this? Drugs? I don't do drugs," I said.

"No, silly, it's my phone number. Please call me, I really like you." I left the club as high as a kite and just couldn't believe what had just taken place.

The next day, after recovering from the previous night's escapades I nervously built up the courage to call her. Even though she'd given me her number I thought it was just a wind-up. I dialled the number she'd given me and after six or seven rings, an elderly chap answered the phone.

"Hello, there. Can I speak to Morgan, please?" I asked.

"Sorry, I think you have the wrong number," he replied and put the phone down. I thought *Okay, that's that then, she must have given me a dodgy number.* Suddenly my phone started ringing and it was the number I had just dialled.

"Hello?" I said.

"Hi, is that Jonathon? Sorry, that was Granddad. He doesn't know I call myself that. My name is actually Lindsey. Morgan is just my stage name." We went on to arrange to meet each other on the Tuesday night back at her club, as she worked most nights.

We met up at the club and just spent the whole night talking, while every now and again she would go and dance for some of her regulars. During her moments of absence, I would sit there waiting for her to return, and sinking a few nice cold Budweisers. A lot of people would think this was strange, but it didn't bother me. I wasn't looking for anything serious anyway, just a bit of fun really.

We left the club together and shared a taxi home. She only lived about five minutes from me. So she said she'd drop me off and then go home. The taxi pulled up outside mine and I kissed her good night. We spent a minute or so glued to each other's lips, until the driver cleared his throat. She then whispered that she really wanted to come in but didn't want me to think she was a slag who went with guys on the first night. I reluctantly peeled myself from her addictive body and watched on disappointedly as her taxi pulled away and out of sight.

A couple of nights later we ended up back at my house and the obvious happened. After we'd been together she said that she needed to come clean about something. She told me that she'd been lying about her age. I frantically started to think, *I'm fucked. Here we go. She's going to tell me she's under age or something and I've just committed a crime.*

The first night we met she told me she was twenty two, but now she was about to tell me her real age. Thankfully she went on to tell me that she was eighteen and I took a huge sigh of relief. For the rest of my leave we were inseparable, spending every hour of the day with each other. I don't think I ever fell in love with her, it was more like lust. To be honest, at the time I probably did think I loved her, but knowing what real loves feels like now, I can say that wasn't it. Maybe she was more like a class A drug I was addicted to. I just couldn't get her out of my mind, even dreaming of her. Finally, it was time for me to return to Northern Ireland. This time it was extremely difficult to leave her and return, but reluctantly I boarded my flight and returned to camp.

The following week was spent in Scotland on a training exercise. While I was begrudgingly away I was unable to contact her, because I had no phone signal the whole time I was there. When I returned to Northern Ireland on the Friday I turned on my phone and to my surprise found a shedload of text messages and voice mails from her. The messages said how much she had missed me and how things had been difficult since I had returned to NI. She also said that she was thinking of ending it all. I quickly rang her, hoping it wasn't too late, but thankfully she answered the phone in her very sexy voice. I was glad to hear her and apologised for not replying to her messages and calls. I explained that I'd had no signal and told her I was glad she hadn't done anything stupid.

Before we were deployed to Scotland the company asked if anyone want to replace Tim B. on a sailing week down on the south coast of England, and I'd asked to be considered. When we returned from Scotland, I found that I had been accepted. To be honest, I only volunteered to get out of work and thought it would be a load of bullshit. How wrong was I!

We travelled back to Scotland on the ferry, and then we drove the ten-hour road trip to Portsmouth, where we spent the night at a Navy base before heading out the following morning on the open water towards Guernsey. After arriving at the camp, we immediately did what us soldiers do best and found the nearest and liveliest night life and headed that way. Two girls from the battalion had also come on the course and one of them, Sarah, had taken a bit of a shine to me. She kept asking if I would cheat on Lindsey with her, to which I replied no. She then made a bet with me, by saying that she would definitely be able to get me into bed and to cheat on my girlfriend within the week.

Anyway, we all headed out to the local bars and straightaway I knew this was going to be an epic week. Everywhere we went, the bars were just buzzing with ladies dressed in next to nothing, and there were great offers on drinks in every bar we came across. What else could you ask for as a red-blooded male? Well, apart from being single at the time, of course. That night we ended up in… well, I think it was Flares or somewhere like that. Can't really remember, because I was a bit the worse for wear at that point. I just remember cheesy eighties tunes and dodgy squaddie dance moves making an appearance.

Anyway, the whole time I was in there, the same beautiful blonde kept looking over in my direction and eventually she strutted her hot self towards me and spoke.

"I've been looking at you all night. How come you haven't come over and said hi? It's not like you're married, because I can't see a ring on your finger. What is it, don't you find me sexy?" Her hot breath and moist lips pressed up against my ear sent shivers down my spine.

"No, no, I think you're gorgeous, I just wish I was single right about now."

"Where's your girlfriend?" she playfully asked.

"Birmingham."

"Well, she isn't ever going to find out, and trust me, you wouldn't regret it. In fact, you'd probably dump her afterwards and want to marry me. That's how fucking good I am." Not too many times in my life had I been completely blown away by what a bird had said, but this was definitely one of those times. I just couldn't believe what was coming out of her mouth and she really didn't look the type. After she gave me a lingering kiss, she said, "Think about it. I know I will. Come and find me later if you change your mind," and with that, she turned and took her sexy ass to the dance floor, but not before giving a final cheeky look back over her left shoulder as she disappeared into the dancing crowd.

The following morning, we got our first taste of sailing, with us all learning the basics, so we didn't kill ourselves. Then we headed back to shore to stock up on supplies. The skipper had planned for us to head out into the English Channel, stopping off at the Isle of Wight for the night, before eventually arriving in Guernsey, hopefully twelve hours later. We stocked up with enough cans of lager to supply a small Army, and we motored out into the deep blue sea before erecting the sails.

The journey to the Isle of Wight was a very relaxing one, with the yacht just drifting along on the breeze at a steady rate of knots, and with us all just taking in the breathtaking surroundings without a care in the world. The sun was just beautifully reflecting on the rich blue sea, and it made it look like a mirror. I was so glad that I'd put my name down for this adventure. After a few hours of daydreaming we reached our destination and like a well-oiled team, we moored up for the evening. After a quick reminder from the boss, Second Lt H., about what was expected of us and how we were representing the Army, we were finally allowed to explore the island, so we followed our noses to track down the scent of a local pub. After I gobbled down my cod and chips with tartar sauce, and I'd washed it down with a few cold Stellas, we then hunted out a livelier venue to finish the night in. This turned out to be a very difficult task indeed, because for those readers who don't know, this place isn't the most exciting in the world.

After finally finding somewhere to rest our weary bones, the place in question was a small pub-like place. Luckily, we only found this cosy establishment after following a couple of mini-skirt-wearing young ladies in. Now, usually when a bunch of young, fairly decent looking soldiers with enough confidence to try it on with most women, come walking into a random place with a good number of ladies in there, the odds of at least one of us pulling would be very high, or at least even. Somehow that night, in that place, it was like there was some form of conspiracy against us. As if all the ladies in there had ganged up on us and were now making us look bad.

I remember one of the lads telling a really saucy bird that he had a thirty-foot yacht out in the marina and asked her if she fancied coming back to have a look. Her answer was priceless.

"Look around, love. Everyone on the Isle of Wight has a yacht, so you're nothing new, Babe." The look on the guy's face was just one of utter disgust and surprise, and with a quick flick of her long blonde hair and a wriggle from her ample bum, she was gone. We watched her return to her friends and exchange a few words, then on cue they all exploded into a fit of giggles, with some even turning and pointing. After striking out more times than a no-armed baseball player, we reluctantly returned to our female-free yacht and turned in for the evening, with only our dreams and the annoying snores from our nearby companions to keep us company.

The next leg of the journey was across the open ocean and towards France. We would then head south-east towards Guernsey, probably a ten-hour journey if everything went well, the captain told us. It turned out the weather would have a few things to say about that. Things started well and to be honest you couldn't have wished for a better day for an epic sailing adventure. The only distraction was a nice steady breeze that swept across the bow, which at times was a nice relief from the baking sun beating down on my unprotected alcohol-seeping skin.

The first six hours or so sailed by (excuse the pun), but with rumblings of thunder in the distance and with the sky above us becoming darker and darker, we knew that things were about to become a bit more interesting, to say the least. The first spots of rain were mistaken for spray blasting off the front of this streamlined yacht, and it wasn't long before we were all reaching for our waterproofs. The rain had now intensified, so it was like a wall of water which was hitting us head on. The captain quickly adjusted the sails and our safety was now firmly in his rugged hands. After nearly being tossed overboard like an unwanted catch onboard a French fishing trawler, I thought it was high time to clip my steel carabiner onto one of the many safety lines.

What had previously been beautiful calm waters twenty minutes ago had now turned into a raging monster, trying to pick us off one at a time. With every powerful wave that came crashing into the port side of this now tiny bath tub-like yacht, it felt as if it was only a matter of time before the sea would claim six more victims. One of the worst feelings you can have is when you become reliant on somebody else to keep you safe, and that was exactly what was playing out at this point.

After what felt like a lifetime, we passed through the storm and with every metre we travelled, the sea became less and less life threatening. After our close call we finally reached calmer water and headed for the safety of nearby French shores. But because we had now lost a lot of time trapped in the tight grasp of the powerful storm, we would have to reach an overnight spot. Luckily, the village of Cherbourg was our nearest destination, so the quick-thinking captain made the adjustments and headed that way.

As the wind was no longer in our corner, we had to rely on the measly power of the yacht's diesel engine, so now we faced another gruelling adventure. The maximum speed of our craft was five knots, nothing special really, but with the tide now hitting us bang on the nose at four, sometimes five knots, we spent the next four hours not really going anywhere. Sometimes it felt as if the city lights from Cherbourg were in fact fading, making us all think that we were going backwards, and that was a demoralising thought.

Finally, the great sea showed some mercy upon us as the tide changed ever so slightly, releasing us from its tight, evil grip. While the tide was on our side we made a break for it and gunned the engine, heading for the safety of French soil. The captain skilfully positioned the yacht amongst the crowded craft in the marina and found us a welcome mooring slot next to two giant boats. It was now that I realised how lucky we'd all been to have made it here in one piece. I think everyone on board had the same feelings as me, as we all tried to jump onto dry land as soon as possible, and it came as a shock that we now had to negotiate the swaying decking before finally reaching solid ground.

We spent the night in this strange fishing village, with a few of us braving the local cuisine. The place seemed to be locked into times gone by, and we were met with confused and bewildered stares from the locals. It was either our dodgy attempts at the local language or maybe our weird and futuristic dress sense, but I don't think we were welcome in our overnight spot.

The following morning, we were woken at the crack of dawn to finally finish the rest of the journey to Guernsey, and we arrived at last a few hours later, much to the relief of everybody onboard. The Captain had told us that we were allowed to go out for something to eat, but that we should be back by one for knot-tying lessons. As usual we all had other plans. Well, apart from the boss, who inevitably did his best to put a dampener on our visions of an all-day drinking binge. After much persuasion and a great deal of pestering, we finally talked the boss around to our way of thinking with the promise of a few drinks. I think he just wanted to shut us up and that's why he agreed. So with that, we headed towards a local drinking house.

The next few hours were taken up with booze and a few games of pool, before our drunken escapades were interrupted by the Captain, who had finally caught up with us only five hours after we had promised to return to the yacht for the aforementioned knot-tying lessons. We were all now in no fit condition for a lecture. So instead of that, he joined in with the drinking by ordering a round of pints, which was quickly followed up with a round of aftershocks.

After heading back to the marina, I spent the next half hour drunkenly struggling to locate my boat, nearly falling head first between two moored yachts on more than one occasion. After eventually finding my living quarters, I then tried to refresh myself in the tiny, cramped bathroom. We got changed and headed to a nearby night hotspot to continue the drinking binge.

A few hours later, after sampling a few of the local bars, we ended up in some dodgy looking club, where the locals were all drugged up to their eyeballs. I somehow ended up losing the lads and after searching the club, I found Sarah, who was sitting at the bar looking spectacular in her usual effortless way, knocking back shots. I squeezed by a group of wasters at the bar and sat down next to her, brushing her smooth tanned right thigh by accident. She flashed me a beautiful smile and pushed a shot glass in my direction. So I took her up on her invitation and joined in with the tequilas and a few bottles of blue Wicked.

She was still trying to tempt me into cheating with her and God only knows how I resisted her full-on attack. Got to be honest, that night I really fancied her and if I'd had any inclination of how my relationship would soon be coming to an end, I wouldn't have bothered being so loyal and would have taken her back to the yacht there and then.

After knocking back an evil shot and the rest of my bottle, or what I thought was mine, I staggered to the toilet. But business achieved, I started feeling unusual, like I was high on something, even though I hadn't taken anything. I put it down to a nicotine rush or something, but as I tried to take a step, my legs nearly buckled underneath me. I started to think it was something more sinister, because I'd never felt like this before.

The room started to spin out of control and it took all of my strength and willpower just to keep myself standing. After battling with my jelly-like legs I managed to drag my unresponsive body into a nearby toilet cubicle and locked the door behind me. I got my drugged frame onto the toilet and before I could do anything else, I passed out. I'm not really sure what happened next, because I couldn't tell the difference between reality and what my mind was playing back to me.

Finally, my unwanted buzz started to wear off and I was now feeling as if I could stand up again. After a few failed attempts I finally got my legs to co-operate with my brain's orders and stood up, much to my relief, as I'd started to panic a little. My shaking hand unlocked the cubicle door and I walked over towards the row of white sinks that were littered with drug paraphernalia. I then threw a wave of cold water across my heavily perspiring forehead to try and liven myself up.

After a few strange looks from the rowdy drugged-up partygoers, I returned to the bar where Sarah was still sitting necking a bottle of Wicked.

"Where the fuck have you been? Can't believe you left me here on my own, had some right strange lads trying to buy me drinks," she said. I told her that I thought my drink had been spiked and the pair of us started to put two and two together. She now realised what these bastards had been up to, and fortunately for her, they'd spiked the wrong drink. We decided it was probably time to go back to the yacht, and we walked back arm in arm.

The following morning, I woke to a stinking headache, which had probably been brought on by last night's drug attack. The Captain forced us all to take part in the knot-tying lesson, much to everybody's anger. Finally, after a few hours of torture, we were allowed to go and do whatever we wanted. As this was our last night here we had planned to make the most of it. So we headed straight to the pub and continued from where we'd left off the previous night, without the body- and mind-altering drugs this time in my case.

Before we'd left the Captain's company he told us that we would be sailing off at five in the morning, so we could get back to England in good time. He also said as part of our course, we would have to sail the yacht back ourselves, so we shouldn't have too much to drink. After a good twelve hours of heavy drinking we headed back to the yacht and continued the session on board with a bunch of young ladies. After finishing off our alcohol stash we sneakily stole Mr H.'s hundred-pound bottle of fancy whisky, much to his later anger. The boat party continued into the small hours, as we all took it in turns to guzzle mouthfuls of nasty tasting, expensive whisky straight from the bottle, and sing random songs from our drunken thoughts, until I collapsed into the arms of my busty drinking companion.

After probably only an hour's sleep, I was rudely woken by the Captain telling me it was time to head off, and that I had twenty minutes to be ready. I rolled over and tried to make myself comfortable on the wet wooden floor. The smell of whisky was thick in the air, which almost made me heave. My friend from a few hours previously whispered in my ear that she had to go before her husband got suspicious, and she said she was gutted that I wasn't single. She kissed me on my cheek and left, with only her lingering perfume stain on my shirt as evidence of her night onboard.

After the Captain had safely negotiated the early morning

traffic in the harbour, he erected the correct sails for us to make this journey, and then he handed over the responsibility of the beautiful vessel to a bunch of drunken soldiers, which turned out to be a very bad mistake on the captain's part. Even though this should have been a straightforward journey back, just following the compass, it turned out to be a drunken escapade across dangerous waters.

Firstly, we ran the boat across hidden rocks when trying to take a short cut between two areas of coastline, and if that wasn't enough, we then, after heading in a completely different heading from our instructions, nearly snapped the mast clean off, after the boom swung round violently. This was the final straw for the captain, who relieved us of our command until we had all sobered up. It was a good call, to be honest, because the way we were going, someone was going to get seriously injured or even killed. I had visions of us having to be rescued by the RNLI.

A couple of hours passed, and my whisky-induced hangover had started to fade a little. The problem I now had was that with every incoming cruel, evil wave that crashed into us, it would send me rushing to the side, head first, to remove the previous night's liquor. We were now trusted to be back at the helm and with the English coastline in sight, it was only a matter of time before we were on dry land and enjoying a few swift Stellas. After a few bearing issues we final arrived in Poole just before six o'clock, much to everyone's relief.

That night we headed to the main drinking area and after giving H a friendly warning about not causing any trouble tonight, we found ourselves a nice lively drinking establishment and ordered a round. We located a table in the corner that had good access routes to the bar and the toilets, which also gave us a good watch over the dance floor, where we could keep tabs on the local women. H so far was keeping to his word about being on his best behaviour, but when I saw a group of confident lads stroll in, acting like they owned the place, I knew it wouldn't be long before they experienced what H could do.

The cocksure looking group grabbed some drinks and took a seat at a table nearby. Just as I thought, it wasn't long before one of their group came over.

"You lot Navy?" a bald-headed man asked.

"Fuck, no! We're all real soldiers here. Army, mate," I replied. He was taken back a little by my response, but eventually stuck out his hand and shook mine. It turned out this rowdy group were in the navy (Fucking remfs). At first, they were friendly enough as we all took part in the usual banter, until one of their guys took exception to Callum's derogatory comment about their role. The next thing I knew, tables and chairs were flying in all directions and some big oaf tried to manhandle H. Big mistake, this guy had just bitten off well more than he could chew.

The oaf was soon regretting his actions, as H unleashed a beating of epic proportions on him, leaving a motionless and unconscious body flat out on the sticky bar floor. This seemed to spur the Navy lot on, as they sought revenge for H's brutal act of self-defence. Before I could really take stock of what was happening, someone started winging punches in my direction. The first was a glancing blow to the forehead, before I bobbed and swayed from the following three and decided it was time to fire off a few of my own. As my attacker and I wrestled for victory I kept seeing people in the corner of my eye swinging punches that were getting closer and closer, and thought to myself, *As soon as I've dealt with this twat, he's next.* Luckily for us, we had H on our side and before not very long there were no more enemy left standing. The bar floor was littered with knocked-out members of the British Navy. Our ace in the pack had taken care of everyone who had foolishly tried to take us on.

The thing with H was that once you'd pulled his pin, it took a lot to try and calm him down. So you had to buckle in for the ride and God knows where it could take you. He had now turned his bloodthirsty attentions towards the shouting and angry looking doorstaff, who had the dangerous task of trying to remove us from their establishment. So now it was the ballsy bouncers who were experiencing what it felt like to be thrown out onto the street like a piece of rubbish, as H took it upon himself to clear the bar of anybody who dared to try and confront him. Inevitably and unfortunately for us, the police arrived, and it took all our efforts to tame our out-of-control monster, before the police fell victims to his brutal and devastating ass-kicking spree. Eventually we managed to remove him from the bar before anybody else got hurt, and we walked down the seafront to find ourselves another drinking den.

The night then took a very strange turn. I'd ended up with two women back at their house, God knows where that was. After sharing a few drunken kisses with the pair, my conscience started telling me I shouldn't take this any further and that I shouldn't cheat on my girlfriend. So after battling with my alcohol-fuelled thoughts, I removed myself from the situation, went back to the yacht and then turned in for the evening.

A few hours later I was woken by a loud angry argument which was taking place out on the deck. I thought, *Here we go again, what's H done now?* Just as I was about to get up and investigate the reasons for the noise, the door to the sleeping quarters suddenly swung open and a large angry woman walked in.

"Is this him? Is this the man who raped you?" she shouted. I was in utter disbelief as she dragged the girl I had kissed earlier by the arm and into my room.

"What the fuck are you talking about? I only kissed her and realised I was making a mistake and left it at that, and that's all that happened, I promise you," I replied. Her Mom then turned and started to interrogate her and shouted at her to tell the truth for once. Finally, she did and backed up my side of the story. I was left utterly shocked by the whole event and started to think about what position I would have been in if I'd them taken up on their inviting offer.

The next day we headed back to Portsmouth before we made the long journey north up the motorway, and we arrived in Belfast via the ferry the following day. It must have taken me two to three days to recover from the alcohol poisoning my body had just suffered.

Chapter fifteen – Things could have worked out differently

The next three weeks I spent counting down the days till I got to see Lindsey and it wasn't long before we were together again. This time though, something was completely different with her, it was as if her personality had changed. I'd gone on leave thinking that I wanted to finish with her, because of the fact that I was always away, and it wasn't fair on her or me to keep putting us through the separation. This, though, was put on hold when she started telling me stuff about when she was a kid, and I thought about what kind of guy would break up with someone after she'd revealed such dark secrets about herself.

One night she had come around and straightaway I knew something was on her mind that was obviously bothering her. At first, she did that thing that women do best, saying she was fine and all that good stuff. So I had to keep pressing until I finally got her to say what was on her mind, and with that, she confessed that she wanted to end things. I was still trying to get my mind around her reasons why when she left.

Even though it had been my intention to do the same before she had revealed her past to me, quite honestly, I was still a bit gutted and spent the next couple of days dealing with the situation the only way I knew, getting smashed with my old friend Mr Southern Comfort. I think maybe deep down she had affected me more than I realised, and one night after a heavy drinking binge with the lads, I somehow thought it was a good idea to head to her work and have it out with her.

I was met at the door by two burly bouncers, who refused me entry. This only angered me more, so I kicked off and started to make a bit of a scene until the manager came out. As I'd been here many times over the years we had got to know each other very well. I told him that I just wanted to talk to her and that I wouldn't cause any trouble. He let me in on the proviso that I kept my word, but my promise only lasted thirty seconds after seeing the bitch chatting up her next victim. I was quickly set on by two security staff and roughly escorted to a waiting taxi.

The next year or so we would meet up every now and again when we were between partners, or in her case whenever she was bored in one of her current relationships. I remember a time when I was on leave and she had sent me a message about meeting up. I wasn't doing anything special, so took her up on her seductive offer. She told me to meet her at some random car park in Solihull at ten that night. I arrived, and I sat in my car, waiting for her sexy ass to appear, when through my rear-view mirror, I finally set eyes on her walking towards my car, hand in hand with some guy. I started thinking something funny was about to go down, so I began to prepare myself for any eventuality, when suddenly the courting pair stopped, turned towards each other and kissed. Then she walked towards the passenger door and opened it, and with a quick wave to her onlooking boyfriend, we were gone. Small-talk followed, and I started to think she only needed me for a lift. I turned off the main drag and into her estate, when she suddenly piped up. "Where are you going? I thought we were going back to yours for the night."

"Okay, that's sound. If that's what you want, it just looked like you were loved up back there," I replied.

"We have an understanding," she said, and with that I took her back to mine. Events like this sort of just fizzled out until she eventually she moved away and that was the end of that.

I returned to Northern Ireland and to be honest, I was glad to be back and far away from any dramas she could cause me. The company had taken over the role of two hours' notice to move from A company a couple of days after returning from leave. While stuck on this shit, alcohol-free cycle, the company had been deployed to

Newry on a training course, which turned out to be an actual operation down on the border. We were tasked with checking vehicles coming across from Southern Ireland to make sure they were carrying what they said they were, and not full of guns and drugs. The company was kept in the dark to make sure no one opened their big mouths and told their Irish girlfriends what operation they were about to take part in.

We stayed at the camp in Newry, practising drills and making sure all our kit and Land Rovers were ready to go. The plan was to wait out there, until it was time for us to head to the border in force. The company was told nothing about what was going to happen or when and where we were heading. Only a select few knew anything and we would only be informed what was going on when we were on the way to the job. This is the only way operations stay secret until they are actually playing out.

I was in Lance Corporal McN's (Mac) vehicle and we shared a few jokes with each other on the way down, as we usually did. Our banter was legendary. Don't think anybody took the piss out of each other as much as we did. The multiple we were with consisted of four Land Rovers. The role we were tasked with was to be spread out down one road, keeping a look-out for anybody trying to take alternative routes to avoid the road blocks on the main roads.

My platoon was situated next to a group of old farm buildings, which it looked like the local wildlife had started to take control of. The walls of the buildings were completely overrun by a mass of twisting and winding green ivy. The area was quite a heavily-wooded location and with our green and brown camouflaged fatigues, we fitted in nicely amongst the tall trees and bristling bushes. The platoon probably couldn't have asked for a better observing advantage, as we had a great over-watch of the surrounding roads. From our vantage point we could monitor anything or anybody looking suspicious and could cut them off quickly if we had to. The best thing about our position was that incoming vehicles couldn't see us until it was too late, and the drivers had no option but to stop or take a deadly risk and run straight through. Well, that was if they had the balls and the speed to outrun 5.56mm bullets.

We had been there about four hours and not seen a single vehicle pass through our check point. Mac gestured for me to come over to his position and then told me he needed a crap. He was standing there fidgeting about on the balls of his feet and said he didn't think he could hold it in any longer. I was disgusted.

"What the fuck do you want me to do about it, push it back in?"

"No, you dirty tramp. What you take me for? Just want you to come with me to that old outhouse over there and cover the door while I deliver a brown package." I agreed to go with him and followed behind, keeping my distance from his disgusting farts. He was out of control. Every step he took, another eye watering brown methane cloud sneaked out.

We approached the outbuilding, and I could see straightaway we would have to break the lock. I had to take care of this because Mac was now hopping about, telling me he was touching cloth and desperately telling me there was no more time. I kicked down the door with one of my size tens and he raced in and crouched down in the far corner, delivering what he had promised. The smell hit me like a wave of floating shit, almost making me gag.

"Fucking hell, Mac, what the fuck have you been eating? You fucking stink." The rotten stench forced me further from the door, when Mac started shouting that he hadn't any loo-roll and was trying to purloin mine. I told him there was no way I was giving him mine, just in case I had an emergency of my own later. But I did mercifully throw one of my old notebooks in for him to use. I always thought about the poor old farmer doing his rounds and finding a giant turd living in one of his outbuildings. After the shit incident we returned to our checkpoint and got back into our normal routine.

As it usually did in Northern Ireland, it started to rain and when I say rain I mean a torrential downpour. This continued for the next couple of hours and the only thing that got us through it was the arrival of a brand new silver Audi TT. I knew straightaway that we were going to have some fun, because as the driver dropped his window his first words were, "You a bit wet there, mate?" As we had the power to search any vehicle we wanted, I thought I was going to teach this young lad a very valuable lesson.

"Can you get out the car please?" I asked.

"What do you mean? It's pissing it down," he replied.

"Under the terrorist act two thousand, I have the powers to search this vehicle, as I suspect you are carrying prohibited items," I proudly recited.

"Are you taking the piss or something, you fucking ass hole?" he shouted angrily.

"Come on, Sir, there is no need for bad language. If you have nothing on you, it won't take too long," I explained.

The lad was not best pleased, but eventually joined us in the downpour. Now deep down I knew he wasn't carrying anything, but no one takes the piss out of us and gets away with it. So I spent the next half hour searching every last nook and cranny of his tiny car, just trying to pass some time and of course piss off our now piss-wet-through cocky Audi driver. After replacing his foot-mats, which had been sitting out in the rain, I told him he could be on his way and as he was about to pull off, I lent in through the window and quietly said, "You a bit wet there, mate?" All I'm going to say about his response is, if looks could kill!

A few days later, after returning back to Palace Barracks I was called in to company Sergeant Major P.'s office. He told me that he had found a place for me on an external Junior NCOs carda and wanted me to take him up on his offer. He then said for me go away and think about it and give him an answer in a couple of days' time. This offer had come just before I was about to go on leave and I would have definitely lost it if I had accepted his proposal. So from the get-go my heart was never really in it, because I'd also made so many plans with my friends and family back home and I felt like I couldn't let them down. To be honest, looking back now, I should have gone on this course. It would have been the perfect time to get promoted and I would have easily passed. I just couldn't see it then, and it's a decision I slightly regret now.

I returned to his office a couple of days later and told him my plans. I informed him that I didn't think my heart was in it and I would only be taking a place from someone else that was up for it. He didn't appreciate my honesty as I thought he would have, and he unceremoniously threw me out of his office and out on to the landing.

"Get the fuck out of my office, you useless piece of shit," he roared in my direction, "Don't you realise I have stuck my neck out for you and this is how you repay me? Don't ever expect anything from me again." I was then made to stand outside in the car park to attention for the rest of the day, during great British summer showers. I stood there as proud as punch, trying not to show him any weakness. My relationship with him never really recovered after that. No matter how good a soldier I tried to be, he would always find a way of sticking me on guard on a weekend at the drop of a hat.

Thankfully I only had a couple of days before my leave was about to start and if only I could stay out of his way till then, I would be able to escape any further punishments from him. I avoided any evil acts of discipline from my aggressor and returned back to Birmingham to start my two weeks' leave. I was chuffed to be back and couldn't wait to realise all the plans I'd made with my mates. Although saying that, sometimes leave never went as I'd planned and I would end up doing something completely random.

The weather was amazing, with temperatures up in the mid-twenties, and I decided that my tan needed a bit of work. So I spent the morning in the garden, chilling with a few ice cold cans of Stella. I'd been texting a girl I'd met in Darlington while in training, and she had been begging me to come up and see her for ages. I started getting a vision of a road trip, but at the time I wasn't driving, so I rang my mate Mark, to see if he could borrow his Dad's car for a couple of days. Even though he also didn't have a current driving licence, he somehow convinced his Dad to hand over the keys. With this, the dream of the road trip became reality. I rang Dave and told him of our plans and he was onboard straightaway.

We left that same day, stopping off at a nearby petrol station to grab some fuel and supplies, before getting on the motorway to start our epic journey. The plan was to head up the M1 to Darlington and meet up with this bird, who had also said she had some mates for my friends, and that we could stay at her place since her parents were currently away on holiday.

About half an hour from Sheffield the car starting to play up and after pulling up at the next service station we realised there was a small leak in the radiator, which we tried to fix with some rag-weld. We made a plan that we would cut short the journey to Darlington and head to Sheffield to find somewhere to stay till the following morning. We would assess the situation when we knew the condition of the car.

We drove around the city centre in search for an overnight spot until we found a nasty old bed and breakfast, which turned out to be just over the road from the Crucible Theatre, where the world championship snooker is played, and we booked in. There was a bar downstairs, so we headed that way and enjoyed the evening with some of the locals. After a skinful we retreated back upstairs, before we were abducted by some of the older women who were on the prowl looking for some young meat. We woke nice and early the following morning and started to come up with ideas for how the rest of the road trip would continue. Our plan was now to abandon the idea of going to Darlington after all, which pissed off my date to say the least, and we decided to travel across country to Liverpool, where Mark's ex-girlfriend Mary was studying at university. She had told Mark that the place was rocking on the piss and we would have a great time there.

We headed west along the A628, which cuts straight across the Peak District National Park, and what a drive it was. I think we all had our breath completely taken away by the amazing and picturesque views that this part of the country had to offer. It was just mind-blowing that an area like that was carved into the land between two great cities. The journey flew by in no time and we arrived in Liverpool just after ten. For the next twenty minutes Dave and I pestered Mark to pull over somewhere for us to have a drink. We had a real urge for a pint of Stella for breakfast.

We found somewhere to quench our thirst, and we located a hotel for the evening. After checking in we went and dropped our bags in the room and started spying on a group of women through the window, who were situated in a smoking area just across the street. Mark was getting a really good look, standing up against the window, so I thought it would be a good idea to get their attention.

"HELLO," I shouted. With this, Dave and I dropped below the window level, leaving Mark just standing there not knowing what had just happened. By now the group of smoking hot ladies had all spun about and caught Mark in mid-perv, pressed firmly against the window. Dave and I were just in a fit of hysterics, almost to the point of tears. Eventually Mark found the funny side of it all and started joining in with the laughter. After my prank we headed out to start the drinking session proper. We ended up on Mathews Street and were enticed into one of the bars by the promise of free shots, where we were then set upon by a group of women on a hen party, whose wandering hands were out of control. A man's perfect night, really. What else could you really ask for?

The next few hours were a drunken blur of tequila shots and blonde-haired women dressed in nurses' uniforms. The place we had found was absolutely rocking and the blondie that I'd got friendly with wasn't too far behind. Her seductive scouse accent made me want to marry her right there and then. The session continued long into the night until we finally headed back to the Formula One hotel a little the worse for wear, arm in arm with our hot blonde companions.

Mark had met up with Mary and taken her back to his room, but he returned shortly to ask me an embarrassing question.

"Have you got any Viagra on you? The drink has affected my you know what." I laughed to myself as I went and fetched my wallet, retrieving one of the little blue night-savers. I handed it over to him, telling him to take it straightaway and he returned to his room. I continued with my business until an hour later when I was disturbed again by a knock at the door. I angrily swung the door open, only to find a frantic looking Mark standing in front of me.

"What the fuck have you given me? This tablet's trying to kill me. Feels like I'm having a heart attack or something," he gasped.

"Don't worry about it," I told him, "Sometimes it happens, just got to plough through. It's happened to me a few times before. It's nothing to worry about." With that, he staggered back down the hallway and into his room.

The glistening early morning sun bursting through the half-drawn curtains and burning my eyes brought me back to life, and the reality that I had to get rid of last night's conquest was front and centre of my mind. Thankfully, and luckily for me, she had to rush off to meet her boyfriend, which worked out well, as we now didn't have to deal with the awkward small-talk that usually follows these nights. We rendezvoused with a recovered Mark and made the long hungover journey back to Birmingham with only our drunken memories keeping us going. After a few pit stops or sick stops at service stations along the way, we finally made it home and I headed straight to bed for a quick power nap. I had to recharge my batteries, because I was due to meet up for another night on the town with some of Army pals.

After returning to Northern Ireland the battalion was ordered onto the parade square and briefed that a company was going to be deployed to Iraq for a six-month tour. It sounds crazy, but every man in every company prayed it would be theirs. Opportunities like this don't come around that often and when they do, you want to be part of it. It was soon apparent that C company had been chosen and were due to be deployed in four weeks' time. I then volunteered myself to be part of the tour as a back-up, just in case anybody got injured or lost their bottle and went sick. Nothing came of this and I was disappointed that I couldn't go and serve my country in one of the most challenging and dangerous environments at the time. This was the kind of thing that we'd joined the Army for, and to be really honest I envied the lads that had gone.

My disappointment didn't last too long. As it turned out, one of the lads who had been deployed was due to get married half-way through the tour and I'd been chosen to relieve him. I spent the next couple of weeks sorting out my kit and making sure my fitness was up to scratch. I didn't want to turn up there looking like a shower of shit or blowing out my ass like some asthmatic Remf.

At the same time as all the Iraq business was going on, there had been a fad for people in my company to own BB guns. People would find themselves being attacked in their rooms by other lads from the company. Up until this point, luckily, no one had been hurt, apart from maybe a few bruised egos. I had two days before I was due to fly out to Iraq to start my three-month deployment and was just chilling in my room, really looking forward to doing what I'd been trained for, to go to war and maybe pay the ultimate sacrifice.

I'd gone into the toilet when suddenly I heard a disturbance in the hallway. I started to expect the worst when the bathroom door flew open, revealing two lads carrying BB guns, ready to engage. As soon as they saw me they opened fire and I started taking shots all over my head and body. I covered my face and used a small gap between my arms to view my enemy. I charged the first lad and wrestled him to the floor and disarmed him with ease. I now had his weapon and started to return fire at Mac, who was taking cover on the other side of the bathroom door.

He made a break for it, but as he did, he fired the weapon backwards and one of the pellets hit me flush in my left eye, instantly filling my eye with water and blinding me. I shouted at Mac to stop firing and he rushed to my side. At first, I thought I just had blurred vision and was laughing and joking with Mac, although after thirty minutes my vision had still not improved. In fact, it had become even worse, with my eye now closing. I was rushed down to the med centre, but not before telling the company duty Corporal some stupid story about someone shooting me from behind the bins by the block and then running off laughing. I didn't want to get Mac into any trouble, as we were good mates. If he'd been caught as the perpetrator, he would most likely have been demoted.

When I arrived at the med centre it quickly became apparent that the condition of my eye was worse than I first thought. I was told by the doctor that I would be required to go to the hospital straightaway. She said that I needed to return to the block and arrange an escort, as the hospital was on the Falls Road. Callum volunteered to take me, so along with a nine-millimetre Browning high-powered pistol shoved in his waistband, we went on our way.

I was given a fake address to give to the hospital staff and used a shortened version of my name. I struggled into a seat as my peripheral vision was now non-existent, and I waited to be seen. A doctor came out and called me through. Callum stood up and helped me to my feet and we headed her way. As we went to walk through the open door to her examination room she stopped Callum and said only I was allowed past this point. Now Callum and the doctor started to argue about why he'd been stopped. He explained in no uncertain terms why he was not going to leave my side, and he asked her if she understood what he was trying to say to her. Finally, the penny dropped, and she realised who and what we were. After what felt like a lifetime since the incident, I finally sat down on the bed and she took a look at my swollen eye. She said it was too early to tell what damage had been caused, and that she would need time for the swelling to go down before she could give me an honest answer on whether I would be able to see again. If not, it would probably be the end of my Army career.

The next day I woke up and slowly came to the realisation that my dream about being posted to Iraq was over. I would be very lucky just to get the sight back in my eye. Two days later I went to my appointment with the eye specialist and was told that I had detached my retina. Now it would be a waiting game to see how it repaired itself, before they could tell me if it would go back to a hundred percent. I headed back to camp and after returning to the block I was summoned to Company Sergeant Major P.'s office to explain what had happened and who had shot me.

He told me he had heard rumours about who the perpetrator was, and he was also aware that I knew who it was. He said that the whole story about someone shooting me from behind the bins was a load of bollocks and he wanted me to think carefully about my next statement. I braved it out and kept to my account of the night and hoped he was just bluffing. After going back through my story, he looked at me.

"Okay, you're sticking with that then? Fair enough, I understand that you don't want to get anybody into trouble. Especially not Lance Corporal Mc., as I know you are mates." He sent me on my way and I returned to the platoon office. I sat down with Sergeant I. and explained that I'd been put on the sick for three months and I was to take no part in any physical activity.

A couple of weeks later news broke that a patrol in Iraq had been caught up in an explosion, but there were no reports of casualties. At the time I think a lot of people around the battalion started hearing rumours to the contrary, and that two soldiers had been seriously injured in the blast. At times like this the camp could be overrun with Chinese whispers, everyone having a story about what had happened, and this time it was no different. Somehow people just found out what had happened and to whom. I had good friends in C company and just hoped it wasn't any of them, and to be really honest I wished the rumours were false altogether.

One day, on a crisp sunny September morning the battalion was ordered to form up on the parade square and it was now obvious that something had happened. There was just a feeling that was swirling around and every now and then I caught the glimpse of two higher ranking soldiers whispering to each other. On the way to the square I started to mentally prepare myself for the tragic news that was waiting for us.

After forming, we quickly learnt that two soldiers, Fusiliers Me. and Ma. had been killed while patrolling in Basra. Even though everyone probably had some idea that this news was going to break, I could feel the whole battalion just sigh and deflate instantly. This was devastating news for everyone to take and especially for those who had called the two heroes friends. Even though I didn't really know the two of them, I spent a moment in my thoughts, thinking about their families and how they would be feeling. And even though I'm not a religious person, I said a quick prayer for them and their loved ones.

I later learnt through friends who had been deployed to Iraq that Fusilier Ma. was the lad who I was to replace before my injury. I felt devastated to learn of this and couldn't help but think of the what ifs. If that BB pellet had been an inch higher, maybe it would have been my family getting the knock at the door and having their world come crashing down around them. But sometimes life is weird like that, maybe it just wasn't my time.

While I was recovering from the eye incident, Sgt Major P. had told me that due to the fact I couldn't take part in any of my normal duties, I would have to report to the Sergeants' mess and work down there. Some of my duties involved being a member of the bar staff and waiting on the senior NCOs. At first, I hated the idea, but as I still had ages before I was due for my medical review, I was stuffed.

I had worked on the Friday night and was given the Saturday off by Colour Sgt B. He told me that I was due back at work on the Sunday night, so I should keep hold of the bar keys. I decided I was going to go over to the NAFFI on the Saturday night and as it had been a while, I planned to really get on it. The problem with that idea is that when I was pissed I did stupid things.

I walked in the NAFFI, and straightaway noticed a couple of older women sitting at one of the tables. One of them started to look in my direction and then unbelievably, she winked at me. I thought to myself, *Here we go. Should be a good night.* I headed for the bar, got a pint of my favourite tickle and sat down so I was facing my admirer. We exchanged a few cheeky glances until she stood up and walked over, sitting her amazing body elegantly next to me. Wedding rings hadn't usually bothered me before, but this time I was sober and started to ask questions about how her husband would feel about her talking to me.

"Don't worry about him," she told me.

We were all over each other and just couldn't keep our hands off one another. It felt as if we were the only two people in the room, if you know what I mean. Her friend kept coming over and trying to get us to calm down, because people had started to stare. With the drinks flowing and the in-house DJ playing some cracking tunes, I stupidly suggested we went back to the Sergeants' bar as I had the keys. I promised her we could get a few more drinks and finally be alone. She responded within a second.

"Come on, let's go. I hope you have protection." We made our way in to the little office behind the bar, where I poured us a couple of drinks. One thing led to another, until the door swung open and CSM P. walked in and caught us in the act. He was absolutely furious. I really thought he was about to kill me and it didn't really help his mood when he realised he knew my naked partner's husband.

He ordered me to put my clothes on and sent me on my way. I thought he had finished with me, until he shouted that he would deal with me on Monday morning. Out of all the dumb and stupid things I'd done in my drunken escapades, this was definitely one of the worst. Don't get me wrong, I had a very good night up until I got caught, but man, it was crazy.

I was called to his office on the Monday morning and read the riot act. He was as mad as anything and I think if I hadn't been on the sick, he would probably have filled me in. He was going crazy, shouting and screaming. I don't think I had ever seen him this mad, the whole two years he'd been in charge. After about thirty minutes of bad language and threats, he sent me to the guardroom as punishment. I was made to clean the whole complex inside and out and commanded to just stay there until told otherwise, which eventually came about a week and a half later, when he had found me some other crappy jobs to take over.

I later found out that the husband of the woman I'd been fooling around with was in charge of the physical training of the battalion. Luckily for me, he couldn't touch me, as I was still on the sick with my dodgy eye. About three weeks later, just before I learnt the fate of my eye issue, he got posted off to Germany before he got a chance to get his hands on me.

My review board assessment day with the medical staff came and thankfully I was given the all-clear to continue my normal role as a fully-fledged soldier. Now I didn't have long to wait until the battalion was to be posted to Dehkilia garrison in Cyprus, about fifteen minutes from Ayia Napa, which turned out to be a nightmare situation for the battalion. Imagine a camp full of horny, drunken soldiers living in the sun. Not a very good recipe really.

Chapter sixteen – Danny

I arrived in Cyprus in November 2005, and what hit me first was the heat. Even though it was still their winter it was absolutely baking, although it was probably the fact that we had just come from the minus conditions in Belfast that made it feel that hot. I'll always remember the day after we arrived. The whole company was ordered down to the battalion's private beach for a barbecue and a few drinks. Even though the temperature was in the low twenties, the locals were in hats and scarves, while we were running around like idiots in shorts and flip flops.

From the very start I had a strange feeling that this might be my last residential tour, and for the first time in my life I felt homesick. I'd always thought that the Army would be a career for me, but I felt things had suddenly shifted and no longer did I have that burning desire inside me that had driven me on this far to fulfil my dream. I still had a year and a half to push before I could become a free man. So I pushed those thoughts to the back of my mind and got on with what I was getting paid to do: being the best soldier I could be.

The company was placed straight onto guard, with one platoon taking over the duties of protecting the garrison. Another was posted to the Royal Air Force camp called Aiya Nikalis, which was about a fifteen-minute drive down a highly dangerous road, and the final platoon was on cover for any incidents taking place at either location.

I had been on guard for a few weeks when tragedy rocked the battalion and the hardest hit was B company. Lance Corporal Mark Dryburgh (Drys), Fusiliers Danny W., Ray R. (Robbo) and Craig G. (Gibsie) had been involved in a road traffic accident while on a routine patrol from Dehkilia Garrison to Ayia Nicholias. The Land Rover they had been travelling in left the road at speed, turned over and hit a tree. The accident had fatally wounded Danny and left the driver, Drys, in a critical condition and in a coma. Gibsie was also seriously injured with a broken back and he was left paralyzed from the waist down. Robbo luckily survived without any serious injury, just badly bruised, but having said that, he was affected very badly by the crash mentally. I think after a life event like that, when you are the only one to walk away without any visible injury, maybe you start to question a few things. Like how did you escape this terrifying crash with your life?

This was the first time that I had lost someone I would have called a good friend and the whole company was absolutely devastated. I will never forget it. Our platoon commander sat us down in the guard room and broke the news to us. Everyone just sat there in silence and I just reflected on how such a great young soldier, sorry great person, could have been taken from us in such a tragic way. At tragic times like this I have been always capable of retreating into my mind and keeping my emotions in check. Something that has probably caused me more harm than good over the years, because I still struggle to this day to deal with what has happened in the past. A harmful trait of mine that maybe needs addressing one day soon.

For the next few days the battalion mourned its loss, but as always, things had to move on. Never try and get stuck in the past. Trust me. It will eventually try and consume the present. The company was called on to parade to discuss the funeral arrangements. Company Sergeant Major D. emerged from his office and asked if anyone wanted to volunteer to be one of the pallbearers. I think everyone in the company raised a hand and through a sea of worthy and brave candidates he picked out ten guys, with me being one of them. I saw this life-changing duty as such a great honour. Carrying my friend to his final resting place turned out to be a moment in my life that I will never forget.

It was a week or so before the funeral was due to take place in Newcastle, but before that could take place, the battalion had a repatriation service at the garrison church to arrange. So the funeral party spent the next few days practising with CSM D. the drills needed to carry out this service in the correct manner. We would spend six hours a day with a coffin filled with sandbags, making sure we knew what we were doing, so we could give Danny the best send-off possible. During this period the families of the injured soldiers had arrived in Cyprus to see their sons and we had been tasked to be their escorts around camp. I took up this task with pride and wanted to show them that we were all thinking of them in their time of need. I also told the family members that if there was anything I could do for them, not to hesitate to ask.

The day of the service arrived, and I felt sick with nerves. I still just couldn't believe that this was reality and not a totally horrendous nightmare that we had all been part of. I had now started to really struggle with my emotions and kept having to take deep breaths to control them, but I knew I had to pull myself together and be the professional soldier I was capable of being.

We arrived at the church dressed in full ceremonial uniform and waited in a state of trepidation for the dreaded black hearse to arrive. I was one of two rear guys, so I would be carrying the head of the coffin into the church with Chris B. We were of similar size, so our shoulders matched up nicely with each other's, which made a firm, level platform for the heavy and uncomfortable coffin to rest on. I saw the black Jaguar appear and watched it as it started to make its way up the steep, winding hill. Luckily, before any more unwanted feelings could take over my already nervous body, CSM D. drilled us to our starting positions.

The hearse carrying our friend slowly approached the church and stopped just outside the giant wooden doors. Under orders from CSM D. we proudly marched towards the back doors, which were then opened, ready for us to slowly and correctly remove Danny and take him into the church for his repatriation service.

The first two lads nervously started to remove the coffin. Their shaking hands reached in and slowly started shuffling it backwards, until all six of us had hold of him. Under further orders from CSM D. we slowly raised the coffin until it reached in line with our chests. Then in one fluid movement we carried out an inward turn, with one arm reaching out to go over the shoulder of the man next to me and at the same time the other hand resting palm first on my left-hand cheek, and with my thumb awkwardly placed just under the coffin for extra support.

After this difficult manoeuvre was complete we were slow-marched up the concrete steps and into the stiflingly hot and uncomfortable church, with Chris and me struggling to keep the head of the coffin above the feet under the unbelievably heavy strain. The funeral party worked as if it was a single entity and glided down the aisle, proudly carrying Danny to the front of a packed-out church. We then slowly lowered the coffin and placed him onto two wooden plinths. CSM D. then left-turned the funeral party and marched us back outside to a welcoming cool breeze. After the service finished we were marched back in and collected Danny. Then he was returned to the hearse and he was taken to RAF Akrotiri to be flown home for the final time to be back in Newcastle with his waiting family.

I spent the Christmas of 2005 on guard. During this time, I kept finding myself thinking of my family back home and how they would be spending Christmas. I knew they would all be with my Nan and Aunt, a family tradition that went back years. I also spared a thought for the family of Danny and how they were going through hell without him. This in turn would make me think of how things could change in a blink of an eye and you never knew what was waiting for you around the corner.

I went on leave knowing I still had to head to Newcastle to do Danny proud. I also wanted to show his family what he truly meant to us all and how devastated we were for their loss. I saw in the New Year with my family. Still, I couldn't really celebrate anything with the funeral deep in my thoughts, but I did privately raise a glass for my friend.

I was collected on the morning of the funeral by Sean and we made the long journey north. The mood in the car was of one of reflection, with us all recalling stories of how we first met Danny and how we would all miss him. I remember meeting him in Belfast when he first turned up at the battalion. He was a really likeable lad and fitted in with B Company straightaway. Usually when new lads turned up there was a little bit of time when the new lad got ignored. He'd be sort of getting assessed by all the other lads, to see what kind of bloke he was, but with Danny it was as if he had been with us for years. That's the kind of lad he was, a real character.

I recall two songs that came on the radio that we all hoped the family wouldn't use for the service. They were *The World's Greatest,* by R. Kelly, and *Goodbye, My Lover* by James Blunt.

We arrived at an old TA centre where we would spend the night. After we'd been shown to our sleeping quarters, CSM D. gave us our final rehearsal to make sure we were up to scratch. He then told us to go out and enjoy our night, but not to do anything stupid, and not to turn up the next day stinking of booze. Otherwise, stand by when you return to Cyprus. We went out for a few drinks in honour of Danny, but didn't go crazy, which was a bit of a surprise from a bunch of soldiers, but this tragic event meant so much to us we didn't want to let anyone down.

I woke the following morning in the freezing cold hall that had been given to us as accommodation. I very reluctantly removed myself from my warm and cosy sleeping bag to go to the toilet. I grabbed a quick wash and shave and then met up with the other lads down the road in a small cafe and scoffed down a full English breakfast, or as we were in this part of the world so close to the border, a full Scottish. We returned to the hall and made ourselves presentable in our ceremonial uniform, but as this dress was made for Cyprus weather and we were now in Newcastle in January, we were bloody freezing.

Sean drove us to the church and waited for everyone to arrive. The weather conditions had not improved at all, and all you could hear from our group was the sound of chattering teeth. Before we started our duty, CSM D. reminded us that we were here representing the battalion and not to show any emotion during the service. He told us to just keep it inside and let it out once it was all over.

After Danny arrived and everyone was in position we approached the back of the hearse and prepared ourselves to remove his coffin from the gaping boot space. Like a well-drilled machine, we gradually started to lift him to the correct position, but this time there was a problem. We had been standing around for that long in the cold, that my arms were just not taking orders from my mind. I pleaded with myself to find some form of extra strength that might have been buried deep within, but to no avail.

Then suddenly, as if from nowhere, my body finally agreed to do what I had been asking of it and with one fluid motion I helped lift him on to our waiting shoulders. This was a very moving and difficult time for us all for the obvious reasons. I could really feel the tension radiating from the coffin, as it gently shook from the nervous energy that was slowly seeping out from the pores of the six of us; soldiers who were struggling to hold back our emotions beneath our friend.

We slowly turned the coffin so it lined up with the double doors, and under the orders of CSM D. we slow-marched our way towards the church. My heart felt as if it was about to burst clean through my chest and I felt as if everyone could hear its unbelievably loud beat. My emotions were trying everything to take over, but I battled back, forcing them deep inside where they belonged. About now my shoulder and back were starting to wilt under the enormous strain that they were under. Don't get me wrong, the coffin was heavy, but it was like I was breaking down from the stares of the onlooking mourning crowd. His family had now formed up behind us and the tears falling freely from his mother's sore red eyes kept me motivated to do her son proud.

As we entered the church our previous day's fears of song choice materialised, with the sound of R Kelly's *World's Greatest* vibrating around the tall church ceiling. Now with Danny's family and friends behind us, it felt as if we had been given extra strength from their flowing tears, as we headed towards the church altar and for the final time placed Danny down. We then, as we'd practised many times, folded the union flag into a tight and neat triangle and handed it over to CSM D, who in turn politely passed it over, along with Danny's beret and belt, to his distraught mother. We were left-turned and marched to the rear of the church from where we would watch the rest of the service.

The place was packed to the rafters, which just showed how many lives this young soldier, who we all called our friend, had touched in his short twenty two years. If you have ever heard the last post being sounded on a bugle, then you will know what I'm talking about. It is moving at the best of times, but to hear it being played at a friend's funeral is completely soul-destroying. I could feel a wave of emotion building up inside me and had to fight like crazy to keep my feelings in check.

I will always remember his sister bravely standing up and, while fighting back the tears, reading out a moving piece that depicted Danny perfectly. At the end of the service, as the tearful crowd paid their final respects and headed for the exit, the unmistakable sound of the first few bars from the piano of James Blunt's *Goodbye My Lover* rang out, and I just looked at Sean and said quietly, "It must have been a sign," to which he just nodded his head and said,

"Definitely, mate."

We followed the family to a nearby pub where the wake was taking place and noticed Danny's Dad just waiting outside alone. As we approached him he stopped us and told everyone that Danny would have been so proud to see his friends here and giving him such a great send-off. He also wanted to shake each one of us by the hand and thank us for what we had done today and also in Cyprus. I said that it was a huge privilege and a massive honour to carry his son. I went on to say that I was deeply moved by the courage of his daughter, to have been able to stand up, and in front of everyone, to deliver such an amazing eulogy for Danny. It showed that even through the most difficult of times, she wanted to be there for her brother.

We stayed at the wake for a few hours, paying our respects to this great and strong family and after saying our goodbyes we headed into Newcastle. We found ourselves a hotel for the evening and after a quick wash we headed out. We now wanted to go out and have a right proper knees-up for him and knew that was what he would have wanted us to do. I woke the following morning with a stinking hangover and prepared myself for the long journey home. I think the past fortnight's events had finally caught up with us, as we hardly said a word to each other the whole journey back. Everyone locked in their own soul-searching thoughts.

You were such a great bloke, Danny, and were taken away from your family and friends far too early, before you got chance to realise your full potential.

Chapter seventeen – The Musketeers

When we returned to Cyprus you could tell that everyone was still struggling to come to terms with the recent events, and with Drys still in a coma, the higher ranks were still none the wiser as to how the accident had occurred. There were rumours that an oncoming vehicle had made him swerve out the way and lose control. Although until he woke up and told his side of the story, what had truly caused this tragic accident would remain a mystery.

Battalion life continued as it always did, and the weather was really starting to warm up. A bunch of us started to enjoy what Cyprus really had to offer. The beautiful beaches and the fantastic night-life started to draw us in. There were four of us who would always go out together. Chris, Steve, Evo and I, we ended up calling ourselves the four musketeers. We would go everywhere together and in Northern Ireland we were in the same room. Chris was probably my closest friend and we still have contact with each other now. Even though we can go years between seeing one another, it's like it was only yesterday that we did. We still have a strong bond and I would do anything for the big-eared fool.

I first met Chris in North Luffenham and from the off we didn't seem to get on with one another. In his words, he referred to me as an arrogant fucker, but it wasn't long before we became good friends. After moving to Northern Ireland, and being sent to B company, I ended up sharing a room with him, Steve and another lad called Kev, who was again a close friend. But after Kev got married and moved out of the block, he started doing the stuff married folk do.

Chris will always tell a story of me when I was on leave and my brother had got himself into a spot of bother while in prison. He'd asked my Mom to drop some money off to some guy whose friend had been hassling Richard on the inside. I went with Mom but as I didn't know who I was dealing with, I took a weapon with me, a nice 9mm pistol which I had got from one of my dodgy acquaintances.

I rang Chris and asked him if he could meet me at the location as a bit of back-up and it was only when I was there that I revealed my new piece of protection. He still talks of this event and calls me a crazy bastard, which we always laugh about. Chris and I would always play-fight with each other at any chance we got and if he were brave enough, he would still try his luck now.

I recall a time in Cyprus when we had been on a heavy drinking binge and after returning to camp, we started fighting with each other outside the guardroom. The knobhead ended up taking full advantage of my drunken state and chucked me head-first into a thorny bush. After stumbling to my feet and removing unwanted thorns from my hand, I sought revenge for his early cowardly act of aggression. I took my chance for revenge while he was on the phone to his mom.

I snuck up behind him and with a firm right hand, slapped him clean across his laughing face. Can you believe he was actually telling his Mom what he had just done to me at four in the morning! I left him where he dropped and legged it to his room, locking him out in the process. After getting his sorry ass up off the ground he gave chase and returned to his room, only to find that he was locked out and that I'd taken a picture of his Mom off the wall as a hostage and threatened to please myself to it.

He was absolutely furious. Probably the angriest I have ever seen him, and he demanded I opened the door to him, which I flatly refused to do until he'd calmed down. After about thirty minutes or so, he had calmed himself sufficiently enough for me to feel safe from attack. So I carried out my promise. Unfortunately for me, as soon as he was inside he attacked. We then spent the next ten minutes rolling around the floor fighting until we were both exhausted, and we finally put an end to this childish horseplay.

Steve and I met for the first time in Northern Ireland. He was in my room and in the bed space opposite mine. At first, we didn't really say much to each other, just a small acknowledgement of each other's presence every now and again, as it was kind of one of the unwritten rules. No one really spoke to the new guy when they first turned up. They would just get ignored for the first few weeks until they got to know you and that was no different with me.

Then one day, out of the blue he popped his head into my bed space and said that he was going the NAFFI for a few drinks and did I fancy it. After that we sort of just clicked. He was a Geordie and a diehard Newcastle fan, and we would spend ages just ripping each other about our favourite football teams, depending on their current league positions. He had a massive forehead, so he was nick-named Bomb Head, which he didn't seem to mind too much. The fact he had a way with the ladies suggested his bomb head didn't seem to affect him too much in that regard.

Steve and I would take part in this game of trying to get each other to flinch by pretending to hit the other one in the balls. Well, it wasn't just our game. At times it felt as if the whole battalion was playing it. If you flinched, then he would give you two punches to the arm, and if he hit you in the balls, you would then have ten punches to hand out to him or one to his gentlemen area. This could go on for hours and then the drunken game would quickly escalate. The next morning, we would find huge bruises all over our arms.

Out of the four of us, Steve loved going out the most and when we were based in Cyprus he would head to JJ's every night and get on it. I mean, when we went out on the piss I would probably end up drinking the most, but he just hated being in camp. He hated it so much that sometimes he would not return until later the following day and one such event affected me directly.

He'd come to my room one night and persuaded me to join him on the night out with a promise that a girl he was seeing had a mate who wanted to meet me. He didn't have to twist my arm too much and after a quick shower, I excitedly went to meet my date. The night was fantastic and after spending a few hours with her at her hotel I returned to camp, but stupidly signed us both in.

I woke the following morning slightly hung over, but in relatively good spirits after last night's conquest. I wanted to thank Steve for doing me such a good turn, so I walked down the corridor and headed for his room. The little sod wasn't there, and I soon realized when we were on parade that he hadn't returned to camp at all. At this point I'd completely forgotten that I'd signed him in and went about my day as usual with a big smile on my face. How things were about to change for the worse! Thank you, Bomb Head.

Eventually after a few hours and still no sign of the elusive head, the CSM got wind that someone had signed him back into camp. Unfortunately for me it wasn't too long before he put two and two together and I was quickly called to his office to explain my actions. It went without saying that I received a right good bollocking from him, but I was sent on my way thinking that was the end of that. As was usually the case, things were about to take another turn for the worse.

Unluckily for me, as I was leaving his office I marched right past the Provo Sergeant. (He's the guy who is in charge of discipline, and that's where you get sent to for extra special beastings.) I addressed him as I marched by and thought that was the end of it, up until I was about to head down the stairs and get out of sight.

"Oi, you stop there!" he shouted. I halted and about-turned. As he started to approach I knew I was in for it and just prepared myself for the upcoming beasting I knew I was about to experience.

"Are you the twat that signed your mate in?"

"Guilty, Sergeant," I answered. He then shouted for me to wait for him downstairs and get ready for some punishment.

He quick-marched me to the battalion parade square where in the blistering heat he ragged me all over. The sweat was dripping from me as if someone was spraying a hose at me. I was in a really bad way and I could now smell last night's alcohol pouring out of me.

"Left, right, left, right," he shouted. My legs just couldn't keep up with what he was demanding I did. Even the fantastic memories of the previous night's womanising couldn't help me through this, and at some point I started regretting even going out. After finally being sent on my way and told to return after lunch, I headed to my room and rang Steve, telling him he needed to return straightaway as I was getting fucked for him. After lunch I returned to the parade square and was given a brush to sweep the square. The Provo then told me that he didn't want to find one loose stone on there when he returned.

My day took an upwards turn when I saw the returning bomb head walking down towards company HQ. It wasn't long before I happily witnessed him receiving the same punishment as I had. I even took a second to watch and a small grin appeared on my sweaty face. After Steve had joined me to finish off the cleaning of the parade square, we were told that we needed to report to the guard room at the weekend for extra duties, which turned out to be to clear the beach of sea weed, where I spent the whole time cursing Steve for getting me in the shit. This turned out to an even shittier task than the parade-sweeping one. As you can imagine. the sea brings in weed with every wave. So it turned out to be a continuous task of cleaning the beach from one side to the other. Even though we were told in no uncertain terms we were not allowed to leave the camp that weekend, we still managed to sneak out on the Saturday night to have a few drinks down on the strip. Although this time I made him return with me, so there was no repeat of the day from hell.

Evo joined about a year or so after me and moved into my room after the others had been sent on recruitment. He was few years younger than me and after getting briefed up for loud music, we got on well. I sort of introduced him to Steve and Chris when they returned and that's how we all became friends. We all just clicked and would do anything for each other. Some of the nights we had together were legendary and it's such a shame that we sort of drifted apart after the Army.

The four of us would go out most nights, but unlike the rest of the battalion we hated going to places that were full of soldiers. So instead, we would seek out more clandestine places and keep them secret from the rest. One night we stumbled across one such place. After a company beach party, we headed down on the Dehkelia strip and found a bar named JJ's. The beat of classic eighties music drew us in like moths to a flame. We headed through the glass doors and walked into the bar. Once inside, we were greeted by the most beautiful creature you could be lucky enough to lay your eyes on called Margarita. I remember the four of us singing *Lady in Red* to her every time it got played and she just lapped it up like it was a nightly occurrence. She was so beautiful I would find myself just staring at her, until she would catch me and say in her amazing Latvian accent, "Everything okay?"

Pete, who owned the establishment, took a shine to us pretty much straightaway and would spend the night having drinking competitions, with us knocking back shots of black sambuca. Most of the time after a night in there I would wake up the following morning with no recollection of what had taken place, until I went the next night and to my utter horror saw pictures of me all over the many TVs that were around the place. I would end up reliving the embarrassing night, sober and in front of a sniggering audience. The number of pictures of me asleep in random places was unreal, but there was nothing you could do but laugh at yourself.

One night we had headed to our usual haunt and after a good many drinks we decided to sit outside and enjoy the beautiful warm air of this Mediterranean paradise. Chris had disappeared to the toilet and the remaining musketeers were just sitting at a table with a cool Carlsberg in hand, reminiscing about the many fun-filled previous nights we had all experienced there. Then suddenly, from virtually nowhere, a jet-like stream of warm alcohol-flavoured piss fired from the uncanny aim of Chris's cock struck Evo on the back of his head.

At first, we thought it was just some random idiot who was looking for an ass-kicking until we looked up to see Chris hanging out of the window, cock in hand and laughing his head off. As you can probably imagine, Evo on the other hand was out of his mind with anger and headed in Chris's direction to seek revenge. Steve and I were doubled over with laughter and tears. Evo, at this point, had caught up with his aggressor and was trying to teach him a lesson for his earlier humiliating crime, only to find himself in a kind of wrestling hold that we had nicknamed the Breenarge.

Chris would pin you to the floor with his knees holding down your arms, then with his free hands try and undo his jeans and attack you with his manhood. Very funny when it was someone else, but not so when the victim was yourself! If I ever found myself in this embarrassing predicament, I would threaten to bite his dick off if he dared remove it from his pants. That would usually get him off me, as he was always unsure if I was joking or not. After five minutes the pair returned and now Evo was seeing the funny side of it, but he'd warned Chris that he would return the favour in due course.

These kinds of nights were a regular event, but the hangovers were not the most enjoyable experiences. The number of times I found myself coming back to camp at five in the morning and having to go on parade at six for an eight-miler or some other buzz-killing event was almost a daily occurrence. Although the hangovers were the worst I had ever experienced, I never seemed to learn my lesson. I remember one night we'd been told that we could go out for the night of the England vs Sweden game in the 2006 world cup. The one when Joe Cole scored that screamer.

The company commander had told us that we didn't have to parade until ten o'clock the following morning.

"So go out and enjoy yourselves, but just make sure you're in a decent state when you do, and stay out of trouble," he instructed. The number of times I'd heard that saying. With this great news still ringing in our ears, the four of us headed to JJ's for the night and found a table right in front of a TV. I called over to Pete to bring a bottle of our favourite, and five glasses and we started the night the way we wanted to continue. Even though it wasn't the result we wanted, with England only getting a draw, we still made the most of the late parade and got absolutely hammered.

Steve and I ended up singing all our favourites on the karaoke and we must have sung *Rockin' All Over the World* about five times after demands from the rest of the bar. At the time Chris was fooling around with some old bird called Viv. That night while we were singing, Steve and I kept slipping in references to their relationship between lines of the songs. Chris was going crazy, saying he was going to kill us when we returned to our table, but eventually he would find the funny side of it. No matter how much we teased him about Viv, he still kept messing around with her and once to our horror, we even found the Madonna-aged women in his room back at camp.

I would never say I woke up after these kinds of nights, it was more like just coming to, not knowing if I was dead or alive. That morning, after my resurrection, I could hear shouting coming from around the block for people to wake up and get out on parade. It wasn't long before the duty corporal came into my room and told me the same. I rolled over to look at my phone, thinking I must have slept in and missed the ten o'clock parade.

At first, I thought I was seeing things, but after rubbing my eyes I could now clearly see it said six thirty five. I rushed from my bed and threw my PT kit on while heading for the door. I stumbled down the stairs and made it outside, where I could see the three platoon commanders standing there laughing with each other.

After the rest of the company arrived we were taken to the football pitches and given a beasting to remember. This time, though, everyone, including most of the Corporals and Sergeants, was still drunk. Not even hung over, just completely pissed. We were crawling by each other, laughing as someone else was being sick and at the end there were more piles of Carlsberg-smelling vomit than there were soldiers. Suddenly from the other side of the football pitch came the company commander.... and he was furious. He gave his platoon commanders a complete dressing down in front of everyone, but as we were all still pissed, no one took much notice. We were then sent back to our rooms to recover and reminded about the real ten o'clock parade.

Chapter eighteen – Iraq

We flew into Basra airport and what hit me first was the overwhelming heat, and even though I'd been in Cyprus for six months it choked me with its intensity. After the heat had finished with me, the next thing that nearly knocked me off my feet was the unbearable stench of raw sewage. It was utterly horrendous. Every breath I took would result in me getting a mouth full of thick polluted air and the taste would make me gag, almost getting re-acquainted with my aeroplane food.

We were shepherded into the main terminal building and made to wait until a flight to Shaibah air base was authorised. I sat on my kit reflecting on how I had missed my leave, and the fact that my Mom and sister had planned to visit me in Cyprus for their holidays was even more of a downer.

A week previously, I'd been looking forward to my leave and finally spending some quality time with the family in Paphos, when suddenly the company was ordered to parade outside company HQ and then informed by the company commander that we were going to be deployed to Iraq in a week's time. He went on to say that our role while we were there would be to cover two battalions swapping over, and we should be prepared to be there for six to eight weeks. This had come completely out of the blue, with none of the usual rumours circulating the battalion.

At first, I was well chuffed, knowing that I was finally getting deployed to Iraq. The very thought of heading to this dangerous land excited me, but I was soon brought back down to earth with the thoughts of how I was going to explain this to my Mom. I had no idea how she was going to react to her son missing the family holiday and of course, how she would react to the news about where I was heading. Later that day I reluctantly made the difficult phone call home and broke the news to an upset mother. Obviously, she didn't take the news that well, but she'd known this was always a possibility. Especially now being based in Cyprus, and the Middle East only a couple of hours' flight away.

For the next few days the company was thrashed from pillar to post, as the battalion hastily reacted to B Company's deployment. As I said, this had come completely out of the blue and we were totally unprepared for the task in hand. The company was issued with new kit, everyone looking strange in our new desert-coloured camouflaged uniform and boots.

After heading back to the block, I started to try on all my new kit and when I saw myself in a mirror the realisation of actually going to Iraq finally hit me. Since the war had started in 2003, for some reason I knew one day I would end up going there. Saying that, after my eye injury had got me out of the last tour, the British government's attentions were aimed more at the war in Afghanistan. I thought maybe I had missed my chance.

The Merlin helicopter I was in took off and headed east towards Shaibah. As soon as the chopper had cleared the perimeter fence the Merlin started making evasive and tactical manoeuvres and firing chaff grenades from out of the back. We had been fired at from an unknown location and now stinger missile lock-on was in the thoughts of most of us onboard.

The skilled pilot aggressively made the helicopter climb and then suddenly lose altitude. It was like being on board one of the scariest roller coasters you could imagine, but in the back of your mind you knew it could crash or get shot down at any moment. The worst thing about this situation was that all our kit and weapons had travelled separately, so if I had survived a crash, I would have been easy pickings for any nearby enemy. Then I would probably have found myself on the Internet, dressed in an orange jumpsuit, with a head-removing knife placed firmly against my throat, and the following day knowing my captors would be asking the prime minster if he would give into their demands and kindly save my life. Thankfully, the Merlin finally settled into a normal flight path and touched down safely to the great relief of the nervous passengers onboard.

The first few days in our new home were just like any other usual routine of wake up, wash and shave, then grab some breakfast before heading to the ranges to zero the weapons. Shaibah was absolutely massive, nothing you could ever imagine. Well maybe Camp Bastion could probably top it. You know a place is big when they lay on coaches, so you can travel to the American side of the camp, where they sell all the good stuff. Then you have all the little market stores where the locals are allowed to peddle their goods. You can pick up almost anything from these little establishments, from dodgy DVDs to memorabilia from the Iraqi Army.

On the second night, however, things started to heat up, and we got our first experience of indirect mortar fire. It had been a long, hot day so I headed to the wash-rooms to take a shower and then into one of the many disgusting portable toilets. I was just daydreaming really and not actually thinking about anything apart from the muffled conversation coming from a nearby tent. The camp was deathly quiet, when suddenly the crisp silence was broken by three loud thuds. This was followed up by a whistling noise that weirdly made me duck down. Like that would have made any difference! Three explosions shortly followed about a hundred metres away. I found out the next day that they had destroyed one of the cookhouses.

The mortar alarm burst into life, so I stayed in the toilet to take some form of cover. Admittedly not the best I know, but sometimes something is better than nothing. A further six mortars blasted their way into the camp, but now all I could think of was that there was no way I was going to get blown up in one of these horrible sweat-boxes. I calmly started to think of ways out of this embarrassing situation, so I decided I was going to have to make a run for it.

I dashed across the pitch-black camp, across uneven rocky ground with a tiny Army-issue green towel wrapped around my waist and a pair of stupid, unsafe flip-flops on my feet, heading for the relative safety of my tent. Once inside I found everyone huddled under their camp beds, with body armour and helmets on. I quickly followed suit and listened in to a succession of mortars detonating nearby.

I looked around the tent and started to giggle uncontrollably to myself. I just couldn't help thinking how crazy this would all look to people back home. Everyone taking refuge under an uncomfortable canvas camp bed, like that would offer you any form of protection from an unwelcome life-changing mortar that might find itself piercing your tent roof and exploding inside. Finally, the mortar alarm silenced itself and after about half an hour we removed our protective gear and started joking with each other. The conversation then turned to how I'd run across the camp in just a towel and flip-flops, while mortars were falling all around me.

For the next week this seemed to be the nightly routine with everyone starting to get used to it. I remember one night a few of us had gathered outside the back of the tent with a white polystyrene cup filled with an Army brew in one hand, and Hav-a-tampa vanilla flavoured cigar in the other, chilling there and just reminiscing on Northern Ireland and Cyprus. Discussing the best places to go out on the piss and which place had the hottest birds. Got to be Cyprus for me, birds from all over the world flocked there. Then, nearly as predictable as clockwork, the usual mortar firework session started. We just carried on as normal, casually donning our helmets and body armour, then complaining as if it were an inconvenience to put something on that might just save our lives. Once we'd protected ourselves we would carry on with the conversation, completely oblivious to the overhead dangers. Then when one landed nearby we would just shrug our shoulders and laugh and say, "Fuck, that was close." That's the thing about mortars. If you have no hard standing to get undercover, then you're stuffed. So sometimes it's best to stay still and hope they passed by.

It wasn't long before we were tasked to take over the guard. This added a little bit more excitement because we were now a lot more in harm's way. Don't get me wrong. Guard could be the most boring thing in the word and trust me, I have spent plenty of time experiencing it, but every now and again something crazy happened and it made me glad I had chosen the infantry that day in the recruitment office.

It turned out that we didn't have to wait too long before one of those crazy moments materialized and we experienced a suicide attack at the front sanger. A man had approached the guard tower where the Iraqi Army were situated, and he detonated his crude homemade bomb vest. The blast took us all by surprise, with everyone preparing for a follow-up attack, which was usually what happened in this situation. Once the dust had settled, people started scurrying about, checking the well-being of their lads. Luckily for everyone on guard that day he hadn't got close enough when detonating and the only fatality was himself.

This seemed to be the catalyst for things to come and over the next few days we saw the number of attacks intensify. Luckily, throughout this period no one got hurt. Well, apart from the attackers, anyway. As quickly as the attacks started, they dissipated, leaving us bored and stuck on guard without a hint of trouble on the horizon. Thankfully though, things were about to change for the better, with all three platoons to be deployed to different locations around our area of control.

My platoon was deployed to Um Qasr, a British forces' base not far from the border with Kuwait. The task we had been given was to provide security for the docks and the surrounding area, where huge amounts of supplies came in from the Persian Gulf. This seemed like a good tasking and I couldn't wait to get there and finally leave the boredom of Shaibah behind me. We took the short journey in a Merlin helicopter to our new destination, hoping that we would finally get to see a bit of action that wasn't mortars or suicide bombers, but maybe some good old-fashioned gun battles that we all craved so much.

As I watched Iraqi territory flash by from the open rear door of the Merlin, I started reflecting on all the shit I had been through and what was about to unfold in my future. My thoughts had started me questioning my decisions about joining the Army in the first place, and I wondered if I should re-think my plans of leaving. First things first though, I needed to carry out my role as a soldier and hopefully get back in one piece.

We landed on a dusty heli-pad just outside the camp and rushed out into all-round defence. After a minute or so the giant green bird lifted off and we waited until it was clear of the area before moving off. The down draft from the main rotor blade was so powerful it felt as if an elephant was climbing on my back. The call came over the radio and we headed off down the long freshly laid tarmac road and towards the camp.

As we were close to the coast we'd been informed that mosquitoes were rife at this location and told to make sure we continued taking our malaria tablets. This blood-mutilating threat was never more apparent than when I glanced up at one of the many swarms of mosquitoes that were congregating around the camp security floodlights. Luckily for me, it turned out the biting little blighters didn't enjoy my dodgy AB positive blood and turned their bloodthirsty attentions to the rest of the normal blood carriers. Much to their annoyance and my enjoyment!

The camp wasn't such a bad place to be based, apart from the many occasions when the air con decided to break down in our tent and there was no possible way we could endure the sixty-degree temperatures that had been recorded in there during the day. So we would spend most of our free time in the little NAFFI area, where we would spend hours playing table football and trying to beat two local interpreters who were out of this world at it. The pair took the piss. I have never seen anything like it. Every now and then it looked as if someone was about to beat them, but no, it was like they were just making us think we had a chance.

Our duties consisted of guarding the camp, going on small patrols around the local area or going to the docks to provide security for the drivers and workers. I can tell you now things can get very heated between the two and there was many a time when we had to intervene before there was violence.

On one occasion we had been tasked to remove a few of the drivers who had outstayed their six o'clock curfew and had refused to leave. Their reasons were that it was too dangerous for them to leave now, due to bandits on the road to Baghdad who would try and steal their load and most likely kill them in the process. This was a very real threat for the drivers and most were looked at as if they were in cahoots with the coalition forces, when in reality they were just trying to make ends meet. We had to negotiate a truce between the two raging parties and luckily before anyone was hurt, we found a way for the trucks to stay, but we would have to provide two vehicles to make sure they didn't get up to any funny business.

My fire team was one of the two Land Rovers that were picked. So we spent the evening staging on and making sure the lorry drivers kept to their side of the bargain. They were only supposed to leave their cab when going to the toilet and they would make their presence known when doing so. I was woken in the night for my stag and headed out with Jacko on a quick patrol of the area to make sure we didn't have any intruders sniffing around.

Apart from a few nearby floodlights, the dock was pitch black and was as quiet as a grave yard in the dead of night. Even the cool refreshing breeze that had been rolling in from the Persian Gulf had now died down, as if trying to aid me in listening out for intruders. After every ten paces or so I would have a quick check through my night-sight to make sure none of the drivers were wandering about or that we didn't have any unwanted intruders who were in need of a rough arrest and search.

As I approached one of the trucks I heard someone's shoes rustle on the gravel. I placed the butt of my rifle firmly in my right shoulder and went into full alert mode. Now I was trying to place every step carefully, trying to be as covert as humanly possible. Every eventuality was running through my mind and I had to battle with my senses to keep moving forward to find the source of the noise. As I rounded the corner of the truck the driver was squatting down, taking a crap.

"For fuck's sake, I nearly shot you," I gasped. Not that he understood a word I said, so I gestured for him to show me his ID, which he did after wiping his stinking ass.

After verifying his identity, I spent the next couple of minutes scrubbing shit stains from my hands with a wet wipe that I had hastily pulled from my webbing.

"Fucking wiping his arse with his bare hand, fucking animals!" I muttered to myself. With shit stains removed and hands clean, we headed back to the vehicle to wake the next two up for their stag. Then I made myself comfy in the liner of my sleeping bag and settled in for an uncomfortable night's sleep on the hard metal Land Rover floor.

The following morning, I woke to the chatter of people moaning about their mosquito bites and the fact I hadn't received any angered them more.

"It must be the aftershave you're wearing," I jokingly goaded them.

While we were stationed at Um Qasr the platoon befriended two stray dogs which would keep me company while I was on guard at the front gate. When I say befriended, I mean more like as long as you didn't try and stroke them, they in turn wouldn't bite you.

Anyway, they were excellent guard dogs and would warn me if anybody came strolling past the front gate. Sometimes they would even chase the locals off, who were just minding their own business and going about their daily routine. One night I had been on guard probably ten minutes when I heard the pair strolling down towards the front gate and then casually they both sat down next to me.

Then suddenly the bigger of the two, which I had nicknamed Arnie, pricked his ears up and started to snarl and growl as all his senses went into overdrive. This in turn had now set off the smaller one, which I had nicknamed Milo. The unmistakable sound of a local's flip-flops slapping off his bare rough soles drifted in on the warm night's breeze. This made my companions take a defensive stance and they started to scratch the gate and growl to be released in search of fresh meat. I thought they might know something that I didn't, so I unbolted the catch and sent them on their way. Unfortunately for the innocent local, they headed straight in his direction, barking and snarling.

Screams from the unfortunate passer-by broke the dark, quiet night. Then he started shouting.

"Mister, Mister, please get your dogs." Trying not to laugh I answered back.

"Sorry, mate, but they are not my dogs. They just do what they want." Looking back now, I probably should have gone over and helped him, but I was too busy laughing. Plus, I knew they would most likely have turned on me and I didn't fancy shooting two dogs that night. After a few minutes of screaming and shouting, the evil pair returned with blood and pieces of the man's dishdash dripping from their dagger-like teeth. Unbelievably, they then just lay down next to me as if nothing had happened, and they went to sleep. It was like their night's work was complete. I thought to myself, *It's alright for some.* I still had four more hours until I could have the comfort of my dreams.

A few nights later I was back at the front gate. This time, however, I was missing my usual back-up, but I thought nothing of it. They were probably out attacking the locals or something like that. I heard gunshots from the east, but as this was Iraq and a nightly occurrence, I just got on with things and ignored it. Suddenly Milo returned to the camp and started scratching at the gate. I slid the steel bolt over and opened the heavy metal gate to allow access to our fearless pair. It was at this point I saw Arnie hobbling towards me with thick red blood dripping down his side.

I ran towards him and for the first time, without any defensive attacks, he allowed me to touch him. I tried to see what had happened to him and it was quickly apparent he had been shot after I noticed five holes that looked like bullets wounds. He was in a bad way, so I just tried to guide him towards the safety of the camp. Once he was inside he just collapsed next to the guardroom door, and now I thought he was dead. Milo was frantically trying to get a response from him. He started nudging him with his wet nose and occasionally calling him with short sharp barks.

The guard commander came out and starting to try to help Arnie. As you can tell, we had become very attached to our four-legged friend, but as neither of us had ever been in this situation before, we were sort of just standing there hoping he was going to pull through. The camp medic was called, and he rushed to our location thinking he was dealing with a human casualty. After arriving and realising he was in fact dealing with a dog, he said he wasn't sure he could help him. After a short conversation, though, we convinced the doc to try and do what he could for him. Arnie must have known we were trying to help him, because he allowed us to manhandle him into the back of the Land Rover and he was quickly taken to the med centre.

During this time Milo never left the entrance of the med centre. He just lay there whimpering and calling for his best friend. After an agonising few hours it turned out that the doc had saved

Arnie's life, and within a couple of days he was back, unbelievably doing his old things with Milo by his side. We found out later on that the pair had tried to attack an Iraqi police officer, who drew his side arm and shot Arnie five times at point blank range, but this dog was hardcore and needed more than bullets to finish him off.

There was a huge compound next to our camp which at times held a massive fleet of tanks, warriors and other fighting vehicles. They would arrive by sea, then stay the night before being deployed to different areas of Iraq to continue the battle. So on the days they arrived we would have to guard the compound and make sure no one got access to the multi-million pound fleet.

One night I was sent to the back sanger to provide cover for more vehicles arriving later that night. The boredom had really started to kick in and I was now in a serious battle with one of a soldier's biggest enemies, the dreaded sleep. My eyes were now closing on their own and even standing up wasn't working. My body was falling asleep whether I was standing up or sitting down. I was in big trouble and losing this horrible battle.

Then from nowhere I thought I saw two shifty looking people hanging around a small dwarf wall on the other side of the perimeter fence. At first, I thought I was losing my battle with sleep and seeing things. So I strained my eyes to try and get a clearer look at the target, but still I couldn't quite make out what I was really looking at. Then I took a look through my night vision sights to get a better a view, but just couldn't seem to locate them. By now I thought that maybe I'd been seeing things, but at least I was now alert and fortunately awake.

Thanks to my scare, I was now fully concentrating and taking my guard seriously, when from the aforementioned wall I could clearly see someone sticking their head up above it and looking in my direction. Then I witnessed a second figure stand up and rush towards the fence. He hit the deck as if he thought I had seen him. I got on the radio and called the guard commander, who turned up at my location shortly afterwards with a 51mm mortar.

I gave him a quick brief of what had been going on and the direction of the two elusive prey. Mac quickly removed the dust cover and with a loud blast, fired an illumination mortar into the warm, dark night. It was bang on, detonating perfectly above the wall, which sent the men running in separate directions. They were like cockroaches after someone had turned a light on, scurrying to try and find the first place to locate a suitable hiding position.

The rest of the evening passed without incident, but it had put everyone on edge, because this was the first time that something had happened at the camp since we had arrived. Even though it was probably only a couple of local scum-bags trying to mess about, it gave us hope that maybe we would see some proper action soon.

Our stay at Um Qasr had come to an end, so we headed back to Shaibah, before returning to Cyprus. Before we flew back to Basra and then to Cyprus we had a couple of days to wait before our flights were authorised, so we spent those days hanging around camp. Saturday 13th May 2006 was a day I will never forget. It will always be remembered by Liverpool fans as the day Steven Gerrard scored two screamers in the last few minutes of the F.A. cup final against West Ham to grab a draw and take the game into extra time. We had been given the day off, so a bunch of us had headed down to the NAFFI to enjoy the football. We found a nice viewing area and took a seat and got ready for the match.

The game hadn't been on that long when we heard Bang! Bang! Bang! The familiar sound of mortars rang out and everyone in the NAFFI looked around in disbelief. A further eight explosions reverberated around the camp and it was now clear that we were under a more severe and sustained attack. The only thing we could do in this situation was to put on our helmet and body armour and hope the mortars missed our location. The attack continued for a further half an hour, with a few mortars exploding just behind the NAFFI.

The whole time we were under siege we continued to just take in the epic final that was playing out in front of our eyes, not really worrying about what was taking place outside. Finally, the mortar alarm was switched off and after a further half an hour the camp was deemed safe, which meant we could remove our protective clothing and return to a normal state of mind.

These events really summed up Iraq for me. Either I was stuck in some camp somewhere under indirect fire or patrolling around in vehicles, hoping the Snatch Land Rover I was situated in didn't activate a road-side bomb. The enemy never really made a full appearance while I was there, but preferred to stay in the shadows, attacking from a safe distance. Was I disappointed about this scenario? Maybe yes, but I wouldn't have to wait too long to get up close and personal with an enemy who wanted nothing more than to see me return to England in a box. With nothing more than my dog tags to identify my body.

Chapter nineteen – Downtime

The plane touched down shortly after 1500 hours local time at RAF Akrotiri and we were taken back to Dhekelia garrison by coach. As it was Friday, talk on the journey back was where everyone was going to head once we were stood down. I just couldn't wait to head out to get a few beers down me. It had been way too long since I'd tasted the sweet and stress-relieving golden nectar. But when we arrived back at camp our dreams of a good old knees-up were quickly dashed when the Regimental Sergeant Major informed everyone that we had been gated and were not allowed to leave until eight o'clock the following morning. Everyone was gutted. All we wanted to do was get on the lash and deal with a stinking hangover the following day.

I headed back to the block, while Chris made a quick detour to the camp shop and picked up a crate of beer for a night trapped in camp. The four musketeers hung out in Chris's room all night, with more people joining as the atmosphere and the music started to take off. This went on until there was a good group of us just squeezed in wherever we could sit. Someone then stupidly (Probably Cards) thought it would be a good idea to get some waxing strips and wax from their room, and then see how painful it really was.

Most of us just put strips on our arms and legs, but as the evening heated up and the lads became more pissed, Chris decided to up the ante. He stripped down completely naked and got Cards to put strips on his 'Ass, Crack and Sack'. Then three people each took hold of a strip and yanked them clean off. Chris screamed and rolled around in agony, not knowing which of his delicate areas to hold first. With everyone rolling around in laughter, Cards struck again and quickly slapped on another strip on Chris's left eyebrow. With one smooth fluid motion his eyebrow was no more. This sent the room into another fit of hysterics, with people barely gasping for breath and folk must have been able to hear the laughter from the other side of the camp.

The following morning, I went to Chris's room to see if what I could remember of the previous night had actually happened, or if I'd dreamt the sadistic prank. But then, when I saw Chris's one eyebrow and he showed me his bright red balls, I suddenly had a clear vision of the whole event, which sent me into a fit of laughter. The memory of that night will live with me forever.

The gated ban had been lifted and we were now allowed to leave the camp. The four of us headed down into Dhekelia and straight into JJ's for a reunion with Pete, the manager. Just before we'd been deployed to Iraq, I'd sort of been seeing a holiday rep called Charlie, but I wanted to try and finish with her, so I came up with a devious plan. Something I am not that proud of. I told the lads to tell her that we'd been caught up in an explosion while on tour and that I'd suffered a head injury, which had resulted in my losing some of my short-term memory. I would then just act as if I'd never met her before. After seeing her wander by the window, I nudged Chris and put the plan into motion. It worked like a dream. She completely bought it, but later on after a few drinks, the wankers told her that I had been bullshitting her. When alcohol is involved, one thing leads to another, usually the case with me, and I inevitably ended up in bed with her that night. Much to my despair, I woke the following morning in her bed, and now she thought we were seeing each other again.

When we'd got back from Iraq we'd been told that we would have to wait ten days before our official leave started. The company was briefed that we'd been placed on stand-by just in case something happened back in Iraq, but brilliantly we were off duty until we flew home. The only stipulation was that we couldn't leave the Island and would have to be within two hours' drive just in case anything happened.

This was fantastic, maybe even better than actually going home. The weather was incredible and with Aiya Nappa just down the coast I knew this would be an epic ten days. Chris and I headed down to the strip to hire a car and ended up with a rusty, old, white Suzuki Vitara convertible thing, which we ended up using to drive down to Nappa every couple of days. The plan was to cruise down there, leave the car on a side street somewhere and then head to the beach and just see where the day would take us. Then if we got lucky we wouldn't need to fork out on a hotel room and if we didn't, we'd just fall asleep on the beach and wait for the sun to come up. Then start again. Great routine it turned out to be.

Don't get me wrong, the four of us were always proud soldiers but would always try and stay away from where the rest of the battalion would go, as they always caused trouble. Saying that, I could be a bit of a knob at times when I'd had a few drinks, but the last thing you need when you're trying to pull some bird is a load of lads with the same confidence levels as yourself. We'd ended up in Coyotes, but after the place filled up with a load of raving troops, we decided it was time to find somewhere else to continue the drinking binge.

As we walked down the street in search of a fresh and untapped watering hole, an attractive beat pumping out of a nearby bar suddenly got our attention. We took a quick glance to make sure no one we knew was in there and followed the mesmerising beat inside. Straightaway we realised that this was going to be a good night, because the place was full to bursting point with half-naked birds and most of them were absolute stunners.

Chris and Evo headed for the men's room, leaving Steve and me to get the drinks. I turned to take a look at the talent on the dance floor, when I noticed this beautiful blonde bombshell gliding seductively towards me. I couldn't quite hear what she said, so I stooped my tall frame to get a bit closer to her inviting red lips. Then from out of nowhere she just started kissing me. I felt like I was dreaming and couldn't believe what had just taken place. When we finally came up for air, we formally introduced ourselves. I looked around quickly to see if any of my mates had seen what had happened. After a quick scout around I caught the confused face of Steve staring in my direction, mouth ajar.

She went on to say she was just going down the road to another bar to meet her friend and would be back shortly. Her every word made me fall for her even more and I started to get that feeling that told me I might be in for some big trouble. A woman like that could make you bankrupt in no time at all. After recovering from the sexy blonde's lip assault, I made my way to the toilet, but before I reached the door a brunette stepped out in front of me and with one hand, she gripped on to my gentleman area. Before I knew what was happening she grabbed my right hand and pressed it up against her hot body. She looked me straight in the eye and smiled and then started to kiss me passionately until a point where I was struggling for air. After releasing me from a sexual grip and with a quick flick of her beautiful brown hair she headed for the dance floor. I was completely bemused with what was going on in this place, but with her advances luring me towards the dance floor, I headed her way.

I was joined by the rest of the musketeers, who had each found as much success as me. The place then erupted when a crazy song in a foreign language burst onto the insane stereo system. Everyone around us was just going mad. Other nearby women just started kissing me, then the bird who'd sexually attacked me on the way to the toilet started kissing the girl who had just come over and snogged my face off. It was just out of this world, like nothing I had ever experienced before.

After the song had finished, the place calmed and we all headed for a smoking area outside to just take stock of what had taken place in the last thirty minutes. We made a pact that no one breathed a word of this place to anybody else, because this was going to be our hidden gem, and no one was stealing our action.

We spent the next few days returning to our new local and each night we were never disappointed, but it wasn't long before somebody passing by one night noticed us having a ball and before long the place was overrun with soldiers ruining our night. The fun had to end at some point, so we headed back to camp to give our livers some time to recuperate before we died of alcohol poisoning. The four of us then spent the next day or so just hanging around recovering before our leave was due to start.

The next two weeks flew by as I enjoyed spending time with my family and friends. It felt like a lifetime since I'd last been home. So much had happened since New Year so I just wanted to soak up every last minute of being home before I had to return to Cyprus.

While I was on leave Big Dave and I went out up town for the night. During the taxi ride on the way home we decided to stop off at a chip shop in Sparkhill, probably not the best idea in the world, as the place didn't care too much for strangers of a certain skin colour. Anyway, the taxi pulled in and out we jumped, heading for the door. Once in, I knew that there was going to be trouble of some sort, because the place was packed with lads, all of whom had given us dirty looks as we had come in.

We walked to the back of the queue, trying to ignore the alarming glares, and we waited to be served. At the front of the queue was some big ugly tree, standing there mouthing off about his food. The guy was really starting to piss me off and after he started intimidating two customers who were just sitting, minding their own business I took action.

"There's your fucking food. Now take it and fuck off," I shouted. As soon as the words had left my mouth I started to slightly regret it.

The bear slowly turned and took a step towards me, but as he did, Dave burst into action. He quickly grabbed him by his face and unceremoniously hurled him through the open door and out onto the street. As the man was flying through the air I rushed past Dave and karate kicked the guy clean in the face, leaving our new friend unconscious on the cold concrete floor. Suddenly one of the group came rushing outside and started to confront us. Luckily, they just wanted us not to give him a further beating, which I hadn't planned on doing anyway.

I now headed back into the chippie to grab my food. Dave thought we were probably in a little bit of danger being where we were so he, on the other hand, wanted us to leave the area. I grabbed my kebab and chips with chilli sauce and I stepped over the still knocked-out bear from earlier and headed down the road. Suddenly from behind I heard someone shouting obscenities at us. I spun around and it turned out the bear had woken from his slumber and was standing there, swaying and yelling abuse.

"You fucking white bastard. You're a fucking dead man," he shouted. This angered me more, so I headed in his direction to have it out with him.

"Listen, mate, I didn't hit you because you're Asian. I hit you because you're a fucking knob and you deserved it," I said. Dave now took hold of my arm and started to walk me back down the road, saying we needed to get the fuck out of there.

As we rounded the corner a people carrier mounted the pavement and a group of lads started to open the doors. We just legged it, but as I ran past the opening passenger door I chucked my Kebab straight in the guy's face. I always think about how angry he was after that. Imagine you think you're about to kick some guy's head in for bashing up your mate, and you end up with a kebab with chilli sauce straight in the kisser.

We headed into Bank Side and then into Sarehole Mill, which at three in the morning can be a bit of a spooky place. We laughed about that, and then we went our separate ways home, but I told him to call me once he got home.

It took me about thirty minutes to get home, mainly because I thought every approaching car was the revenge-seeking mob. Finally, I put the key in the front door and headed up to my room. I'd just sat down on the bed when my phone started to ring, so I reached into my pocket and noticed it was my sister, Liz. She asked whether I was still with Dave. When I said no, I then started to think our friends from earlier had caught up with him, so I began frantically trying to call his phone, which he never answered.

I was getting no response, so I started to get myself dressed again and loaded up my air pistol, ready to go and search for Dave. As I reached the front door my phone went off and thankfully it was him. He said that while he was on his way home, one of his friends had called him and he had gone round for a few drinks.

After we got back to Cyprus there was this strange feeling swirling around the camp and before long, rumours began that one of the companies was about to be deployed to Afghanistan. Their role was to bolster the numbers for the Parachute Regiment, who had been under constant attack for the past few months while based in Helmand Province. While the rumours continued, we would all watch the news every day and see that they were drastically short of numbers. The news crew also reported that a battalion in Cyprus was about to be deployed.

With the deployment rumours still circulating the camp, the Commanding Officer took it on himself to muster the whole battalion onto the square to dismiss any speculation that one of his companies would be deployed.

"Listen. Whatever you have heard about Afghanistan, it's a load of rubbish. I have not been contacted by anyone and there is no way any of you will be getting deployed." We were sent on our way with everyone really gutted that the gossip was incorrect, but an hour later we were recalled to the square to be told that A Company was going to be deployed and that they would be heading to Helmand Province in a few weeks' time. Further news that got my attention was that they would be looking for volunteers from B Company to make up the numbers.

After returning from the square for a second time we were told to parade outside the company lines. We were told that whoever wanted to put themselves forward should go to see their Platoon Commanders afterwards. They would then make the decision about agreeing it, if they thought you were up for the challenge.

Straightaway I knew I had to go on this dangerous tour. There was no way I was missing out on something like this, and so I headed straight to the boss's office to make my intentions clear. He then broke the news to me. Because I'd handed in my notice, they wouldn't listen to any offers until I had retracted my termination papers. This left me devastated.

I headed back to my room, cursing that bloody stupid asshole who had refused me a massive opportunity. But luckily for yours truly, my disappointment was short-lived. After a couple of days thinking for some of the A company lads, suddenly the med centre was inundated with soldiers that now needed a few weeks off sick. My boss called me to his office, and he said if I really wanted to go, he would make it happen, but it was at my own risk. I accepted his offer as soon as the words had left his mouth, and I thanked him.

"Don't thank me. Thank those sick notes over in A Company," he said. I didn't give a damn how I had got on this tour. I was just glad I had and couldn't wait to get out there. To be honest, there was no way I was going to miss out on the chance of going to war. I probably would have signed back on, if that had been the only way of going.

The next couple of weeks consisted of preparing ourselves for the arduous tasks that clearly lay ahead. I'd been studying the news daily ever since I'd been given the all-clear. I'd seen from the reports that the Taliban were determined to get territory back that they had lost after the bombing campaigns which had taken place in the wake of the September 11th terror attacks. It was also pretty clear that they were prepared to spill blood in doing so. We were briefed that we would be heading to Helmand Province and this time we should be under no illusions, and that we would face stiff resistance from the local enemy.

The night before we travelled, as the whole battalion was gated. I spent the evening in my room, just going through all my kit and making sure I'd packed everything. Chris had come over and we talked about how dangerous a place Afghanistan was. Then we decided it would be a good idea to write farewell letters to our parents, and how we would deliver them to each other's if the worst thing happened. It was extremely difficult to start a letter like that. I spent an hour just typing and then deleting passages I had written. As the letter wasn't getting anywhere I started to just flick through different menus on my laptop, hoping for some inspiration. Then suddenly I discovered a letter addressed to me. I was intrigued, and so I opened it.

Unbelievably, it turned out to be a letter that had been saved on my computer, and which had been written by my two sisters. They told me how proud they were of me and how I had turned my life around and followed my dream to become a soldier. They went on to say how they missed me terribly when I was away from them. This letter now gave me the inspiration to write. So I went on to tell them how much I loved them and Mom, and that if anything happened to me it was the greatest honour of my life to be their son and brother. I also added messages to their respective partners, telling the pair that they needed to look after them now that I was gone, and that I would be watching over them to make sure they did a good job.

I wanted to let Mom know how glad and grateful I was that she was my mother, and I thanked her for everything she had done for me; for all her sacrifices and the struggles, but I had finally become a man. I continued to tell her that if this war was to take me, then not to feel anger, but just to carry on, knowing that I would see them again one day. The letter brought emotions to the surface that I hadn't felt in many a year and I'm not ashamed to say it, but it nearly broke me, and I still get the same feeling now, recalling that very moving moment in my life. The thoughts that I might have seen my family in this life for the last time scared me. I wanted to call them and hear their soul-soothing voices, but I would have broken down, no question, and I tried never to let them see that side of me. Maybe they would think I was weak and that I shouldn't be a soldier at all.

I'm not a religious man at all, but that night I did say a little prayer between tears. I hoped that my family never got the chance to open that letter and have their world crushed, but if they did, please could God give them the strength to continue without me in their lives and not to just continue, but to prosper and use my death as a way of making their futures brighter.

The company paraded outside the block at five in the morning and with all our kit packed, we took the three-hour drive to RAF Akrotiri, where we boarded our carriage that would take us to one of the most dangerous places on earth. I'd lost my scared feelings from the previous night and was now totally focused on what was going to be a difficult and demanding, and maybe life-changing five months. I also took a moment and hoped everyone on board this Tri Star would make it back in one piece.

Chapter twenty – Danger ahead

We landed in the capital, Kabul, and after a long delay we were herded like cattle into the back of old Bedford trucks with nothing but canvas sides protecting us from the evil that was loitering around the back streets of this dangerous city. As we drove to a new destination I couldn't help thinking about being ambushed, and how vulnerable we all were, rammed in the back of this bullet magnet. But luckily for us, that night the hidden enemy stayed just that and let us arrive without incident.

After we were unloaded from the trucks we were taken to a small hangar, where we would wait for another flight onboard a Hercules to Camp Bastion. As I approached the thirty plus-year old thirty five tonnes of metal, I wondered how the British Army still operated in modern wars with kit that was older than me. We headed onboard in single file, where I took a seat just opposite the landing gear. After being given its clearance, the giant green monster barrelled its way down the dusty runway, eventually taking off into the pitch-black night sky heading for Bastion. Being in these old planes you can really feel turbulence and with every shudder I felt as if the gaffer tape holding this thing together was about to give way, sending us spiralling towards a certain death.

After what felt like an eternity, the landing gear slowly started to creak into position and the plane started to descend towards the unknown. Suddenly the beast started to gain height again and the landing gear struggled back into its previous location. My inner compass started to detect that we were turning around. After ten minutes the landing gear lowered, but again the thoughts of being on solid ground were short-lived as we started to climb, and we turned around.

This routine happened three more times before word was passed down the line telling everyone that they couldn't land due to a massive sandstorm that was currently making the Bastion runway an impossible landing site, and we would now be returning to Kabul. The last thing I wanted was to spend any more time in the belly of this monster, but unless I found a parachute I had no other options. After landing in Kabul, we were taken to the cookhouses to try and grab what was left of the food that had been cooked many hours earlier, but all I craved was a nice brew and a Benson and Hedges silver.

The following morning, we were back onboard my friend from last night and mercifully, this time we landed without trouble on a landing strip just outside Bastion. Straightaway the heat was unbearable, everyone trying to find cover behind anything they could to save themselves from the sun's intense heat. The camp was huge. I mean massive. I remember one night I'd been over at the phone room making a call to my Mom to let her know that I had arrived. When I finished the call, it took me an hour and a half to find the tent I was staying in. The place was colossal and that was back in 2006, before all the expansion had taken place.

The next week we spent the time just getting used to the heat, but I found the altitude more of a problem, especially in morning fitness. It felt like my lungs had shrunk since I'd arrived, but the fact I was smoking sixty a day probably wasn't helping. It just felt impossible to breathe. We would spend the days just learning about new pieces of kit we would be using out here. Like the new fancy rocket launchers and the Browning fifty-calibre heavy machine gun that seemed to be bolted to the top of every single Land Rover, along with general purpose machine guns mounted on the front.

This was going to be a right proper war. No arsing around with rules of engagement and the sort of bullshit that had suffocated us on previous tours of Iraq and Northern Ireland. This time things would be different. No bastard shooting in our direction and then dropping their weapons and thinking they would just get arrested.

This time the enemy had better be aware we hadn't come here to fuck about and play police.

After a few weeks I quickly started to adapt to my new routine and the place suddenly became like a second home, now I could actually find my way back to the tent after making a family call, without taking a detour around this vast establishment. It didn't take us long before we found the NAFFI and we would spend all of our free time there, drinking tea and smoking cheap fags while we waited to see what the tour had in store for us.

Our first role here was taking over the security of the camp. This involved the normal guard duties, and we would also be providing cover for any planes landing and taking off from the nearby runway. My platoon had been placed on providing cover for the runway, and I was part of a nine-man patrol in three WMIK Land Rovers that were armed with fifty-calibre machine guns and GPMGs.

Thirty minutes before flights were due to land we would head out and secure the local area around the runway and keep an eye out for anything suspicious. As we left the camp we noticed a silver Nissan, with the three occupants on board acting strangely. We headed in their direction and pulled up alongside them. With our best Afghan and their broken English skills we warned them that they needed to fuck off from the area. Before they left, we told them that maybe next time we wouldn't be so kind. They took our warning onboard and drove off over a steep hill and out of sight. We were left to continue on our patrol and waited for the incoming Hercules to land.

I was now just surveying the area to my front, and as I spun the turret on the fifty-cal, I noticed the same silver Nissan driving down one of the nearby gravel roads. Dean immediately gave Etch the thumbs-up to give chase and I locked the gun in place before heading off. We headed in their direction at high speed across the rocky dessert, trying my best to keep eyes on the Nissan. It took us a while to catch up with them as we had to head off-road down a couple of steep banks, before hitting the gravel road that they had escaped down. We could see dust trails from the other side of the valley and then from nowhere the Nissan reappeared from behind a mound and headed north back towards camp.

Etch floored the Land Rover as we hurriedly tried to cut them off, but now we were taking more and more dangerous risks trying to catch up to eliminate their unknown plans. After nearly rolling the WMIK twice, we finally cut them off and pulled up alongside. I spun the fifty-cal in their direction and placed my finger on the trigger.

"Please. Please don't shoot," the driver begged.

"Listen. I told you earlier about coming round here. Luckily for you I'm in a good mood today, but next time, he will shoot you dead. Do you understand?" Dean shouted. Finally, they got the message and accelerated away to safety before we changed our minds. We would get stupid people like that sometimes, but if I opened fire every time we encountered them I would be known as a serial killer who enjoyed the killing.

I first met Joseph 'Etch' Etchels in Northern Ireland after he arrived from training and he was immediately placed in six platoon. From the get-go you just know what lads are going to be like, and I could tell Etch was going to be a flyer (somebody who flew up the ranks). He was just an incredible soldier. Really knew his stuff and was fit as a fiddle. A fantastic example of an infantry soldier and not just that, a great bloke too. Even though he wasn't in with my closest group of friends we spent many hours together, either through work or out on the piss, be it N.I. or Cyprus. We would later even spend hours and hours in the cricket nets just having a laugh. For someone so slight he had a really great bowling action and would often surprise me with a really quick ball that would smash through my batting defence or hit me plum on the pad, bang in front.

In Afghanistan we were placed in the same fire team together for patrols and we would split the driving duties when one would get tired or bored of driving. During this tour Etch conducted himself with absolute professionalism and I would sometimes look on with envy at how he made being a soldier look so effortless. Sadly, while serving Queen and country during a later tour, on Sunday 19th July 2009 Etch was killed by an explosion while conducting a patrol in Sangin. Very sad to those who knew him well and a massive loss to the Army itself.

Camp Bastion would have shedloads of lorries delivering all sorts of things on a daily basis and one of the duties we were responsible for was the searching of the loads. The trucks were first forced to wait in a holding area for twenty four hours, and after that they would arrive at the main gate, where they would be searched.

One morning I was tasked along with a member of the dog-handling team and his search dog to start making our way through the backlog of vehicles that had arrived the previous morning. Having the search dog with us made this task a lot easier and it would have taken two men so much longer than it would one of these super dogs. While searching a lorry that was delivering supplies for the NAFFI, I noticed a red car coming down the drive towards me. I told the dog handler to finish off, and I made my way to the now stationary car.

The driver looked nervous, so I shouted at him to get out of the car and keep his hands where I could see them, but for some reason he just sat there gripping the steering wheel, staring in my direction. He gripped the wheel so tightly I could almost see his brown knuckles turning a lighter colour. I repeated my previous order, but this time aimed my fully loaded rifle in his direction. This seemed to get his attention and slowly he opened the door, taking a step onto the red-hot sand.

"Keep your hands where I can see them," I shouted. The man was just not acting correctly. There was something just not right about him. Everything about him was wrong and at this point I flicked the safety catch off and waited for him to make the first move.

We just stood there staring at each other, eyes locked into a weird sort of trance. Suddenly he started walking towards me with his hands now down by his sides.

"Stop fucking moving, mate, and put your hands in the air. I won't give you another warning," I demanded. He didn't seem to be getting the message and now there was only one more option I could use. That would be lethal force. I had given him enough chances to obey my commands. I even started using my limited Afghan language skills, but still he moved menacingly in my direction. I took a knee and aimed directly at him. Looking through my SUSAT rifle sight, I picked a place to send a 5.56 mm bullet and casually placed my index finger on the trigger. I could see his chest moving in and out. As I watched him taking what might be his final breaths, I readied myself to take my first life.

My feelings were mixed. On one hand this wasn't the way I would want to do things, but he just would not listen to what I was saying. On the other, I knew if he got any closer it would not just be my life he would be sending to the other side. I took a deep breath and with my finger now squeezing the trigger, the moment had come. Then from nowhere the interpreter shouted for me not to fire and started angrily talking to the emotionless man. Azim, the interpreter, then told me he was a local man from his village who was a bit slow and didn't really understand what he was doing.

Maybe another soldier wouldn't have given him the chances that I had, but a few more steps or if I had squeezed the trigger harder then he would have been gone. No questions. After sending the man away with a flea in his ear, I returned to the trucks and continued searching, not really thinking of what had just taken place, but keeping a professional stance. The Army made you think of things in a completely different way, so you never really tried to overthink situations, just continued as if nothing had happened. Problems only occurred years later when I started to think about all the shit I had done.

There was an American camp next to Camp Bastion which we would stag on from time to time. Nothing really ever happened there, just the usual few days bored out of our minds looking out into the vast desolate area. One night I was situated at the rear guard tower, just daydreaming really, when a number of gunshots broke the monotony of the usually mundane guard duty.

A further burst of machine-gun fire now got my full attention and I frantically looked round to try to locate the source of this disturbance. The radio fired into life and I recognised the calm northern accent of Sgt I., my Platoon Sergeant, trying to give a fire control order. He was obviously struggling to locate the hidden enemy in the unhelpful darkness. He made me aware that the patrol was heading back to camp and would use my location to enter the relative safety of the camp.

Through my night vision goggles I could just make out two blurry, green shapes that resembled WMIK Land Rovers, so I ran down to the gate to grant them access. The hidden enemy resurfaced and now a number of bullets whistled past my location, with two puncturing holes in the steel gates inches from me.

While under fire from an unknown location, I started to unlock the gate. Then, Snap! The key snapped inside the lock with a now angry Sgt I. on the other side, demanding to know why the fucking gate was still closed. I tried everything to unlock the padlock, but I failed with every attempt, until finally he lost patience. He jumped back into his WMIK and headed to the front gate and stormed towards me. He demanded an answer.

"What the fuck were you doing."

"It just snapped, Sergeant. I tried everything," I explained.

The following day he eventually calmed down and found the funny side of it. He started joking that I must want him dead, but nothing could have been further from the truth. Chris, who was in the rear WMIK, said that tracer rounds had just flown between him and the commander, missing his head by millimetres. After returning to Cyprus, rumour broke that it was friendly fire and there was some form of cover-up. Apparently, higher ranks knew who the poor shot was, but they didn't think taking him off duty would help our situation. That night around thirty rounds were fired at two vehicles and the only casualty was the rear gate. I suppose the truth will never come out. It might actually have been a Taliban attack, or just a very nervous and crap-shot soldier.

A few days later the company was split into two, with two platoons being sent to a small compound in the dangerous village of Nowzad, a real hotbed of activity in one of the Taliban's last remaining strongholds. My platoon was then split into two with one half being deployed to a small FOB (Forward Operating Base) in a village called Gereshk, and the other half being tasked to Kajaki to protect a huge, important dam. If the Taliban ever got their bloody hands on that place they would have ended up with a massive bargaining tool.

My platoon was told to rendezvous at twenty hundred hours that night, when kit was going to be handed out for this task. The amount of ammo I was given was unbelievable. Just in my webbing alone I had nine magazines of 5.56mm ammunition, two grenades, one bandolier of another one hundred and fifty rounds of 5.56. Along with all that, I then had one hundred rounds of 7.62 for the GPMGs, rounds for the fifty-calibre machine gun, plus all my other essential gear, which included rations and water.

Then our bulky bergens were also rammed with extra ammunition, water and more rations and anything else I could fit in there. I was also given the 51mm mortar and rounds for that, which added even more weight to my personal load. It was unreal how much kit we all had. I felt like a one-man Army. Days of running around my house when I was ten sprung to mind. I would storm about with pretend weapons strapped all over me, trying to recreate amazing battle scenes from Arnold Schwarzenegger films. But I wasn't even sure if I could move with this amount of kit.

It turned out that we would spend quite a bit of time in Gereshk over the next few months, and it became like a second home to us all. At times it was an absolute nightmare of a place, which we all loved to hate, especially me. We would end up doing incredibly long guard duties, with eight hours on and two off being the standard shift.

The following morning, we were driven to the heli-pad by Bedford trucks and waited for our flights to our new home. We were told that when the Chinook was approaching Gereshk it was going to come in hot. As soon as the wheels hit the ground we needed to be ready to move. The plan was then to charge from the rear door and into all-round defence. So we would need to keep all our kit on during the flight, as there wasn't time when we landed.

The loadmaster called us forward and like a steady stream of ants we followed in single file. There were no seats onboard so we sat in lines of three on the uncomfortable metal floor facing the rear door. With a quick blast of the powerful twin engines we were a hundred metres above the ground and racing towards the unknown. From where I was sitting all I could see was the back of people's heads. My mind started thinking about what was waiting for us at the other end. Would we be met with a hail of red hot 7.62 rounds bursting from the barrels of AK47s or would it just be a nice peaceful landing? But, as always, I was mentally prepared for any eventuality.

Another thought then entered my head. How the hell was I going to stand up with all this kit on my back? It had taken two people to lift it on to my unhappy back and now I was expected to stand up when it felt like I was carrying everybody else's kit. Two minutes to landing was passed down the line, and now my earlier fear was realised, but this was not just my problem. The way the

Chinook was coming in to land and with the sheer weight of our life-saving kit, not one person could stand up.

We must have looked a joke, but eventually the first three guys took off their bergens and then pulled the three men directly behind them to their feet, so creating a system to foil the laughing stock we had become. After everyone had made it to their feet, the wheels of this flying taxi touched down and as previously mentioned, everyone disembarked and rushed to their pre-rehearsed positions. We must have looked the dog's bollocks, everyone hitting the ground in sync. In a storm of stand and stones, our lift disappeared into the sky and we were left monitoring the surrounding area like a pack of lions surveying their territory, looking for any signs of prey.

As the dust settled I noticed something very strange. We were actually inside the wire with people just milling around, with tops off trying to bask in the early morning sun. You should have seen it. They all stared in our direction with bemused looks plastered all over their boat races. It soon came apparent that the Intel on this place was incorrect and we had just made complete prats of ourselves in front of members of the Parachute regiment. The same soldiers we were supposed to be backing up.

After the Paras headed to new locations we had the place to ourselves. Well, apart from a unit of American special forces, who we didn't see that much. We quickly learnt that we didn't really have enough manpower to protect the place efficiently and there were going to be times when other members of the British forces, like the chefs and medics, were going to drafted in to help pick up the slack.

There was one time when I was on the front Sanger with a female medic and I had asked her if she was comfortable with the GPMG, The General Purpose Machine Gun.

"Yeah, I've had some training on it," she replied, while pointing at the radio. On another occasion which cracked me up, one of my good mates, Martin Butts B. told me that once, while staging on with one of the chefs, he (Martin) had gone down to talk to one of the locals who had turned up at the front gate after something or other. When he returned, the chef, with clacker in hand (the firing device) told him to his obvious shock that he had him covered with the claymore mines, which were directly in line with Martin. Gereshk was a strange place where you wouldn't see action for days on end and then suddenly a burst of activity would remind you of the dangers we were all up against.

The platoon was in the middle of one of those aforementioned quiet spells, and we were starting to get frustrated by the endless guard cycle and zero action. I'd been on in the morning and completed a ten-hour spell, moving to each of the four Sanger locations. I'd spent two hours in each of the first three, followed by a gruelling four-hour stint in the last, when I was on my own with only the local irritating biting flies keeping me company. I had a cigarette every thirty minutes to try and break up the monotonous tasks of this sun-baked day.

I was released from my hell at twenty past six, a whole twenty minutes later than I should have been. People who know about this sort of thing will probably know just what I mean when I say how highly infuriating it is to watch the guy who is replacing you just strolling down towards the sanger without a care in the world. Especially annoying when I knew that I still had to complete a handover/takeover and walk back to the guardroom and get unloaded. That could easily take another twenty minutes, so when I'd finally get myself off stag, I'd have lost an hour of the two-hour rest period. Sometimes it could be even worse than that and I might as well just have stayed on.

I returned to my tent and grabbed a quick wash, before the recurring routine started all over again. I was just relaxing on my bed reading a copy of *Zoo* that I'd stolen from Chris, when a rumbling of gunfire got my full attention. I grabbed my kit and headed for the guardroom to see what the hell was happening. Dean, my section commander, was there and he explained that a few of the police checkpoints had been attacked about kilometre and a half away. He told a group of us that we should be prepared for similar attacks where we were.

I headed back to my sleeping quarters and grabbed a quick power nap before I had to begin another devastating eight-hour stag duty. My alarm woke me, and I returned to the guardroom with Phil W. to replace the guys at the front Sanger, who in turn moved to the sniper tower to continue their routine cycle.

Phil and I started our usual chitchat; what we were going to do when we were finally on leave, and then we started to joke about how much time we'd spent here on guard. I'd even started a tally chart to show how much time I'd spent in the Gereshk sangers. I was up to nearly two hundred hours. Then, from nowhere a succession of loud bright explosions lit up the coal-black night sky, which sent the pair of us into an alerted state, trying to locate the source.

We thought that it was a mortar attack, so we waited for the detonations, wherever they might be, which never happened. This event was followed up with machine-gun fire that came from the other side of the camp. The guys that were positioned at the back Sanger alerted everyone over the radio that they were witnessing a small fire fight out to their fronts, roughly two kilometres away, but at that point there was no real threat to them.

It came our time to move to the next stag position, which was the sniper tower. At this point we really wanted something to happen closer by so we could engage the enemy. Again, rumblings of gunfire and small explosions broke the silence and we observed the area through our night vision capabilities, hoping to spot any Taliban fighters out in the open. The intensity of the nearby battles started to grow, along with our morale, but we were again soon left frustrated by the lack of action closer by.

We were replaced and moved to the last stag position, the rear sanger and almost instantly started to witness battles raging between the local Army and police together against the Taliban, but now they were a lot closer and had started to come in range of the brutal General Purpose Machine Gun that we had at our disposal. I started to fire Schermulys into the star-filled night sky. (A hand-held flare that you would fire into the sky, which was attached to a small parachute that gave us about thirty seconds of light.)

While I was carrying this out, Phil kept his eyes on the ground to our front, ready to unleash a wave of 7.62mm bullets on any aggressors who were foolish enough to pick a fight with us. Suddenly the attackers began to turn their deadly attentions towards us and we started to receive a small amount of incoming tracer rounds that pinged off the razor wire that was situated just to the front of the sanger, Luckily for us, though, they were falling short. We both looked out for muzzle flashes in the distance, so we could return fire, but a clear shot never materialised.

The sound of moving vehicles from behind us grabbed our attention and we quickly realized it was three Humvees that belonged to the American Special Forces that were based here with us. I heard the unmistakable sound of the Browning fifty-calibre heavy machine gun being cocked, and I got ready to be deafened.

Bang! Bang! Bang! Bang! Bang! The guy on the gun unleashed it Rambo style and started to engage targets out in the distance. Waves of red hot tracer started to sting the enemy like a swarm of angry wasps, but suddenly the unmerciful gunner started identifying new targets that were in the same arc as the guard tower we were positioned in. Now those same angry wasps which were once our friends started getting closer to our position and zipping through the sanger just feet from us.

We both tried to take cover in the corner, huddled together, but it was only a matter of time before one of us got stung and with those types of bullets there were no second chances. I started to shout at the gunner.

"Mate, what the fuck are you doing? We're in here." I repeated myself three more times before finally getting the excited gunner's attention. The commander of the nearest Humvee dismounted and ran to our location.

"Sorry, guys we didn't realise anybody was in here," a thick Californian accent explained. He stayed with us while the Humvees continued to obliterate anything that moved, and I started to think they were probably shooting friendly targets in the process.

The radio on our American guest burst into life and it was a from a nearby jet that was in the middle of a bombing run. We listened in disbelief as the pilot and a Sergeant based at a camp somewhere argued about the pilot's intentions. The pilot was adamant he had sufficient fuel to complete his mission, but the now angry-sounding Sergeant argued otherwise.

At this point our guest placed a firefly (a beacon of light only visible to the planes above) on the roof of a sanger and said, "Don't want the pilot to make any mistakes here tonight." Those were his very words. I couldn't help but laugh, although maybe it was only nervous laughter, and I thought about my Mom, and how she always said to make sure the Americans were always in front. That night they were behind and above, a bad cocktail really. The argument on the radio continued, with the crazy pilot now saying he was dropping his two five-hundred-pound bombs and that was the end of it.

We didn't even see the jet, but two huge explosions in the distance finally silenced the attackers and the night fell quiet, almost boring really. We continued our guard and waited to be relieved, which came bang on time, a rare event. We made our way back to the guard room and explained what had been going on to the guard commander. There was a myth in the Army about fifty-calibre bullets, that when they went two feet by you, they could rip your skin off, which we now knew was a load of bullshit, as they had been a lot closer than that to us.

The next day after everything had calmed down and returned to normal, I sauntered to the guard room to start another mind-numbing shift. I hadn't been on too long when one of the locals approached my position carrying a small child. In Gereshk we would open our medical centre up for the local villagers to get basic first aid and every now and again a more serious casualty would turn up. Today was one of those days. I met the guy half way down the drive, before he could get any closer to the front gate and pose a threat. I shouted for him to halt and not to make any sudden movements, with which he complied. I moved closer and started to talk to him with the help of the interpreter.

The upset man started to cry while he was explaining what had happened to his four-year-old son. They had been caught in the middle of a fierce battle between a local militia group and the Taliban. During the bloody battle his son had been shot in the chest. At this point the visibly shaken parent removed a bloodied bandage and showed me his son's injury. The bullet had hit him in the centre of his chest just above the sternum, with the exit wound just below his left shoulder blade. I could hear the air leaking from his chest and knew things were bad, so I quickly called the guard room and informed them of the current situation, to which they replied that a medic was en route.

I now had the difficult task of explaining to the broken man that I had to search him and his dying son. He looked on in disbelief as I started my search. I placed my hands gently on his son and started to feel for any hidden objects, of which there were none. At difficult times like this I would always try and detach myself from my emotions. Although, saying that, when you see children badly injured like this it becomes a very arduous task. After checking the young boy, I turned my attention to the dad. I started with his upper torso, shoulders and arms then continued down his body until I reached the awkward area.

People will try and secrete items anywhere on their person. So you have to be extremely thorough when searching, even though sometimes moving someone's wedding tackle from side to side can be a little embarrassing, but that day it wasn't the case. With the two now searched I gestured to the waiting medics to move forward. The lead medic gave me the thumbs-up and they both made their way towards the badly injured boy. I quickly explained the situation and the pair were hastily taken away.

I continued my guard and started to talk with Steve about how things like this would stay with us forever. I then said how this was the real cost of war. As we were talking, I looked down and noticed blood on my hands. This only reinforced in me the understanding that we were supposed to be here to try to protect this country's future, and not to be in any way a destroyer of it.

A car approached the front gate, so I greeted it in my usual way, weapon pointed at the driver. I instructed him to stop and get out, which he did, so I began doing a search. I then asked him his intentions. He told me he was a relative of the injured boy and wanted to know his condition. I told him that I hadn't any news of the boy's welfare, but deep down I knew this would turn out to be a sad day for the family.

Ten minutes passed before the med centre ambulance came trundling towards us from the rear of the camp and stopped in a cloud of dust just short of me. The rear doors opened, and the local man appeared first. I knew straightaway from the look in his eyes that the young boy had sadly passed away. Then a stretcher bearing the young victim appeared, carried by two soldiers and it was slowly carried to the waiting car.

The man and his relative picked his son up and placed him in the back of the car across the back seats, and then they closed the door. He returned and unbelievably shook the medics' hands and said thank you for trying to save his son's life. He added that he feared that this wouldn't be the last time he would experience a tragedy like this. Before getting in the car he glanced in my direction and gave me a look that has lived with me till this day. A look that I didn't truly understand till the day my first child, Isabella, was born. A look only a loving dad can give.

At the time, this tragic event obviously stunned me and made me really think about what life was all about. But it's true to say that it has caused me even more pain since the arrival of Isabella. I sometimes think of how I would have reacted if this had been my situation. Would I have been able to thank and shake the hand of a soldier who was a member of an Army that in a way had caused the death of my beloved son? I don't think I could have had the strength or the control to do so.

Chapter twenty one – Coming face to face

My soul-destroying guard of the Gereshk camp continued for the next few weeks. During this time, we started to spend time with a small local militia group who were being paid by the Americans to protect the first guard tower. They were made up of about thirty men, in ages ranging from about fourteen up to the head guy, who was in his forties. I remember once when one of the young lads turned sixteen he was given an AK47 for his birthday and was told he was now allowed to join them on patrols, which I thought was just crazy. But they looked at life in a completely different light from the way we did.

They were a nice group of guys, to be honest, and the elders would bring us bread when we were staging on, even though it took us about a week to finally trust them not to have laced it with anything funny. There was a time when one of the guys gave Chris a smoke, and instead of tobacco it was some of the local ganja. It left Chris flying for a couple of hours, which we all thought was hilarious.

One unbelievably hot day I was in the front sanger with Steve, while Chris was in the tower just behind us on the General Purpose Machine Gun. We hadn't been on long when I noticed an Afghan Army vehicle blasting straight through the heavily guarded militia checkpoint and heading our way. I shouted for the vehicle to stop and moved in the direction of the Afghan commander.

"As Salaam alaikum," I said, to which he replied, "Wa alaikum us salaam." We exchanged some broken English and some of my recently learned Afghan phrases until our masked interpreter joined me. I used the interpreter to advise the crew that they shouldn't think they could just drive straight in there without stopping at the checkpoints.

At this point the militia had made their way to my position and started to confront the soldiers about refusing to heed their instructions on stopping. I could tell from their body language that the militia were not happy, and soon, raised voices in a language I couldn't understand erupted. It wasn't long until other members of the militia turned up from a nearby camp and joined in with the heated argument. I knew this wasn't going to end well and now I was stuck in the middle of the two raging groups. I tried everything to calm this volatile situation down before any blood was spilt. It kind of reminded me of that scene from that Nicolas Cage film called *The Rock*, when they had that massive stand-off in the shower room.

Suddenly, one of the younger fresh-faced Afghan soldiers pulled a Russian-made 9mm pistol from his worn leather holster and pointed it in the direction of the angriest militia member, which prompted the rest of this angry mob to follow suit. I was now faced with a dire predicament. There were weapons pointing in all directions and with me bang in the middle hoping no one would pull the trigger. Otherwise we would all be brown bread and my Mom would be getting a knock at the door a few days later to be informed of her son's untimely and gruesome death. I knew I had to try and remove myself from the danger zone and fast, but every time I moved I got a dirty look from a member of the Afghan Army, who was pointing his weapon in my direction.

I got on the radio to Chris in the tower and quickly briefed him on the current state of affairs. I told him that if all hell broke loose I would go to ground to my left. So at least he would know of my whereabouts, if or when he started spitting fire from the barrel of the GPMG. I now tried to sneakily unclip my sling on my rifle, so I had more movement in case I had to open fire. Then I turned the catch to automatic and removed the safety catch. I thought *If anything goes down now, I'm just going to spray people as I hit the deck and hopefully I'll make it out of this tight spot in one piece.*

My radio crackled in my ear and the voice of Cpl Dean H.

got my attention. I quickly gave him a sit rep and he told me that he was on his way. I watched on in shock as he approached this action-movie-type situation, dressed in only his combat bottoms and boots, brandishing a 9mm Browning pistol in his tightly gripped right hand, with a radio in his left. The pissed-off group had now calmed slightly, so I was able to make contact with Dean before he got to the danger zone. I said that the situation seemed to have cooled down, but there was still some tension between the Army commander and one of the militia.

Dean grabbed the interpreter by his skinny left arm and dragged him to the group, with me to his left side. He then addressed the mob.

"Tell them this," he shouted at the interpreter. "Everyone put their fucking weapons downs. If you don't, we will kill every last one of you." As the words were leaving his mouth I waited for the reaction from the noisy crowd, but there was a delay because Dean was speaking to the interpreter, making sure he heard it correctly, then finally translating it. I just hoped they listened to their stark warning and lowered their weapons before anyone got capped. The interpreter slowly conveyed the message and I looked around into everyone's eyes as the words hit home like a hammer. I couldn't quite believe what I was seeing, but they reluctantly made their weapons safe.

Dean, however, had not finished and started furiously yelling at the Afghan soldiers.

"Next time you try driving in here without obeying our orders, we will just open fire up and finish you off. Do you fucking get it?" They nodded their heads and were sent on their way, and with Dean's threat still echoing in the air, I hoped we had seen the last of them. I think this had shaken *them* up more than anybody else, although saying that, *my* heart took a while to return to a normal beat.

A month or so passed and we returned to camp Bastion.

During this time, we were deployed to different areas of Helmand Province, which I enjoyed immensely, as we never spent too long in one place getting bored. On one such occasion we were deployed on a ten-day operation, moving from different locations, providing cover for the artillery, who were in turn providing long range fire support for the surrounding British Army outposts that were sometimes stretched to their absolute limits.

We could find ourselves driving anywhere in the Province, hastily setting up the gun lines with the artillery, and there was always a constant threat of attack from the Taliban. At night we would find a suitable location to set up all-round defence and then proceeded to dig our fighting trenches. Just in case the enemy felt brave and attacked us while we slept, which they did on more than one occasion.

One night we arrived at a location about ten kilometres south of a town called Musa Qala, which had been brutally fought over for the past year and where a lot of casualties on both sides had been taken. We were called into a half circle in front of the platoon commander and briefed for the following day's mission. We would move in on vehicles under the cover of darkness and take up defensive positions on cliffs and mountains that surrounded the town. At the same time, troops from Third Battalion, the Parachute regiment, would approach in two Chinook helicopters and land on a designated landing site.

The plan was that, under our cover, the elite units would try to secure the town, so that a company of Danish soldiers who had been held down for weeks under intense enemy fire at an old police compound, taking heavy casualties, could be relieved and taken back to camp Bastion. The town, apart from the police compound, was under total Taliban control and it wasn't going to be relinquished from their rugged hands easily. This was going to be a mission where we could easily take significant casualties and I really hoped that someone was looking down on us that day.

I made myself comfortable in my sleeping bag and used a rolled-up combat jacket as an uncomfortable pillow, which I suppose was better than the loose rocks that were the alternative. One thing I will always remember about the dessert was how cold it was. We would find ourselves huddling up to our nearest buddy at night and then getting some very strange looks the following morning.

At times like this I would think of my family back home and hoped I would get to see them again in this life. I also wondered whether, if my Mom knew what I was about to embark on, it would send her grey, if my previous adventures hadn't already. But to be really honest, I tried not to think of home too much, as sometimes it would make me scared of the what ifs, and as a soldier you shouldn't really let those thoughts ever enter your head. You should stay focused on the tasks at hand and make sure you and your mates make it home in one piece. I knew that if the worst thing did happen, Chris, my best mate and I had made our pact and would deliver our final letters home to each other's family.

I was abruptly woken from my slumber by the whispered voice of Cpl H., my section commander, informing me it was time to wake up and that we would be moving off in thirty minutes. He told me to make sure I was ready and on the vehicles in twenty. I grabbed a quick snack and made sure my weapon was well oiled; the last thing I needed now was for that to let me down. We loaded into the vehicles and moved off in single file into the vast, green darkness, the murky view through my night vision goggles.

The ground was unforgiving, and I kept finding myself being thrown from one side to the other and painfully crashing into an unexpected colleague. We reached our first checkpoint just in time to watch the amazing sunrise peeking out from behind the rugged cliffs. Afghanistan has some of the most beautiful landscapes I have ever seen. It's just such a shame about the trouble that has plagued it for so long.

Callum, our driver, another good mate of mine, positioned the truck on a raised area. The steep banks left and right and to the front gave us a great over-watch of the surrounding area. The plan was to stay here for a period of time until the troops behind us had moved into their designated positions. So we took this time to grab a bit of food before moving to the next objective.

The guys in my vehicle were just sitting and chilling, not really concerned about anything happening, when suddenly: Bang! Bang! Bang! We started taking small-arms fire from a hidden location, some of which had struck the ground metres from us. We were now in a bit of a bad spot, so Callum took it upon himself to turn the vehicle around to try to find some cover, which was nearly impossible.

At this point the enemy started hitting us with Chinese rockets that whistled feet above us, to explode on the other side of the ridge. We were now taking fire from two well-covered locations and it was about this time that I started to realise we might be in a spot of bother. With rounds pinging off all around us, I frantically tried to locate the enemy. At this point Callum was still trying to turn around without sending us tumbling down the steep banks which seemed to be working against us. As quickly as the attack had started, it dissipated. It was as if the enemy had melted into the backdrop and like ghosts, just disappeared, leaving us fumbling around trying to locate them to return fire. Don't worry, I'm not going to mention a certain someone's helmet rolling down one of the banks.

After our wake-up call, I was tasked, along with half the platoon including Chris, to climb up a steep cliff and get a better perspective of the area and to provide cover. The climb was utterly horrendous, undertaken in the soaring heat of this unforgiving landscape, and with upwards of one hundred and fifty pounds of uncomfortable kit on my unbending back, I felt as if I was about to crumble. The cliffs were made up of loose stones and boulders that with one ill-placed step would threaten to send me crashing back down from where I had started.

Strangely, it wasn't my back that gave up first, it was a recently purchased backpack which finally decided it had taken all it could and picked the worst possible time to snap. Half way up this monstrous climb I ended up dragging what was left of it in one hand, while climbing with the other, which obviously added another layer of difficulty to an already nearly impossible task. I reached the top just behind Chris and almost instantly we started taking fire from Chinese rockets again, but this time the uncanny firer nearly put a round right on top of both of us. A second one, closer by this time, destroyed a small wall just behind us, so with that we scrabbled into the nearest available cover. An old trench system from when the Soviets had been brutally beaten into submission here back in the eighties. After getting our bearings and checking our underwear, we took stock of our near miss.

In the Army, when on the ranges, there is a saying which is 'watch and shoot'. Usually when hearing this, you're in a pre-built trench and waiting for a small metal pop-up target to appear from a known location. Easy really when you're an accomplished soldier, but hearing this phrase burst into my ear from my radio sent shivers down my spine. A saying I never thought I would hear on the dusty battlefields of Afghanistan.

We moved along the trench system and up into an elevated position where we had great views into a cluster of buildings, and we waited for our chance to punish the enemy. Two guys appeared with Ak47s in hand, one standing in the doorway, the easier of the two shots. He was dressed in a whitish grey dishdash and was clutching what looked like an old two-way radio in his left hand. As I knew there were no civilians in the area I took aim and fired my first round, which hit the wall to left of the unsuspecting man. I made the adjustments quickly with the second round, hitting him in the chest, and with a thump he stumbled backwards into the room and out of sight. My feelings of that moment were of nothing. I was neither happy nor upset. To me it was as if I had shot one of those aforementioned metal pop-up targets on the range.

The radio burst into life again and we were told to take cover as American war planes were about to start bombing runs. The first five-hundred-pound bomb hit the building which was harbouring the dead or injured man who, just a minute before, had been shot with one of many 5.56mm bullets. The detonation shook the ground around us. I then bravely or stupidly popped up quickly, camera in hand, and took a couple of snaps, then ducked back down before a second bomb destroyed a complex of small buildings to my right.

The day continued in this brutal fashion, with American and British war planes and Apache attack helicopters stalking the area. It was a sight to behold. They obliterated anything that moved and at times I almost felt sorry for them. A sniper situated just behind me, firing at unwary prey with deadly accuracy, kept us all motivated. The day started to drag out and the troops became more and more restless when the action started to die out. Every now and again sporadic gunfire in the distance fired the morale of the guys up around me, as if they'd just taken a shot of insulin.

Finally, though, we were left with just the baking and soul-destroying heat to keep us company and for most of us, we would rather a bullet had finished us off! Mercifully, two hours later we were extracted from the area and were back down that crippling cliff. At the bottom we clambered back into the waiting vehicles, which took us back to safety, stopping every now and then, hearing the rumbling of gunfire in the distance.

We returned to the relative safety of the desert and found a suitable area for us to take shelter for the night and reflect on the previous twelve hours. The area was surrounded by cliffs to the east and a dry river bed, also known as a wadi, to the west. After digging our trenches and scoffing down some cold rations, my section was tasked to head up into the nearby cliffs and set up a recce, so we could keep eyes on the surrounding areas. We now expected some kind of attack from the Taliban, as retribution from events early in the day.

The climb was across unpleasant and unforgiving ground, with us all tripping and stumbling over loose rocks and occasionally falling face first over hidden objects. My radio burst into life, almost making me jump.

"Halt."

"Hit the deck."

"Movement from the ridge line to the west."

"Four enemy soldiers spotted."

I lay there as still as possible, watching them looking in our direction. Anticipating a fire fight, I placed my finger on the trigger, ready for them to make the first move. Fortunately for them, they hadn't seen us and started to move off back over the ridge line and out of sight. We waited for thirty minutes before we continued our mission, just to make sure they definitely had moved and weren't planning an ambush while we were in the middle of our climb.

Eventually the coast was clear, so we continued and set up defensive positions at the top of the cliff and then took it in turns to stag on. We had a brilliant vantage point from the top and could see for miles through our sights. Our only concern was that we couldn't get a clear view of the wadi, as most of it was in dead ground. I'd just finished my one-hour guard slot, so I returned to a small rocky area that I'd made into a living area for myself.

The whole place was dead silent when a couple of other lads and I heard what sounded like chatter coming from a ridge just below us. I woke Dean and whispered my concerns. He followed me to the location where I had heard the voices and both of us tried to find a better observation position, without making the enemy aware of our location. Dean then quietly got on the radio and informed HQ what was happening. They broke some worrying news to us that they'd been listening in on radio chat from nearby enemy forces who'd been talking about how they were just about to sneak upon a sleeping unit on a cliff.

These words sent a ripple of horror around the section, and it made us ready for whatever was about to take place. We were in an advantageous position, as we had the high ground, but nevertheless we all knew we could be in a fight for our lives if the information was correct. Every noise now set my heart racing. Even the odd rodent sneaking over loose rocks behind us nearly encouraged me to set off one of the claymore mines which had been strategically set up around us. A few hours passed, and we were informed that another section was headed up the cliff to relieve us and that we would be able to go and grab a quick nap.

I settled in for an uncomfortable and cold night in my new surroundings and as I gazed up at the magical mind-blowing blanket of a million stars, I thought there was no way I was in one of the most dangerous places on earth. I tried to make myself comfortable for a well-earned sleep before I was woken again for another stag, when suddenly a loud burst of machine-gun fire erupted from the direction of the wadi.

At first, I couldn't believe what was happening and even thought I must be dreaming, but as soon as it sank in, I quickly scrabbled around for my helmet and weapon. The radio was awash with panic and confusion, because no one really knew where the threat was coming from. I just stayed in my position and awaited further orders.

Surveying the area to my front through my night vision scope, more and more bullets were coming in my direction, with some even hitting the ground two feet from me. Then a voice that I recognised as Corporal H. shouted for Chris and me to follow him. He told us that we had been attacked from the wadi and that the enemy was trying to breach our lines.

We started to make our way to where HQ was situated to try and get a better grasp of what the hell was happening. We approached with caution, trying not to spook anyone that didn't recognise us as friendly. After getting a quick brief, we headed in the direction of the wadi, hoping to make it there before any more of the enemy broke through. I was now in full alert mode and was trying hard to control myself, as adrenaline was pumping like never before and my breathing was becoming more erratic.

We moved forward under heavy gunfire, trying to survey the area. As we reached the bank of the wadi the intensity of the fire fight went up a couple of notches, so we started to force the enemy back with a well-aimed burst of gunfire. Then, from nowhere: Bang! A huge explosion just metres from us shook us down to our boots. A rocket-propelled grenade had been fired at us. With my ears ringing and my body shaking, I checked myself for any injuries and to my surprise I was completely unharmed.

The radio crackled into life and a thick Glaswegian accent informed us that an Apache attack helicopter was inbound, and he told us to mark our positions as friendly. The helicopter arrived from the north, unleashing hell on our aggressors, strafing the area with its 30mm chain gun. They completely annihilated the enemy with unbelievable fire power and I almost felt sorry for them being overwhelmed by this mechanical grim reaper. It continued on with the mission until the area was declared clear, and then it moved on to its next objective.

As the sun rose on the bloody battlefield, the air was still heavy with the smell of gunpowder. After a short recovery period, our next task was to head into the wadi to check for any survivors, but after the amount of firepower that had been unleashed, I couldn't imagine anyone coming through that. Before heading off we were told to fix bayonets, another saying I never thought I would hear. I was thinking, *Shit, is this for real? It's one thing slotting someone, but sticking a bayonet into an enemy? Well that's definitely another. But if it comes to it and it's a choice of their life or mine, then he's fucked!*

We patrolled into the wadi and with each careful footstep, I hoped the bastards hadn't left any little leg removers hidden under the sand. My section was then tasked to head to a formation of old cave systems and to make sure they were clear of anybody taking refuge in there. Dean and I approached the first one and before he took a step in, he turned and said, "A.P. you go first and I'll cover you."

I bravely went in through the tight entrance. The black space seemed to engulf me and the thoughts of my detonating a booby trap rushed into my mind. I flicked on my torch and moved further into the black abyss. Now all my senses were working overtime, trying to paint a picture of the mysterious cave in my mind's eye. A misplaced step on a loose rock made me stumble and luckily, I just got my footing before heading down a steep shaft head first, which would have almost been certain death.

Small entrances to further tunnels at the back of the cave worried me and I started to feel as if I was being watched from multiple locations. You just seem to get that feeling when someone's watching you, don't you? This was one of those strange moments. Then I heard what I thought was a footstep behind me, so I spun around quickly, rifle at the ready, but as I did so, the light from my torch created shadows that cascaded along the rugged cave walls, which almost made me shoot a ghastly figure that turned out to be a piece of rock sticking out from the wall.

The place gave me the shivers and before long I found my way to the entrance of the cave and squeezed into the brilliant warm sunshine. We continued on to the next cave and repeated the same scary procedure. In the second I found the remnants of a fire and bloodied bandages, which must have come from the previous night's firefight. It was deemed too dangerous to continue the searches. So now we just threw a few grenades in and let them do their work.

The convoy steadily started to head back in the direction of Camp Bastion, stopping every now and then just to check certain routes, and occasionally we would set up a gun line to send in some artillery. This was to prevent advancing enemy troops from mounting sustained attacks against British forces in nearby camps. We finally reached the gates of Bastion and I could tell from everyone's faces that they were well relieved to finally be back there. Everyone was totally knackered. We had spent the last ten days driving all over Helmand province looking for Taliban forces and getting into a few scuffles along the way, surviving on probably only four hours of sleep a day.

Chapter twenty two – Hoping to make it home

After returning to Bastion we were ordered back to Gresehk for a further week to join up with the marines who had taken over from us. It was here where we learnt that the section who had been deployed to Kajaki a month before had taken their first casualty. Fusilier Andy Barlow (Ken) had been taking part in a patrol when they ended up in a minefield. A soldier from the Parachute Regiment had triggered a mine and was critically injured in the blast.

Ken moved to the injured guy's position, when he too stood on a mine which blew most of his foot off and severely injured his leg. This event was made into a film some years later, which depicted the bravery of the guys on the ground that fateful day. Some people never come back from injuries like Ken had received in the same frame of mind as before, but not Ken. After we arrived back in Cyprus he was there waiting to see his mates. He stood at the side of the road with a pair of shorts on, now minus a leg below the knee and wearing a T-shirt that said, "I stood on a land mine and survived!" A testament to what kind a guy he is.

After being told by our platoon commander that we were due to fly into Nowzad for the final few weeks of the tour, everyone was chuffed to be part of what the rest of A Company had been achieving. For the whole time they had been there they had been under constant enemy attack night and day, and now we were due to fly there the following day. We boarded the Chinook the following morning and this time we knew that maybe we would be landing under fire. Unfortunately, this had become the norm for the Chinook crews since the start of 2006.

My first sight of Nowzad came from the small misty window of a Chinook helicopter travelling at speed above this dangerous war zone. My thoughts drifted back to enjoying everything Cyprus had to offer, from the beautiful beaches to the thirst-quenching local beverages. I was abruptly brought back to reality by the voice of the loadmaster.

"One minute to landing." The giant green monster made its final adjustments and in a storm of sand and stones, touched down.

We rushed from the helicopter and into all-round defence, keeping our eyes peeled for any movement. The chopper had dropped us about two miles from the compound, so the rest of the journey was on foot. The feeling amongst the platoon was one of trepidation. Every man knew the risks of patrolling on foot into this village. The Taliban would use this opportunity to hit us, knowing they could fire from buildings in the village and that we were right out in the open, with only larger rocks as cover. I was last man in my platoon, so I had eyes on left and right plus the rear. So if anything happened I would be right out in the open. I was on a constant look-out for enemy and also looking for cover if something did go down.

We made it unscathed to the entrance of the village, which now left us with a thousand-metre run to reach the compound. We raced through the back streets of Nowzad and with every turn I expected to confront an enemy soldier just standing there with an AK47 in hand, about to send me back to sunny old England in a wooden box. It was absolutely crazy. There were so many places for the enemy to hide and it kind of reminded me of the film Black Hawk Down, when they are trying to get to the crash site. But this time there was no enemy or any of the locals visible. It was like a ghost town.

I don't think I've ever moved that fast in all of my life, and with so much kit on too. Plus, it was like forty odd degrees, which made me sweat like no-one's business, but I'm not lying when I say this. It was like I was running around in a T-shirt, I couldn't even feel the weight on my back, down to the fact that my body was buzzing from the effects of the huge dose of adrenaline that was pumping around my swollen veins. I was now just frantically trying to keep up with the guy in front, doing everything not to lose sight of him. I rounded a corner and passed by the old bazaar. Not a single soul anywhere, very strange. I was just waiting for someone to step out and hit me with a burst of 7.62 machine-gun rounds.

Finally, I could see people peeling off into the entrance of what I thought must be the camp, but it was like nothing I thought it would be, just an old police compound slap bang in the middle of the village, completely surrounded on all four sides. As I reached the gates, everyone was sitting down on their kit, awaiting further orders. Now inside, the weighted run finally took its toll on me. I couldn't even breathe. Just coughing and spluttering, trying everything to control my breathing. It was a further twenty minutes before I had finally got myself in good order and was able to take a drag on a fag without coughing my lungs up.

The camp at Nowzad was tiny and from what we had been told, the place was getting attacked on a daily basis. From the get-go we weren't disappointed, it was everything and more than I thought it was going to be. The only problem now was that we were coming into the last month of the tour and the lads were starting to lose focus, daydreaming about going on leave, and I too was sometimes guilty of the same offence. It would take an attack on the camp to kick my ass back into gear. The well-hidden enemy that encircled the camp had balls of steel. They would crawl up undetected, so they were feet from us and would chuck grenades over the old mud walls.

The way guard worked here was that we would stag on in sections, so there would be three or four blokes in the sangers, while the rest of the section would be in the room underneath, ready to go. Then when anything happened they would come up and join in the fire-fight. The buildings that surrounded the compound were all given different names, so when we were being attacked, we could quickly give everyone an easy fire control order. I will always remember one of the buildings called twin towers, two identical buildings standing right next to each other, maybe a little bit of irony there!

The local Taliban forces had taken over the whole town and for the time I was there I don't really remember seeing any of the locals. So if we did see anyone, it was always the enemy. They had cleverly knocked holes in the walls of buildings, so they could quickly change firing positions. They were like meerkats, just popping up all over the place, until a burst of fifty-cal rounds silenced their assault. The front sanger, where I spent the majority of my time, was heavily guarded with a couple of GPMGs, and a mimimi or two. Then if anything did happen, it was all hands on-deck.

I recall one time when I was on guard with one of the other lads and we both kept seeing movement from a roof line approximately one hundred meters from us. It looked as if someone was trying to monitor any patterns we might have. I contacted the guardroom and informed them that we were about to engage with the target and to wait for any further information.

I was watching on through a pair of binoculars while Dan was on the gun, preparing himself for me to give a fire control order. Suddenly, as if on cue, the hidden man stood up with a weapon slung across his chest and he started moving at speed towards a small wall on the far side of the roof, probably only ten meters away from safety. Dan squeezed his index finger and a swarm of angry 7.62 machine-gun rounds headed in the unlucky bloke's direction. Somehow none of the hot metal slugs hit the target and the man now hit the accelerator, trying to escape the next burst.

I watched on as the roof and surrounding buildings were turned into a dust cloud, as bullets ripped through hundred-year-old mud walls and metal corrugated sheeting. The GPMG did what it did best, putting a huge number of rounds on a target quickly, but somehow the lucky man was still moving, and he headed for cover behind a small wall, desperately trying to live for another day. I shouted for Dan to make adjustments and fire right.

I watched on in disbelief as rounds seemed to hit everything but the target. Fortunately, with the last burst of machine-gun fire before the man escaped to safety, his luck finally ran out. A well-aimed group of five to eight red-tipped rounds ripped through the insurgent's body, taking him clean off his feet and through a cloud of red speckled dust. I watched him collapse in a heap probably a meter from his exit.

"Did I get him? "Did I?" Dan asked.

"Yeah, yeah you got him," I answered.

"Do you think he's dead?"

"There's no way he survived that. No way," I responded.

It's a weird thing seeing stuff like that and even though it wasn't me firing the gun, that time it seemed to affect me more than it did when it was my finger squeezing the trigger. I think maybe because I could see the desperate look in the guy's face as he frantically fought for survival, and maybe a part of me hoped he would succeed. It's like when you watch a wildlife documentary and a lion is chasing down a deer or something. Most people want the deer to escape, don't they? That's what it was kind of like, but he put himself in that situation and how would the enemy treat me if I was stupid enough to be out in the open?

Nowzad was just one of those places where these events were not that uncommon, and with buildings so close to the compound we usually got a good view of the enemy's final moments. There were times when our air support seemed to drop their bombs just the other side of the walls, and due to the close proximity of the raging fire fights, it was a real test of nerves for the guy calling in the air strikes.

I remember once talking to my Mom on a sat phone when the camp suddenly came under heavy gun and grenade attack. My Mom was saying things like, "What's going on there? It sounds as if you're getting attacked." I told her that we were doing some range work and there was nothing to worry about. My boss then gave me the signal to finish the call, so I quickly made my excuses and hung the phone up and then raced to go and join in with the defence of the camp.

While I was away on tour I always tried not to think of my family back home, because I wanted to try and stay focused. So I only called occasionally and after there had been a death on our side, just to put my Mom's mind at rest. Back then when somebody had been killed we would be banned from using any phones or the Internet until the unfortunate parents of the brave hero back home had been informed, but for every family member waiting back home this would be an agonising wait until either they got a knock at the door or a phone call from their serving son or daughter.

The BBC would broadcast that a British soldier had been killed in Afghanistan and then usually they would say which area, like Helmand province. So if your family knew where you were based, they would put two and two together and come up with God knows what. It was, a really bad system which did eventually change.

I recall once I rang home after one such event and told my Mom that everything was fine. After being questioned I played down the recent death toll, telling her nothing had been happening where I was based, and that everything was fine. Even though I think she knew I was bullshitting, it seemed to reassure her, but maybe it was just because she had heard my voice for the first time in a while. I spoke briefly to my sisters, telling them it wouldn't be long before I was home and that I should be back in time for my sister Liz's twenty first birthday party, and that changed the mood slightly. Then my sister said Dad was there and he would like a quick word if I didn't mind. For the first time in my life he then told me that he was really proud of me and he wanted me to know that he was trying to change and be a better Dad for all of us. I could tell in his voice that he was fighting back years of emotions that were trying to pour out, and I struggled to find words to cheer him up. It was a very awkward moment as I have never dealt with emotional moments like that very well.

Most of the time I would usually just give my phone cards away to the lads who had children, so they could spend more than nineteen minutes, or whatever it was a week, speaking to them. I would only call when I needed to, and I would try not to speak to people back home except on those occasions. I know it sounds strange, but it sometimes scared me because of where I was. Maybe I wouldn't react promptly enough to the situations I sometimes found myself in if my mind was preoccupied with thoughts of home, and that could ultimately cost me or someone else their life.

The time came for us to leave Nowzad, but predictably the local enemy had other ideas and tried to give us a parting gift. It was as if they knew that our tour was coming to an end and as everyone had leave on their minds, they thought this was a good time to try and hit us.

On the morning of our extraction the enemy was spotted in the area, so American A10 tank-busters were drafted in to give us some much welcome fire support. If you have experienced these combat aircraft in full attack mode, you'll know it's something to be in awe of, and you quickly become very glad that they are on your side, even though the American pilots would sometimes get a little too close for comfort. After a short nerve-wracking delay, we made our way through the tight and twisted backstreets and blood-stained alleyways, stopping every now and then to check on the enemy's position. The plan was to just leave the area and not get caught up in any unnecessary battles. Leave that for units that were replacing us, unless we absolutely had to.

The amount of kit we were all carrying was out of this world, and every time I had to take a knee on sharp rocks and stones just got me more and more angry at the company commander for stopping us every twenty metres or so. Finally, we made it to our pre-designated helicopter landing sight and waited in all-round defence for our taxi to safety. As I lay there in my uncomfortable state, I kept expecting something to go down. It just had that feel about things. Everything up until that point had gone smoothly. It was of those strange moments when I really didn't want anything to happen, and from looking around I could tell most were thinking the same. Previously I would have really wanted something to. It's funny how everyone's mentality had changed the closer we had got to finally going home.

The unmistakable sound of the double rotor blade Chinook mumbling effortlessly towards us caught my attention. Then with a familiar powerful blast of small sharp stones and dust that almost choked me, it touched down. We now formed up into two lines ready to run into the belly of the chopper, while our relief were heading the opposite way and in a very Army way of doing things, we welcomed them with, "Have a great Christmas here, lads. Merry Christmas." The looks we received were priceless and the fact we knew we would be spending Christmas with our families, well, the joy was all the sweeter.

We arrived back at Camp Bastion a short time later and now the feeling around the platoon was one of relief and happiness, knowing that the crazy times were hopefully behind us. However, the following morning the company was told that we might be needed for one last operation before we left, and it would be a very dangerous mission into Sangin. Along with Nowzad and Musa Qula, at the time it was one of the most dangerous places on earth. You could tell from everyone's facial expressions after hearing the news, that no one really wanted any part in this with only a couple of days left in Afghanistan to push. Thankfully, the operation was deemed too high risk and was binned before any planning had gone into it. The company was finally stood down, so we started the long and laborious tasks of weapon and kit cleaning.

The company wouldn't be heading straight back to Cyprus as we'd thought, but would actually be taking a detour to Kuwait, where we would then be put through a decompression process. This was where we would spend a couple of days unwinding, prior to returning to Cyprus and where we would try and get back to some form of normality. We would also get the opportunity to speak with doctors and talk about the things we had experienced. That was, if we really wanted to.

We flew into Kandahar first, an American camp in Afghanistan, where we would have to wait for ten hours before our flight to Kuwait was ready. The place was unreal. Absolutely gigantic! The Americans certainly know how to conduct tours, I'll give them that. They had a little shopping centre where there were places like Subway, and pizza places, Nike shops and electrical shops, just to name a few. I was spoilt for choice and couldn't make up my mind what to eat, so I had a bit from each one.

We found a little cafe place, like a NAFFI, I suppose and ordered four brews. Then we headed outside to enjoy the warm evening and took a seat at a nearby table by a group of female medics. Suddenly an explosion in the distance triggered the mortar alarm. While people sitting by us scrabbled around looking for helmets and body armour, mortars exploded nearby. The four of us just chilled without fear, enjoying our recently purchased cups of Earl Grey. Because we had just experienced nearly five months of this sort of shit, we were all just taking it in our stride, just casually locating our protective gear and putting it on. We continued our conversation while people nearby started shouting at us to find some form of hard cover, but we would hear none of it and saw it as an inconvenience. It just shows what your mind can get used to, if you give it time. Thirty minutes passed and then, thankfully, someone finally silenced the mortar alarm. After finishing my new favourite cigars, we headed back towards the airfield and found somewhere comfortable to spend the next couple of hours. I tried to grab a couple of hours shut-eye before the flight, but I found my mind wandering to all sorts of things: how I would come to terms with everything I had seen and if I would ever be the same person when I returned to civilian life. This was probably the first time I'd started to come to terms with the fact that I would be leaving the Army, and that I knew this would be the last tour.

We arrived in Kuwait and were taken by coach to a nearby American camp, where we would spend the next forty eight hours just trying to be normal again. The place was colossal, thousands of troops everywhere and the shopping area just out of this world. This was the first time I had ever been in a Starbucks. We were told to make sure we were back at the accommodation by two o'clock, when we would be taken to a hall set up for a talk with a doctor about post-traumatic stress and how to deal with the experience of war. To be honest, this was where a lot of us should have tried to talk about certain aspects of the tour, but as soldiers can be stubborn beasts, we would never want to show signs of weakness. Nobody wanted to engage with the specialist staff due to the fear of being ridiculed.

After heading back to our rooms, we were told that a barbecue had been arranged for that evening, but that there would be no drinking. Because we were in an Arab state, this activity was completely forbidden. After the barbecue everyone just headed to bed. This was probably the first time we were all able to really relax without fearing an attack of some kind, and I was gone the moment my head hit the pillow. After spending the next day just milling around camp, we boarded our plane and headed back to Cyprus, knowing this was the final leg back to normal existence.

The Tristar touched down and after finally coming to a halt, I could see a huge banner hanging over the main arrival entrance saying, 'Welcome home A Company'. We headed across the runway and were directed into another room. Once inside I noticed a table stacked with cans of Carlsberg, and I happily grabbed one.

A can of lager had never tasted so good, the crisp flavour refreshing my parched mouth. As I looked around I could tell everyone was enjoying the same experience. Two or three more cans followed before we were ushered onto the waiting coaches and were driven back to *DHEKELIA* garrison.

The whole journey back I didn't really speak, just watched the world go by. Maybe I was drunk or something on my three cans of Carlsberg, but I remember just staring at a group of road workers whilst stuck in a traffic jam. I sat there thinking they had no idea how lucky they were to just have a normal job, something I'd started to crave badly. We arrived back at camp and as the coach turned the corner and drove through the gates, we all noticed that the road was lined with clapping soldiers and family members. I couldn't believe what I was seeing, a real spine-tingling event. I felt like I was dreaming, a really surreal moment in my military career.

I walked down the steps and out into eye-squinting sunshine, where people who I didn't really know that well started to try and shake my hand. People were saying "Well done," and "Great job." Stuff like that. Then we walked over to the cookhouse where a meal had been put on for us, and again I could see a stack of Carlsberg that was just sitting there waiting for us.

We finished our very welcome meal and washed it down with a few more cans, and then the Regimental Sergeant Major got everyone's attention. Once we were all quiet, the Colonel walked in and started talking to us. He went on to say that the battalion was so proud of each and every one of us and how after talking to other commanding officers from different units who we had been working with, he was chuffed to bits that we had done the Fusiliers' name proud. He handed back over to the RSM and then shocked the room by saying that we would not be gated. He said we were allowed to go out tonight for a few drinks, but on the proviso we would all promise to behave ourselves.

Heading back to the block, the place was buzzing. Everyone

was walking around, can of beer in hand, just really enjoying themselves. All kinds of music was pumping out from every room and I had never felt a vibe like it. There were people who hadn't really seen eye to eye before, who were now embracing each other as brothers. After a nice, long, relaxing shower I got myself ready for my first night out in nearly five months. We followed the long stream of people who had the same thoughts and after signing out, we jumped into our booked taxi. There was only one place the four musketeers were heading and that was our old favourite, JJ's, but as we approached the door, we thought we would play a bit of a prank on Pete.

We told Chris to stay outside and come in five minutes later. As we walked through the door Pete shot from around the bar and ran up to us, giving us each a hug and shaking our hands.

"But where is Chris?" he asked.

"Sorry to tell you, Pete, but Chris didn't make it." As his smile slowly disappeared I could feel his hands shaking. After hearing the upsetting news, Chris flew through the door and embraced Pete. At first, he didn't know what was really happening, but finally he cottoned on and after scolding us for such a terrible prank, he went and fetched a bottle of black sambuca, which he had been saving for us for our return. That evening, to be honest I don't really remember it much, but I woke suddenly the following morning lying in my bed, fully dressed and with no recollection of how I'd arrived back. But I just knew I must have had a good evening because of the large love bite I'd received from an unknown attacker. After recovering for the best part of the morning, we rendezvoused over in the NAFFI to discuss that night's plans and as we'd all given such a poor showing on our return, we knew we had to go back to JJ's to give the regulars a real evening. The night was crazy; booze, women, dancing and karaoke. All you could really ask for, but maybe my liver would have a different take on the evening's events.

Chapter twenty three – Scary times

While I was in Afghanistan I started emailing a woman called Shelley, who had sent in her details via one of the national newspapers about becoming a pen pal for a member of the British forces, and I'd got her details from Chris. We stayed in touch while I was on tour, chatting via email whenever I had the chance, and after arriving back in Cyprus in one piece, we decided that we would meet up while I was on leave.

After arriving back in England, a group of us took a taxi and travelled back up the motorway from Heathrow. We dropped one of the lads, Old School, off at Corley services on the M6, before I arrived at my house. Even though it was eleven o'clock at night and absolutely bloody Baltic, as I'd been used to forty degrees for the past few months and it was now November in Birmingham, I stood outside the house just taking in the surroundings, not really sure what to do next.

I was finally home and there had been many times when I thought I would never see this place again, unless I was haunting it. I rustled around for my keys and went in. As I quietly climbed the stairs, trying not to wake anybody up, Mom just stood on the landing waiting for me. We shared a hug, and I offered to make us a brew. After returning to her room, we had a quick chat before I finally turned in for the evening. A strange time really, Mom just sitting there listening to me talk about the past few months. She was just so glad to have her son back home and I was relieved to have finally arrived home. I'd dreamt of that moment for months.

I had big plans for my two-week leave. I was really going to enjoy myself and had arranged to meet up with Shelley. I'd also pencilled in a few nights out with Chris and Butts, like I always did on leave. It was Liz's twenty first birthday, and everyone was going to Solihull to celebrate it and also my return from battle. As I had about ten grand saved from Afghanistan, this leave was going to be something really special, but leave sometimes never really went how I had planned it, and with all my civilian mates either working or broke, I sometimes would spend days on my own, just drinking to pass the time. Alcohol and things on my mind and with no one to talk to, but that's never really a good combination. Some mornings I would just wake up hung over, head to the local off licence, grab a bottle of Southerns and twenty fags, head home and get on it on my own. I never felt so alone as I did on those occasions. I'd gone from spending every waking minute with someone, to spending sometimes eight hours a day lonely and drunk, with only my mind keeping me company. And with some of the horrible things that were swirling around in there at the time, it was enough to send me crazy.

While I was away I would spend so much time in my mind, thinking about how good it would be and what I would do on leave. Then when I finally arrived home, I was so lost and without my mates to keep me company it was an unbelievably scary existence. I had no clue of what to do and my only escape was drink.

A couple of days passed in a drunken blur and it was now time to go and finally meet up with Shelley, the girl that I had got speaking to while away on tour. She was an air hostess from Brighton. From how she talked on the phone and from the pictures she'd sent me, I couldn't wait to meet her for the first time. We had arranged to meet at the Regency Hotel, where I'd booked us a room.

As I sat there in the car park waiting for her to turn up, I couldn't help but think that it wouldn't be the woman in the pictures showing up, but maybe one of her mates. Suddenly her blue Megane pulled into the car park and out stepped this beautiful curvy brunette. After retrieving my jaw from the floor, I walked over towards her, trying to act as cool as possible, but deep down I was nervous as hell, maybe overwhelmed by her natural beauty.

For the next couple of days, we never really left the hotel room, only really going out to get refreshments and me sneaking off for the occasional cigarette, even though I'd told her that I didn't smoke. After she paid the hotel for our stay she gave me a long, passionate kiss and we went our separate ways. I never heard from her again apart from a few drunken text messages. Funny, all the years of me doing that to women and then I got a taste of my own medicine and I didn't like it. Not one bit. I suppose things really do come back to bite you.

The rest of my leave continued the way I'd started it, just drinking heavily, trying to fill the void left from the excitement of Army life, and it was now that I first started to experience strange dreams. At first, they were just maybe flashbacks from certain places I'd been in and things I'd seen, but then they started to become more real and now members of family were taking the places of lads from the Army.

The only answer I had to those worrying dreams was to try and drink more and more. I hoped by doing this my drunken state would mess my subconscious up enough so that dreams would become impossible to create, but this only seemed to add more fuel to the already intense fire. That made the dreams more like nightmares, when I would sometimes wake up in that strange state where I was somewhere between awake and asleep and I couldn't tell the difference between the pair. I would just lie there, shaking uncontrollably, hoping that I was in fact only dreaming. The visions were so powerful that I would sometimes go and listen at my Mom or sisters' bedroom door, to make sure they were still breathing. I knew this wasn't a normal thing to be going through and at that point of my life I should probably have sought professional help to get to the bottom of why I was experiencing this, but as quickly as they started, the nightmares stopped. Well, it would be a few more years until they resurfaced, anyway.

After celebrating my sister's birthday, I headed back to Cyprus. My leave had been split into two parts, so I had just completed two weeks and went back to camp for three weeks, then had a further three weeks off over Christmas and New Year, which would be the first time I had had both off since joining up. The next three weeks passed slowly, with the company not really doing much but fitness and cleaning weapons. I had ended up somehow in charge of my platoon's Wolf Land Rovers and had to make sure they were all up to scratch with their documents and service history. A really shit job, but it got me out of company duties, I suppose.

I now had only a couple of months left in the Army and had really started thinking about my future. To tell you the truth, when I'd handed in my notice ten months previously, I never really thought I would ever go through with it and leave, but now something inside me had changed and I had mixed feelings about staying or going. My decision was made even harder as I was so close to being free. I just didn't know what to do. In the back of my mind I knew the battalion would spend the next year or so going to and from Afghanistan and I just didn't think I could keep putting my family through the nightmare of being posted to a war zone.

I returned home for Christmas and New Year, and after spending it with my family, this only strengthened my thoughts about leaving the Army for good. My second leave took the same path as my first, with some more severe alcohol abuse. I took my final flight back to Cyprus and paraded the following day, when the company was told that they would be heading back to Afghanistan in a couple of weeks' time, but this time they would be deployed to Kabul. I could tell that most of the company was not thrilled with the prospects of spending six months in Kabul, especially as it was winter there and apparently it was bloody freezing. This was obviously not a concern for me as I only had about six weeks to push before I was due to leave, so I just headed back to my room.

Deep down I wanted to go to make sure my mates were okay, and knowing they would be going without me made me feel sick.

A few days later I was called into my Company Sergeant Major's office. He asked me if I wanted to join up with the company on the posting to Kabul and said that I wouldn't have to sign back up, but just extend my service. He then went on to say that the company needed every good bloke it could get and saw me as someone in that category. He told me to go away and think about things for a couple of days, but before I left his office he said one last thing.

"A.P., if you decide not to take me up on my offer, I wouldn't think any less of you, because I know you haven't long before you leave."

I rushed back to the block and headed straight to Chris's room to tell him my news. He was angry with me that I was even considering the offer. He told me in no uncertain terms that I should just get the hell out while I still could and if I did agree to it, he would beat the shit out of me for being so stupid. Chris had made me see sense, so I returned to my CSM the following day and thanked him for the offer, but I said I would be turning it down. I told him that I was not in the right frame of mind to go on a tour and felt as if I would be a liability. He thanked me for my honesty and wished me good luck with my future plans. He then said if I changed my mind I could just come back and let him know.

The following night I headed down to the strip to celebrate the birthday of one of the lads before he was posted, and as usual the night started in JJ's, but unlike most nights, the usual lads I would go out drinking with were doing other things, so I ended up with a different crowd. The drinks were flowing nicely, and it wasn't long before I started hitting the tequila hard, and then we stumbled to another bar further down the strip. What happened next I can't really explain, as I was pissed out of my mind on spirits and I recall the evening through a blurred memory.

I was with one of the other lads that I was out with. You see? I was so drunk that I can't even remember who it was, but anyway, we cut away from the rest of the group and headed to a local strip club where we came across a lone parked car. Now, somewhere along the journey we had got talking about who had the hardest punch and now we thought of a plan on how to decide.

I stood on the driver's side, with my nameless friend standing on the other. We took turns to try and break the windows with punches. After finally breaking mine, I turned to my grinning mate.

"Watch this," I said as I climbed onto the bonnet and started to try to break the front screen, but the bastard didn't want to know, so I jumped off and found myself a massive piece of rock. I then climbed back up and smashed it straight through the window.

Unluckily for us, as the rock shattered the screen, sending tiny shards of glass in all directions, a police car pulled up, sirens blazing. The pair of us legged it in separate directions, hoping to throw the coppers off our trail. I was so far in front of the pursuing policeman I started laughing to myself that he could never catch me. Even if I crawled he didn't stand a chance of apprehending me. Suddenly I was laughing on the other side of my face, as I fell head first into a storm drain. Now I faced a battle to get back to my feet before the angry officer could catch up with me, but the full effects of my tequila session had kicked in. I did everything I could to stand up, but my legs just would not co-operate and when I finally did get upright, it was too late.

He came at me swinging his baton stick, catching me a couple of times, but it was the strike straight to the stomach that collapsed me like an old ironing board. After he dragged me to my feet he placed me in cuffs and with his partner's help, he chucked me into the back of his kebab-stinking cop car.

"Right," he said. "We can make this situation disappear. All you need to do is go to a cash machine. Withdraw three hundred and all will be forgotten." I was still in fighting spirits, so I told him to go fuck himself. He didn't take too kindly to my response and cracked me a few more times with the baton stick. I thought, *Fucking hell. Now I know what it's like being on the other side of it, after my experiences in Northern Ireland.*

He turned the key and drove off, stopping five minutes later at some dodgy looking bank. He then dragged me from the rear of the car by the scruff of my neck and forced me to the cash point, demanding I put in my pin number, which I flatly refused to do. Consequently, he forcefully placed me back into the car, smashing my head off the door frame in the process. Coppers always seem to have that uncanny knack of making it look accidental, don't they? For the next hour or so they drove me from cash point to cash point, demanding I punch in the correct pin number. Then, after what seemed like forever, and with my buzz slowly wearing off, he furiously told me that I had run out of lives and that they would deal with me Cypriot style back at the police station.

When we arrived at the police station, four more moody looking coppers started walking with a purpose towards the rear door and grabbed me by the neck and tried to pull me from the car. I now knew I needed to do something, as I thought I was in grave danger. So with my hands cuffed in front of me I started to try and fight back against my attackers. More baton strikes followed, and I was finally wrestled to the floor, before being carried into the station. Once inside, I was forced to sit down on an old wooden stool, where the six greasy bastards took it in turns to try and interrogate me, saying things like: "Fucking British soldiers coming to my country. Fucking my women, and smashing up people's property. Then thinking they can just get away with it. Well I'm telling you now, you ain't fucking getting away with it. Not tonight. Not ever."

I have always said there is a time to speak and there is a time to shut the hell up. That night I told myself to keep my mouth firmly shut. So for the next half an hour I didn't speak a word and to be really honest, I thought I was about to get raped or something. That's how intimidating they were trying to be. There was one copper who was a right little knob-head, who kept getting in my face and shouting at me. Which wouldn't have bothered me that much, apart from the fact his breath stunk of shit and he kept spitting all over me. It was now a battle of patience with the Sergeant breaking first and playing his final hand. He went on to inform me that he only had one more option and that was for him to call the Military Police. To which I said,

"Call them." The shock on his face said everything. He eventually untied his tongue.

"Are you sure?"

"Yeah, are you deaf or something?"

"Okay, have it your way." Within twenty minutes my rescuers were there.

As I was un-cuffed and taken into military custody I saw my chance to get revenge on the little prick who had been showering me with spit every time he spoke. So I got in his face and told him what I thought of the dirty little tramp. I was quickly grabbed by a female MP and taken outside before I caused any more trouble. After being politely told to get in the car, I returned to camp, where I would have to wait and see if my stupidity had got back to my CSM.

The following day I was on guard and after twenty four hours I hadn't heard a peep. I took huge a sigh of relief, thinking I had got away with my drunken crimes, but as I headed back towards my block one of the provo staff stopped me and said that the Regimental Sergeant Major wanted to see me in his office at nine o'clock. I ran back to my room to get myself ready for my dreaded appointment. I couldn't help thinking that this was the first time I'd ever been in his office for anything like this and I only had a few weeks left in the Army. I knew I was really in the shit this time. No questions. He was going to tear me a new one!

I waited outside his office for his arrival, saluting every now and again as all the higher ranked officers came into work for the day. I was then met by my Platoon Sergeant, who was just passing. I told him everything that had taken place that night. He told me to just tell the RSM everything I'd just confessed to him and said that things should work out okay. After he left I noticed the unmistakable proud walk of the RSM approaching from the parade square, so I gave myself a quick look up and down to make sure I looked presentable before he arrived.

As he walked towards me I stood to attention and addressed him

"Morning Sir." He nonchalantly just looked straight through me as if I wasn't even there, before turning right into his office. I stood there shaking while the blistering heat sent beads of sweat running down the back of my neck that made me shiver when they reached the base of my spine. Deep down I was really bricking it, but I tried to keep myself calm so I was able to try and give some sort of explanation of why I had behaved like such a dickhead two nights ago. It's funny how I was so scared of this one guy that morning, but when bullets had been flying inches over my head I was cool as anything. I suppose it shows what training can do to you.

Finally, he put me out of my misery and I gladly escaped the baking sun that was burning the back of my head. I suppose the phrase 'out of the frying pan into the fire' suited this situation well. I marched into his office and halted before him. It felt like I'd just walked into God's office, where I now needed to explain to him why I should be allowed entrance to heaven, and he knew all my deepest, darkest secrets.

The pressure from his disapproving stare made me feel like I wanted the floor to open up and swallow me whole, but thankfully after a minute's silence, after he just looked me up and down, he spoke.

"Right then. Let me get this right. You are due to leave the Army in three weeks. Am I correct?"

"Yes sir."

"Okay then. I will make this really simple for you. If you don't sort this situation out, you are not fucking getting out. Do you understand me?"

"Yes, Sir," I nervously replied.

"Right then, get the fuck out of my office now. I don't want to see your fucking mug in here again." And with that, he sent me on my way, but not before calling me back to ask if I'd really tried to beat the copper up. I said yes, and he laughed.

"Good lad. No one fucks with a fusilier, do they?" With a smile on my face I agreed and headed out of his office. On my way back to the block I started to think about how the hell I was going to make amends for my actions.

With help from a sergeant from Battalion HQ I was able to track down the owner of the car and apologise for my utterly appalling behaviour. I then said I would be truly grateful if she accepted my apology and I would deliver the money to repair her car personally that day. I was driven to the police station to again apologise to the police sergeant for my actions, and luckily for me he was in a good mood and dropped the assault charges, but not before giving me a right lecture on how I was supposed to be setting a good example for the British Army and not acting like a complete and utter thug. Even though he was rather condescending, I took his advice on the chin, shook his hand and walked out of his office, trying not to make eye contact with that little prick from the night in question. Just looking at him might have just pulled the pin on my temperament grenade.

It was the last but one night before the company deployed to Afghanistan, so we all went out for one last drink as the musketeers. It was a fantastic evening, just reminiscing about all the good times the four of us had been through and I wished Chris and Evo all the best with the tour. Steve, who was leaving not long after me, had also declined the CSM's offer, so he was heading with me to HQ Company after the company left. We returned to camp, where Chris and I had a real heart-to-heart, where he did shed a few tears and he didn't have something in his eye. I on the other hand remained my usual emotionless self and kept my feelings where they belonged, deep down. Even though I will confess I felt the same as Chris. Sorry, mate. It was the end of an amazing era, something that I hold very dear to my heart. Great friends made the Army what it was, and I still miss those days.

The following morning, I met everyone in the NAFFI, where Chris told the story of how I was a heartless bastard that didn't even drop one tear for him. I told him again that I didn't really cry, but inside I felt exactly the same. The next morning, I made my way to the front of the block at stupid o'clock to wish everyone good luck. These lads had been like family to me over the past four years and I wanted to make sure I shook everyone's hand and told them I would be thinking about them. The last person I saw was Chris and I gave him a hug. I told him to make sure he emailed me when he could, and that I would be waiting for him on the other side when he returned. Chris, like me, had handed his notice in, but still had about ten months to push, so he had no choice but to go on the tour. Before any more tears were shed Chris got on the coach and I headed back to my room. Once there, I felt an almost empty feeling inside, like something was missing.

I had about a month before I was due to leave, so I spent the next few weeks handing in any outstanding kit and getting signed off from every department to say I didn't owe anything that belonged to them. After I'd had my final medical and been given the all-clear, well physically all-clear, I was told that I would no longer be required to take part in any company PT and would spend the rest of my time left in the Army working down at the beach. My duties were to assist with some of the adventure training days, which to be honest was a sweet deal, really. The Army, if they'd wanted to, could have had me doing some really crappy duties until I left.

On the morning of my final day, I woke up with a really strange feeling inside me. Strangely enough, the same one I had on the morning of the 5th January 2003, the day this whole journey started, a feeling of sickness and sadness. It was like I was leaving home again and really needed someone to talk to. I felt again as if I was making a terrible mistake, leaving my adopted family. And that's what you are when you join an infantry battalion, part of a massive family that has a huge and unbelievable history, and it made me feel proud and lucky to be part of it.

My transport was collecting me at half past eight, so I slowly got ready, trying to soak in every last second of Army life. I grabbed my two bags and headed to the guard room and took a seat on the uncomfortable red brick wall outside. I lit a cigarette and tried to enjoy the last of the Cypriot sunshine. What a beautiful morning it was. Not a cloud in the sky. It was as if it knew it was my final morning here and wanted to put on a good show one last time before I left. As I dragged on my Benson and Hedges silver, I started to come to the realisation that I didn't want to leave and really wanted to sign back on. But I put this down to the fear of the unknown and after shaking a few of the lads' hands at the guardroom, I said my goodbyes before getting on board the minibus. For years afterwards, I sometimes wished I had turned around and found a way of staying, but you shouldn't ever try and live with regrets. They have a nasty way of trying to eat you up from the inside. The best thing is to just leave them in the past.

It took me nearly eight hours to finally get home. I really wished I'd put my hand in my pocket and paid for a civilian flight home and not relied on the RAF, but after the car window incident and my out-of-control alcohol abuse, funds were running a little low. I finally returned home on the Sunday night and this was actually the first time I realised I needed to do something else with my life and I didn't have a clue what. I'd always thought that I might head into close protection work, but after my previous leave I'd blown all my savings, so that plan had been completely ruined.

Chapter twenty four – Great friends, bad decisions

After leaving the Army my life slowly unravelled. At first, I loved having my freedom back; not being told how to live, what to wear, when and where to be, and it's silly really, but I also liked not being told I had to shave and have my hair in a certain way. That was a real bonus. At the time I had no real idea of how much the Army had affected me. Yeah, I knew I'd been through some crazy things and yes, I'd seen some utterly horrendous things, things that still live with me today, but at the time I really thought I was strong enough mentally to get through them.

I remember after leaving Afghanistan we flew to Kuwait to spend two days conducting a war zone decompression session, just unwinding before we returned to Cyprus. One of the meetings we had was with a doctor who specialized in post-traumatic stress disorder and he said that he knew some of the things we would have seen could affect us. Maybe not straightaway, but eventually thoughts could manifest themselves. We were asked individually if we wanted to talk about some of the things we had experienced, but I declined, thinking that talking about stuff would somehow make me weak. Something I would later come to regret. Sometimes you just need to open up and get things off your mind, but I have never really been like that. I have always tried to deal with things my own way, and at the time my escape was alcohol and later, drugs. I always thought that the problems I suffered with were from a mixture of the Army and the stuff I experienced in my teens. Two separate issues entangled together, making my mind a minefield, and trying to overcome it became the biggest battle of my life.

My first job after leaving was with my sister Liz's boyfriend Dave. He became a really great friend to me and even though I never really opened up to him about things I was struggling with, he was always there for me when I was having problems with alcohol. There were times when we'd been out drinking, and we had returned home. One night, after getting out of a taxi and heading for my house I suddenly became trapped in my mind. It was like I'd been sent back to Afghanistan and we were surrounded by Taliban fighters. They were everywhere and closing in on our position. I then dragged Dave over a four-foot privet hedge and told him to keep quiet, otherwise we were dead. Once undercover, I tried to formulate an escape plan from what my wonderful weird mind had made up. Suddenly, after a minute or so things returned to normal and I was just left sitting in someone's front garden feeling confused. After Dave left, I went home, but only to find my mind wasn't finished with me. So then, for some reason I barricaded myself in the front room and started to send fire control orders for mortar fire, much to the shock and confusion of my Mom and Auntie. These events would happen probably every other time I went drinking and I would find myself climbing over walls and fences trying to escape a made-up enemy.

Working with Dave was a great laugh, we got on like a house on fire, but the job and the management drove me crazy and with the constant call of the Army still fresh in my mind, I would tell Dave every night that he dropped me off not to bother collecting me in the morning and that I was going to the recruitment centre to rejoin, but every morning I would text him to say I was coming into work. One day I made it to the recruitment office, even got through the door, but turned around and walked out before anyone got a chance to talk to me.

The highly addictive drug that the Army was still circulated around my body, but deep down I knew I could never go back, knowing the strain it had put on my family, with deployments to danger spots in the middle east. I knew I would have had to go back with my tail between my legs, with everyone saying, 'I told you so'.

My drinking had started to become a daily occurrence while I was trying to banish the memories of a dying child and other life changing events that had now started to haunt my dreams. On top of that, I'd fallen behind on paying back my many debts, with any spare money I had now being spent on booze and class A narcotics. I would use cocaine to try and give me the high I was missing from the Army, and when I mixed that with alcohol I seemed to be able to escape from my reality, if only for a short time.

These had become very difficult times for me, probably the most difficult I had ever faced. My other battle was now trying to come to terms with leaving the Army and dealing with the memories. Not just the bad times, but the good times too. These could sometimes hurt me more, because I missed them so much and no matter how much alcohol and drugs I consumed, I could never replace those moments.

I'd been working with Dave for about six months and although I was still going through the crazy dreams and drunken escapades, I was starting to feel like I had a nice routine about things. I would work hard all week just trying to keep myself out of trouble as I still felt like a ticking time bomb waiting to go 'Bang'. But then as soon as Friday came along, I would just get crazy, messed up on alcohol and cocaine. I would usually spend all my wages on grams of coke and would sometimes even use what was left of my credit card limit, even though I knew I could never pay it back.

After one of my mad drug-filled weekends I arrived back at work on the Monday to find that some money had gone missing, about twenty pounds, and it seemed that the finger was being firmly pointed in my direction. I was called into the manager's office, where he said that I'd been seen putting this twenty pounds into my pocket and he wanted to hear an explanation. I was so bloody angry that this bold little jumped-up prick was trying to accuse me of being a thief. I've been many things in my life, but a thief was not one of them. I told him that after I'd put the money in my pocket I took it into the office, sealed it in an envelope, and then I put it into the drop box.

The funny thing was that he tried to show me CCTV footage of me putting the money in my pocket, but then the next clip was me heading to the office to drop it off. I told him to show me the video of me in the office, but apparently there wasn't a camera in there. The argument became more and more heated until I was ready to absolutely destroy someone. If it hadn't been for the fact that Dave had got me the job, I would have jumped over the desk and strangled the fat knob, until every last drop of oxygen had left his stupid round face. That was how angry I was, and this guy had no bloody clue about what kind of fire was raging deep inside me.

I jumped from my chair, almost making the two guys in the room jump out of their skins, and I headed for the door. I told him I couldn't be there any longer as someone was in danger of getting seriously hurt, and that if he thought that was the kind of person I was, then I was bloody quitting. I slammed the door behind me and went to find Dave. I told him what had just happened and then thanked him for getting me the job. Even though I didn't have my car and my house was twenty miles away, I told him I was going to walk home. I left him with a confused and bewildered look on his face and started the long journey home on foot, but to be honest I needed the fresh air to calm me down, as I was still rumbling inside. Like an angry volcano ready to erupt at a moment's notice.

The journey was so long that Dave ended up picking me up just the other side of Perry Barr, and he drove me the rest of the journey home. It turned out that the missing money was found a couple of weeks later stuck in the drop box, but I never got an apology for being accused. I never heard a single sodding word from the knob, but I suppose that really summed up what kind of person he was.

For the next few weeks my financial situation became bleaker and bleaker. I was still searching for the illegal highs that were helping me through one of the most difficult stages of my life, and with now only a few hundred quid left on my credit card, things were about to take a turn for the worse. I never thought I would see myself this low again and started to regret some of the decisions I had made.

One night I was in desperate need of a gram of coke and a few drinks to help me through one of my difficult moments, so I raced to the cash point, only to find HSBC had finally woken up and cut me off, and I now had only a few quid left in my wallet. So I headed home gutted, not really knowing what the hell to do. As I wasn't working, and I'd stopped paying my bills, it wasn't long before the bank was demanding the twenty grand plus that I owed them. I had also had my car insurance cancelled and was now, for the first time in my life, driving illegally. I didn't even have a pot to piss in and was in serious trouble. There was no way I could tell anyone how deep I was in, so I just tried to continue as normal.

Finally, one day completely out of nowhere, Marc messaged me and said there was a job at his place making blinds, so I gratefully took him up on his offer and went in to meet the boss. He said that he only had a bit of part-time work until Christmas, but after that he would take me on the books properly, which was better than the current situation I had found myself in, so I snapped up his offer. I was only on rubbish money and my debts were more than I was earning. I'd chosen to spend my wages on drugs and alcohol rather than pay them off. I knew I was in a really bad spot, but what else could I do? Go to Mom and tell her I had messed everything up? Hell, no. I knew there was probably a way out of my current situation, but I didn't know what it was. It was as if I needed a guardian angel to help save me.

I was still struggling to come to terms with leaving the Army and was trying everything I could to act like a normal civilian, but with the things that I'd experienced over the last eighteen months still so deep in my thoughts, I just couldn't leave the past where it belonged. Christmas came and went, and with having a couple of weeks off work with a bit of a Christmas bonus money on the hip, it was an enjoyable one, but things were always more enjoyable when I had some cash; and the snow wasn't the only white stuff I enjoyed that Christmas.

I had been invited to go and spend New Year up in Nottingham, where Dave B.'s girlfriend, Claire, lived, so a bunch of us, including Marc and Lee, drove up on the day, arriving about four. If I'd had any inkling of how the night was going to play out, I would not have agreed to go. A few months previously Marc had started seeing one of Claire's mates called Michelle, but they'd recently split up and were now just messing around whenever they saw each other.

After we got there, we started hitting the booze and the naughty white stuff pretty much straightaway and it wasn't long before I opened one of my favourite drinks, a nice bottle of Jim Beam. The plans for the evening were to have a few drinks in the house before heading to a couple of nearby pubs, then returning to Claire's to see in the New Year. We walked the twenty minutes to the pub and took over a table near the pool table and just started enjoying the night.

An hour had passed when Marc and Lee went outside to have a quick spliff and I was left with the two girls and Dave. The conversation somehow got onto how Michelle fancied me and the night she had met Marc she'd wanted to get off with me. She said she always wondered why I hadn't made a play for her, even though she'd made it plainly obvious she was into me. At this point in the evening I was still thinking with the head on my neck and tried to squash the discussion before Marc overheard, but Michelle was having none of it and said she wished she'd taken me back to her hotel room that night instead of him.

At that exact moment Marc returned to the table just as she revealed her feelings towards me, and if looks could kill, the pair of us would have been struck down. Even though I hadn't done anything out of order up until this point, Marc had now started acting funny towards me. After about half an hour and a few more drinks, everything seemed to return to normal and I tried my absolute best to try and avoid any eye contact with her. I also tried not to spend any alone time with her, because she was really putting it on me any chance she got. Michelle, on the other hand, was trying everything she could to get my attention and every now and again I could feel the weight of her seductive stare from across the table, which was then quickly followed by a dirty look from Marc.

On the walk back to Claire's I stayed up front with Dave and we talked about how this night could turn on its head in a heartbeat. He warned me that she could be trouble and would probably stop at nothing to get her hands on me. He then said I would do well just to stay out of her way and not rock the boat. Marc, on the other hand, was walking at a different pace, hanging back at the rear of the group, trapped in his drunken thoughts, and I knew he was getting screwed up about what he'd overheard. Every time I tried to talk to him, all he responded with was that he was okay, and that he wasn't bothered about what had been said. But I knew that he had strong feelings for her and at that point I fully intended to do my best to stay away from her.

When we returned to the house everything looked as if it had returned to normal, with everyone just getting on with each other. The booze was flowing really nicely and there was no evidence to suggest the night was about to turn sour. I staggered up the stairs to the bathroom and when I finished, I opened the door to find Michelle standing there in the dark. Before I had a chance to question her intentions she pounced and started passionately kissing me. Even though I knew this was so wrong I couldn't help myself. Her luscious lips locked to mine felt amazing and her perfume seemed to entice me even more. I now knew I was in trouble.

A few minutes went by before I came to my senses and tried to remove her from my lips, but God, she was something else. Like a class A drug making me want to keep going back for more. After finally breaking her glossy-lipped grip, I heard someone making their way up the stairs towards us. While Michelle made a beeline for the toilet, I sat down on the floor, my back against the wall, trying to make out as if I was just recovering from the booze and quickly wiped away any offending lipstick stains. Marc rounded the stairs to find me just sitting there and I could tell straightaway that my cover was blown. He knew exactly what had been going on and just walked back down.

For the next hour Michelle became like an addiction. I knew I was doing wrong, but I just couldn't keep my hands off her. Every time I went to the toilet she was waiting for me, her hot body cleverly positioned to make it impossible not to touch her. Even though I'd kept it to just kissing, it wasn't long before she eventually dragged me into a bedroom and tried to take things to the next level. Going to be honest now, I have no real memory of what happened next, until the door swung open and in walked Dave. He told us that everyone knew what was going on and Marc was really pissed off with both of us. He went on to say that Marc had just punched a hole through one of the bedroom doors.

We headed back downstairs to a very unhappy reception, because we'd ruined everyone's night. So I ended up outside trying to talk to Marc about what had happened. Dave and Lee had joined us outside and the conversation quickly became heated, with everyone pointing the finger at me, and to be honest, I probably deserved more than a few heated words. Claire now came outside to try and calm the situation down, but Dave told her to mind her own sodding business, which in turn angered me because of the way he'd spoken to her. It was now me and Dave ready to kick off and as we'd both been here before, we both knew what to expect.

Lee, who earlier had been pissed with me, was now acting

like more of a peace-broker, with Dave and me ready to brawl at any given moment. Then Lee made me go inside and calm down. I reluctantly returned to the house and headed straight back to the scene of the crime. A couple of minutes went by and then someone started knocking at the door. At first, I thought it might be Michelle trying to start up from where we had left it, and because I was now thinking with my brain again instead of with my manhood, I thought it was best I didn't open it. Bang! Bang! Bang!

"Open the fucking door now," shouted Dave. So I walked over and unlatched the door and in walked an angry looking Dave and Marc.

I thought things were about to go down, so I just readied myself for the first punch, but nothing happened. They just stood there with disapproving looks written across their boat races.

"If you're going to do something, then fucking do it. If not, then fuck off," I said to the two of them. It turned out they just wanted to sort things out before it went to the next level, so we ended up back outside to clear the air, which we sort of did. But for the rest of the night there was still that strange feeling lingering in the air and even after a night's sleep it was still there.

After returning to Birmingham the following morning, Marc dropped me off without really saying anything to me the whole way home, but how could I complain really? He should have left my sorry, disloyal ass in Nottingham with a couple of black eyes for my troubles. I had committed the ultimate sin between friends and I knew it would take a while to put right. In some ways our relationship has never really recovered from that night. Sorry, mate, I hope that maybe if you read this, you might be able to understand that I was going through some real shit back then and I know I can't use that as an excuse, but I am really sorry about that night, and if I could go back and change things, I would.

I was due to start work properly at Marc's place after the New Year, but with the whole Nottingham incident still smouldering in both our minds, I decided not to turn up on the first day, to try and give us both some more recovery time from the event. But Marc messaged me that day and said that we should just put this behind us and I shouldn't lose a job over it. To be honest, I'm glad he did because I really needed that job at the time and with the bank now threatening to send debt collectors to my house to remove any items that belonged to me, I needed every penny I could earn.

My New Year's resolution was to try and dig myself out of the huge debt hole I had made for myself and I made a promise that I would start to try and pay back every last penny. My plan lasted until the following weekend, when I ended up spending all my wages on drugs and alcohol. Things were so bad I even sold my car before the bank took possession of it. I remember taking it to a garage just up the road from my place, and the guy asked if I wanted cash or a cheque. Before he had a chance to change his mind, I ripped the wad of fresh crisp twenties from his oil-stained hand like a crack addict collecting drugs from his dealer, and I raced home to spend my new fortune on another blurry weekend.

I knew things couldn't continue in this way because now every time I got drunk I would do something stupid. Like messing around with women I shouldn't, or getting into fights and then being arrested, and it was only a matter of time before I would find myself spending a night in police custody. I had no plans to go out that night and was just going to chill in the house. Big Dave was my usual drinking buddy at that time, and he'd gone away, so I'd planned to just spend the day playing on the computer.

After a couple of hours, I was bored shitless so went to the off licence and grabbed a few beers. But this soon became a mistake because it wasn't too long after that I was ringing my dealer and getting a few grams of the good stuff dropped off. The first line was always the best. It made me forget all the other crap going on in my life, and after sniffing the line I would just chill, my heart beating a little quicker than normal and I seemed to enjoy beer and fags even more than usual. When I was on the white stuff, alcohol had no effect on me. I could just drink until the sun came up, which happened more often than not.

Within an hour I was back at the local shop for another eight Stellas. The problem now was that there was no way I would be able to stay in all night just buzzing, so I started ringing and messaging lads I thought might be up for a session. After a few busy replies Martin B. got back to me, saying he was going up Solihull later that night and asked if I wanted to meet up at his local before we headed up there.

That night had one of those strange feelings about it. You know those ones when you get the feeling that it's going to be either a really great night and you get lucky, or you have a really great night and wake up the next morning in a cold and uncomfortable police cell, gasping for water and having no recollection of how you ended up there.

I remember being in Roses that night and seeing some bird sitting down by herself looking upset. I asked her what was up, and she told me that she really fancied some guy who was there on a night out, but he hadn't even looked at her. She went on to tell me who he was and that he was just at the bar over the other side of the room. After listening to her go on about how much she liked him, I went over and briefed the lad. I told him he should give her a moment of his time and maybe he might feel the same. An hour later I walked past the now kissing pair, and I was met by the lad coming to me and shaking my hand. After a quick exchange of words, he returned to the girl, and I went on to continue the evening.

It was like now I was unstoppable and every woman I tried it on with was game. With the help of my white powdered friend, my confidence was booming, but with that side of me pouring out, it would only be a matter of time before the drama side of my personality would make an appearance. I used to nickname him the Wolfman, or as my friends from the Army called him, Wolfy. The Wolfman is a very charming and carefree individual. He loves the ladies and will stop at nothing in his pursuit of a good time, but for all his good traits there are many bad ones, and that night he showed all the sides of his complex personality.

After we left the club with a few birds to go back to their place, we headed down the street and stood in the queue for a taxi. We waited for about twenty minutes before one became available. As our taxi pulled up, some chavy prat walked out from the crowd and started to usher his friends onboard. He then sat in the front passenger seat and started to laugh. I was having none of this and gestured for him to get the hell out of my taxi and wait like every other bugger else.

We argued through the window and after I threatened him, he climbed out angrily and started swinging punches in my direction, the first catching me flush on the chin, but to no effect. Before he got a chance to reload his hands I charged him. This action sent the pair of us flying over the black taxi's bonnet and crashing on the cold, wet asphalt road the other side of the car, knocking off the door mirror in the process. We both then scrabbled to our feet and continued the fist fight until we were finally manhandled unceremoniously back to the ground by a pair of police officers. We were hand-cuffed and escorted to the waiting police van and taken the short journey to Solihull police station.

As I waited to arrive in the back of the stinking van, I realised I still had cocaine on me and thought there was no way these bastards were taking it off me. So I stashed it in my fag packet and hoped for the best. After arriving at the station, I was taken inside and pushed into a holding cell before I was seen by the custody sergeant. As it was a Saturday night the place was heaving, so I wasn't far from sober when I was finally seen. I was collected from the cell and taken to the desk to be processed and searched. I started emptying my pockets and placing my belongings on the counter, and then one of the police constables started going through everything.

He opened my cigarette box and all I was waiting for now was for him to locate my hastily stashed gram of coke, but after a quick look with his torch, to my surprise, he closed the box and placed it on the counter with the rest of my belongings.

Bonus, I thought, *he hasn't seen it and maybe I'll be out of here soon and be able to finish it off when I get home.*

The next item for examination was my wallet and I knew I had nothing in there that would get me into trouble. Well, that's what I thought anyway, but as the constable starting rummaging through, he pulled out a pack of Viagra I'd stashed in the side pocket. He started waving it about, saying had it got that bad that I needed these. I thought to myself *Who the fuck is this jumped-up little twat trying to take the piss out of?* so I gave him both barrels.

"Who the fuck you trying to take the piss out of, mate? I'll make you look like a right fucking dickhead in front of all your fucking mates." He tried to reply with some smarmy remark about him being a police officer, until I quickly shot him down.

"You dickhead. What the fuck have you ever done for your country? You don't know me, mate. You don't know anything about me or what I've done for this fucking country."

"So, tell me what you've supposedly done then, mate," he sarcastically remarked.

"I'll tell you what I have fucking done, mate. I have been to war. That's what I have fucking done, you fucking prick, and I come home and have to deal with cocks like you running their mouth, thinking you're fucking special because you have a fucking badge and a can of CS gas. I'm a fucking real man, not some twat hiding behind a badge, trying to look clever in front of a few fucking birds." My angry outburst had now brought the custody sergeant to laughter. I was grabbed and taken to a cell and made to spend the whole night there for my troubles.

The following morning, I woke to a banging headache and a mouth that was dryer than the Sahara Desert. After about an hour of complaining, I was finally brought a glass of water. I was taken to an interview room and read my rights. They told me that the taxi driver wasn't going to press charges, but I would be getting cautioned for assault. After what felt like forever, I was finally given back my possessions and allowed to leave, but not before getting a right good dressing down from the station commander, who turned out to be an ex-sergeant major in the Army. He told me I should wind my neck in and keep my opinions to myself if I ever turned up there again.

I walked down the long, badly painted corridors and out through the main doors. Once outside I was met by a bitterly cold environment, which was made worse by the fact I was still in my stupidly thin shirt from the previous night. I rang for a taxi and lit a welcome Benson silver. After coughing up my lungs on the first drag, I checked my messages from the previous night and found one from the girl I was supposed to have taken home. It read: *"Shame you had to act like a prick last night, ended up having to have fun with myself and my battery operated pink friend, something for you to think about when you get out in the morning. Anyway, see you around, sexy." xx.* I was absolutely gutted. What an evil text message.

Chapter twenty five – Emma

The next month or so continued in the same fashion: a mix of drugs, fast women and more alcohol abuse. Sorry, liver. My dire financial situation was growing worse by the day and my crazy, bloody dreams that were sending me mad were back. During all this, I tried to hide all the things I was doing and going through from the people who loved me the most. Somehow my life had turned into a real mess and I had no idea how things had ended up like this. I wasn't even sure if I could ever turn things around. So many times I just wanted to erase the previous year and go back to the Army or chuck in the towel altogether and just give up, but things were about to take a turn for the better. Big Dave's birthday was coming up and at first, we'd just planned to have a session at my place. A few drinks and a bit of gaming, but at the last moment we decided we would head into Solihull and meet up with Marc and celebrate Dave's birthday properly.

The night started in the Masons and before we knew it we were in Roses. A place we all knew very well and somewhere I had spent many a drunken night on the pull. We found ourselves in the cheesy room and started hitting the shots. The place was buzzing and full of forty-year-old milfs. The DJ played some crazy old tunes from the eighties and it wasn't long before Dave had attracted some attention from a group of older ladies. Even though Dave was going out with my sister Liz, I would always try and wind him up a little and encourage the women, especially the larger ones, to dance with him. We were soon in a fit of giggles, well apart from maybe Dave, when one of them had trapped him up against the railing and started to grind on him. I can see his face now, a look of complete horror, and I'm laughing now as I write, just thinking of it. Sorry, Dave, it was very funny, though!

Now, my memory of that night is quite blurred, as I'd consumed a lot of sambuca, but I remember noticing a woman across the bar looking in my direction, and then when I looked she would quickly look away as if she hadn't been looking over in the first place. This continued for the next half an hour or so until I went over and asked her if she wanted to dance, but I was quickly shot down when she told me that she didn't dance. After buying her a drink we started talking, but to be honest I would be struggling to remember about what. At first it was just like any normal Roses night out, and I thought to myself that maybe after a couple of dates things would just fizzle out and we would go our separate ways.

The night came to an end, and like the gentleman I am, I walked her to her taxi. We shared a quick kiss, before going on our way. The next day, after recovering from my hangover, I sent Emma a quick message, saying how much I'd enjoyed the night and that it would be great if we could meet up again the next weekend, a standard Sunday morning message. It took her hours to respond and at first, I thought, oh well, maybe just one of those things, that she wasn't really interested, or I'd got the number wrong. But at about five o'clock she finally replied, saying that she was sorry she hadn't got back to me straight away, but her phone was dead, and she hadn't been able to charge it until she got home to Leicester.

I thought, *Fucking hell, Jonathon. Leicester? That's miles away. Trust me to pick a bird who lived there.* Straightaway I thought I couldn't be arsed travelling to and from just for a bit of fun. We arranged to meet up at her place on the Friday night and she said she would meet me at Leicester train station. All week I kept thinking of just texting her and making up some lame excuse about why I couldn't make it. A thing I had done a hundred times before, but somehow, I don't know what made me, but I became a man of my word. Friday night came around quickly and after the fifty-minute train journey from Birmingham New Street, I arrived. I left the station and kept my eyes peeled for a black Peugeot 207.

After twenty minutes I watched one such car flying into the

station at high speed and braking heavily ten feet from me. After a quick glance through the passenger window to make sure I had the right car, I jumped in. The journey back to her house was very quiet and an awkward one, with neither of us really engaging the other in any conversation, apart from a bit of small-talk about work and the weather. The usual rubbish you talk about when you're feeling nervous. After screaming around a corner into a residential area, with me hanging on for dear life, she stopped the car outside a small terraced house. I unclipped my seatbelt and climbed out of the car, following her towards one of the houses, and walked in.

Due to the fact she was currently in the middle of gutting her house, the only room that was finished was her bedroom, so I walked up the steep stairs and sat down on her uncomfortable French bed. We now had another awkward moment as we both sat in silence, wondering what would happen next. Until thankfully, Emma broke the unbearable silence and asked if I wanted a pizza, so we spent the rest of the evening eating that and watching Footloose. I know, how corny? The next day she drove me back to Birmingham. I made her drop me around the corner because until I got to know her, I didn't want to her know where I called base.

I'm going to have to be really honest now. Never in a million years did I think this would ever go anywhere, but every time we were together I could feel myself falling for her. Even though I never really let my feelings be known. I was able to talk openly about the Army and how things had been for me since leaving. I was also able to talk to her about how things were for me when I was growing up and surprisingly, all the things that I'd revealed didn't seem to scare her off. When most would have run a mile and then changed their address to make sure I couldn't locate them, she stuck with me.

The next few months passed, and I started to think we could really have a future together, but the only thing that was standing in our way was the distance between us, and at that point I wasn't really ready to move to another city. While our relationship blossomed, I had changed jobs again and started working with Mat, collecting recycling around Birmingham. Not the most glamorous of jobs, I know, but the money was great and even after paying rent to my Mom I still had a shedload of cash to blow on whatever I wanted, but now I was with Emma the need to get messed up on drink and drugs to escape my sorry existence had started to evaporate and I could now start to try and live a normal life.

After only six weeks at my new job I was contacted by the manager and told that due to the recession at the time, they needed to cut back jobs and one of them was mine. At the time I was furious, because I had just started to think I was getting my life back on track. I think if it hadn't been for the fact I had Emma in my life I would have just gone crazy and gone on a bender or something. I now look back at this event as a bit of a blessing in disguise. Emma used to come over once a week, usually on a Wednesday night after work, when we would usually go and watch some cheesy film at the pictures, or just grab something to eat.

So that night I told her that I had lost my job. I said that if she wanted, I could come and move in with her and look for a job over in Leicester, much to her delight. I now had the difficult task of informing my Mom and family about my plans to move in with Emma and start a new life over there, but as ever, they were really supportive, and Mom said there would always be somewhere for me there if things didn't work out. The funny thing was, up until this point my Mom and Emma hadn't even met, because I was still keeping things separate. One of the random things I did back then and maybe still do in some ways today.

Before I moved in, we were due to go away on holiday, our first trip away together. Emma had bought me the greatest present ever for my birthday. A weekend away in Monza for the Italian Grand Prix, so all talk of moving away was put on hold until after that.

I remember walking through the secluded and picturesque park that houses that incredible and dangerous fast circuit. We walked between the tall trees and followed the hustle and bustle of the ever increasing, excited crowd. I held Emma's hand firmly in mine and we made our way towards the racetrack, crossing over the iconic banking of the old circuit. To be able to hear the screaming V8s roaring around the legendary track was completely mind-blowing, something I had wanted to experience since I'd first watched F1 as a kid. As we got closer, the noise doubled and the smell of engines and burning Bridgestone tyres wafted towards us on the cooling breeze, making all the hair on my burnt neck stand on end. There were times I nearly had to pinch myself to make sure I wasn't dreaming, a memory that will live with me for my lifetime. That day I knew Emma was the first woman I had ever loved. The day was incredible. The glorious sunshine burnt our unprotected skin and even though this turned out to be a really bad time to break in a new pair of trainers, every painful step was worth it.

The following morning Emma woke me and said that I needed to look outside. I pulled back the heavy blacked-out curtains and much to my horror, it was absolutely lashing it down. Something I never expected in Italy at that time of year, a complete opposite from the day before, when sun cream had been a must. But now it was time to try and source an umbrella from somewhere.

We had rented a little Fiat Panda and because Emma refused to drive a left-hand car, it was my job to drive and hers to navigate, something we would eventually regret doing. Especially when we were lost, and Emma was trying to find our location on the French page in the atlas. Do you remember that, Emma? The journey wasn't that difficult really. There was a ring road which was right outside the hotel. All we had to do was jump on and head north, then follow the directions to Cologno Monzese, and then pick up the signs for Monza, where we would park just outside the village, before jumping on shuttle buses that took us to the track.

The journey each day to the track was a piece of cake, but on the other hand, the one back was a completely different story. On the three occasions we drove back from the track we took a completely different route. Once we ended up on the other side of the ring road, driving through what felt like a million toll stations, arguing like crazy about whose fault it was. It got to a point where we drove into a toll station, spun around and before the gate closed, I floored it, spinning the front wheels in the crappy Panda and racing under the barrier just before it closed. Unfortunately, it was only a matter of weeks before Emma got the bill through the post.

After watching Sebastian Vettel win an epic Grand Prix, we returned from Italy and I moved in with Emma. Things were great and, apart from the occasional bad dream, my time in the Army seemed a distant memory. I started looking for work, but due to the recession the country was experiencing at the time, things were very difficult. The only work I could find was agency work, which at times was soul-destroying.

I remember working for a company that provided car windows for auto glass and to start with things were good, but it wasn't long before some dickhead tried to talk down to me and he quickly had to be put back in his place. After spending four and half years in the Army and being through what I had been through, there was no way I would ever be spoken to like a knob.

It was coming to the end of a very boring shift and the management hated people just standing around not doing anything. So I had just spent an hour or so walking around clearing up any rubbish that had been left lying about, just trying to pass some time really, but as I had moved from my designated area, the supervisor, who was a cock I must add, couldn't locate me and had spent ages trying to, which must have pissed him off.

I went to the toilet and started messing on my phone as you do and before I knew it I had killed half an hour. After leaving the toilets to finish off my area, the supervisor finally caught up with me and started trying to have a go at me, but much to his utter shock and surprise, I opened up on him, almost knocking him of his feet with my verbal assault.

"Who the fuck do you think you're talking to, you fucking dickhead? You're very lucky I'm in a good mood, otherwise I would take your fucking head clean off, you fucking prick," I said.

To his credit he tried to give it some back, but after a second abusive sentence he soon backed down, and while he still had his senses, he scurried off with his tail between his legs. After I'd clocked out and driven home, the agency called, and it came as no real surprise when they informed me that I would no longer be needed at work the following day. This is what the Army did to me. They made me not take shit from civilians and even though I was now one of them, I couldn't leave that bit of me behind.

The next job the agency lined up for me was over at Magna Park, working for a massive drinks company, packing bottles into boxes. A real mind-numbing job, but needs must. The place was so strict. We only got two fifteen-minute breaks during the eight-hour shift and didn't get a second longer. If we did take extra minutes, we got docked for them. They would march us to and from our work stations, making sure we only got the thirty minutes. The worst thing was that in the time it took to get back to my car and grab my food and then get back, I would use up ten minutes of it. It was like being back in the Army, but worse. At least in the Army I felt as if I was part of something really special, but there they just worked us all like a pack of starving dogs. There were so many times I just wanted to flip on a manager and smash their skull in. The only thing that stopped me, I suppose, was that I didn't want to let Emma down. At that time in my life it was all about her. After what she had done for me I could never let her down.

The funny thing about the recession, it was like it wiped out the class difference. It sort of put all walks of life in the same place. Everyone was in the same boat. There were people who I worked with who'd been bank managers or in high-status jobs before the country went bust, but now that kind of shit didn't count for anything. No one gave a damn about what we had done in a previous job. I'm telling you, *no one*. It was what we were willing to do now that counted and that was what I told friends who were still in the Army and thinking about leaving. No one cares about the shit we have done. The country doesn't care, so think twice about leaving.

While I was working for the agency, I was still signing on the dole, so I would do two days a week working and spend the rest of the week off, or sometimes work a full week and just not declare it. I thought, *Fuck it. I've done enough for this government over the past few years and got nothing but medals and memories in return. So having them over a few pounds is the least they can do.*

This sort of routine continued over the next few months at different locations, but it was only when Emma saw an advertisement about a permanent job, on her way to work one day, that things started to look up. The job was working for a timber frame company, building wooden frames for pre-fabricated homes. After ringing up to enquire about the role I was told to email my CV and come in that Friday for an interview. Even though I'd been to shedloads of interviews, I felt so nervous that day. It was as if so much was riding on it. Over the last twelve months I'd sent off dozens of CVs and heard nothing back. Not even to say I was unsuccessful, absolutely nothing. So this was the first bit of good news regarding a permanent job I'd had since arriving in Leicester.

Even after Emma had reassured me that I would definitely get the job, I arrived with that same uneasy feeling in the pit of my stomach that I always got before an interview. As I was sitting in the reception, I started thinking about how I needed that job so much. If I was successful, Emma and I could finally start to really plan our future. Up until that point Emma was carrying the pair of us and we were really starting to struggle financially, especially with a wedding to be paid for in the next few years. We both needed that chance to come good.

I was called into the manager's office and after shaking Dave's hand I took a seat.

"So you're the guy I couldn't wait to meet. I have been really intrigued from what you've put on your CV," he said.

"Oh really?" I replied.

"Yes, I have the greatest respect for soldiers and what they've done for our country, and it would be great for this company to have someone like you onboard." For the rest of the interview we talked about my experiences from my Army days and after realising he was now late for a meeting, he politely showed me to the door and shook my hand. He then told me there was a very good chance I had been successful, and that I would definitely know in a couple of days.

The good news I had been waiting for came via a letter and I was due to start the following Monday. The only downer was that I would be on the night shift. That day I headed to work and was introduced to the night supervisor, Lewis, who showed me around and told me what my duties entailed. From the off I could tell I was going to fit in here, even though at first the other lads kept their distance, just giving me the usual, "You alright mate?" whenever I walked by one of them.

The place was full of young lads and as you can probably imagine, the banter was unbelievable, but to my surprise no one ever said anything to me, which I found out later was because before I'd started Lewis had called the whole shift together for a meeting and had told everyone that I'd been in the Army. He explained to the lads that I'd seen action in Northern Ireland, Iraq and Afghanistan and that I should be left alone and that I was not to be messed with. I was absolutely gobsmacked when Jimmy told me this, because that's not who I am at all. In fact, I love the banter and it turned out that I was one of the worst there and never minded taking it back.

Life was going along well. Well, apart from the fact that I was still in hiding from the bank and the many debt collection agencies that were desperately trying to locate me, but there was no way I was ever going to pay those bastards back. The Army, and the issues that I had developed after leaving, all seemed to have disappeared and I'd now started to be able to watch things about Afghanistan without turning them off, but one night things changed.

I woke after having a bad dream to find Emma holding me down by my arms.

"What the fuck are you doing?" I asked.

"What the fuck am I doing? Don't you mean what the fuck are you doing?" she replied. It turned out that I'd attacked her in my sleep, while trying to defend myself against an enemy in my dreams. These events were not a regular thing, but they'd strike every three to four weeks. Most of the time I didn't even know I'd experienced one, it wasn't until the following morning when Emma would tell me that I'd been acting weird in my sleep, throwing elbows at her or kicking out and shouting. Thank God I was with Emma. I reckon most women would have run a mile, but not her. She has been my angel looking after me.

For the first time in a long time, things had started to settle down and we were both enjoying life. During this time, though, Richard had started to try and make contact. Emma, although knowing about his past, convinced me that I should give him another chance and go and visit him in prison, where he was coming to the end of a five-year jail term for armed robbery at a local bank. At first, I didn't want anything to do with him, after all the years of heartache and bullshit he had put every family member through, but Emma said that everyone deserved a second chance.

Richard, however, would probably have been on at least his tenth chance by then and he has had a few more since then!

At first, I just started accepting his phone calls, but eventually I agreed to go and visit him at his prison over by Rutland Water, funnily enough not far from North Luffenham, my first posting after passing out of training. The visit went well, even though it had been a while since I had last seen him. We talked about the usual: Formula One, football and computer games. He asked how I was dealing with civilian life and if things were still bothering me. He must have been speaking to Mom to know about that and as I didn't really feel that comfortable talking to him about that shit I just said, "Yeah, doing okay. Have my bad days, but Emma gets me through it." To his credit he didn't really try and push me too much for any information. I told him that I would talk about it when we were on a better footing, as there was still some tension from all the previous bullshit. On the journey home I made the decision that I would continue to see him and as he was coming up to the end of his sentence, I would try and be there for him when he was released.

Chapter twenty six – Building our future

Sunday 19th July 2009 was a day I will always remember for the wrong reasons. I'd woken as usual and had set up my laptop to check with the goings on in the Facebook world, as we all do. I quickly noticed a harrowing and disturbing post from one of my old Army friends, which read: Rest in peace, Etch. All of a sudden, I felt as if I was going to be sick, and frantically searched around on Facebook to look for any other comments that would ease and heal my desperate thoughts. But as the day continued, more and more people posted comments and I started to come to terms with the fact that Etch had been killed in Afghanistan. His patrol had been sent in to locate a bomb factory in Sangin, when he had triggered a huge device and died there from his injuries.

This one hurt the most. Although I hadn't seen Etch for years, it felt as if I had lost a brother. A real hero, a soldier, someone who I was very proud to have served with and been able to have called a friend. A man I would have died for, and him for me. Still now his memory lives deep inside, entangled with my spirit. Sometimes he's my strength to carry on when things become difficult, and I remember that I am the lucky one. I got to come home to my family. It makes me very upset just thinking of that day and the memories we shared with each other.

Every year I still think of him around memorable dates. I'm ashamed to say that I just couldn't go to his funeral. Going would have made it feel as if it was definitely true, and a part of me still hoped it wasn't. I hope you can understand my reasons for not going and you don't think badly of me, but it felt so raw. Sorry, Etch, I still miss you, my brother. The soldier I could only wish to have been. Rest in peace.

The next few years went by with relative ease and as more time went by, the less I craved a military career, but just when feelings and memories from my past were dying out, I would be the victim of one of my dreams and all those things would come bubbling back to the surface. Then for the next few days I would think of nothing but the Army.

Emma and I had also during this time become the proud owner of a very handsome, but also very naughty and health-troubled basset hound called Lionel, who has given us so many heart-aching moments, but also absolutely amazing memories too. From the very start we knew we had trouble on our hands, as he seemed to be uncontrollable. While I worked nights, he terrorised Emma on a daily basis. During these years we also decided that we would plan to get married and had set the date for the 14th May 2011. So now it came to the most difficult task of paying for it.

Even though the Army life was well and truly behind me, I was probably happier than I had ever been before, and my past had become easier to talk about, I still thought about the Army and how much I did still miss it. I suppose in reality it took me many years to really get over being in and leaving the Army. It was such a huge part of my life. I was so proud to have served my country in three separate war zones and to have had the privilege of wearing the red and white hackle of the Second Battalion Fusiliers. Well, it was such a great honour and I will always hold the regiment close to my heart, but I knew if I wanted to secure a great future for my family, I needed to somehow relinquish the past and start to look forward instead of backwards, which in some ways I still do to this day.

The wedding was now only six months away and it was time for me to think about who was going to be my best man. There were so many worthy candidates and I knew it would be a very difficult decision indeed, but one that needed to be made. I thought that there was no way I could just have one, so after a short talk with Emma we decided that I would have two.

I started thinking about all the things, good and bad, that I had been through with all my mates and how each had helped sculpt my life in a certain way. Firstly, there were my friends from school, Dave, Marc H., Mark M. and Lee. Then there was Mat, who I had known for just as long. There was also Big Dave, Liz's fiancé and even though I had only known him for a few years, he had become an absolute corker of a best mate. Someone I could talk to about anything and knew that he wouldn't judge me, and there are only a few on that list. He had also been there for me in my darkest days, when dealing with issues from the Army. Then there was Chris B., who had been a fantastically loyal friend from the Army, a real man. I had served with him in Northern Ireland, Iraq and Afghanistan and on more than one occasion we had saved each other's lives. Remember the Chinese rockets in Afghan, Chris? The next one would have hit us if not for your quick thinking and dragging us both into that trench.

So you can see it took a while before I made up my mind and at first I thought that if I asked Chris, then hopefully none of the others would be too pissed off and would understand, but the only problem with that theory was that after Chris had left the Army, he disappeared off the radar and I could never locate him. It wasn't until a few years later when he 'friend requested' me on Facebook that we got back in touch.

After considerable thought, I made up my mind and rang Dave. I asked him if he would do me the honour of standing up there with me, on the proudest day of my life with the woman who had saved me from God knows what. He said yes before the question had really left my lips. He then said he didn't feel that comfortable doing a speech, but he would do it if that was what I wanted. I told him that I was going to pick a second best man and he would probably be happier doing the best man speech. I told him then that I was going to ask Marc if he would stand up there with me.

This was to a lot of people an obvious choice, but as Marc would probably confirm, we have had a bit of a fiery past. So I called and asked him the question. I could tell straightaway that this had come as of a bit of a surprise and after a few silence-filled seconds, he said, "Of course I will, but what about the others?" I told him that I had asked Dave and that even though we had been through some shit, I had always classed him as one of my best mates. I continued to say that it wouldn't be right if he wasn't up there with me. I told Marc that I would like him to arrange the stag do. I also told him that Dave wasn't a hundred percent happy about making the speech and asked him if he'd feel ok about doing it. After happily agreeing to do it, we laughed and joked about what they would do to me on the stag do and he threatened to have me tied up against a lamp post, missing some body hair.

Marc arranged the stag do and he told me that it would be in Torquay. This would take place two weeks before the wedding, which would give me some time to recover if any crazy shenanigans were to take place. But everyone was warned that there would a serious fight back if they tried anything funny. The stag came and went without any serious events taking place and it was an absolute blinder. A right good old drinking session. Cheers, Marc.

We headed out on the Saturday morning after meeting at Mr G's cafe and filling ourselves up on a greasy full English. Everyone who I would have wanted to be there was there. Well, apart from Lee who hadn't been very well after his kidney had failed, and Chris, who I still hadn't been able to track down. Martin B., who I'd met in the Army, had brought his brother along with him and was in our car for the long trek down south. Martin and I chatted for hours about the good old days, maybe boring the others a touch.

Sticking to the rules of the stag do, what happens on a stag stays on a stag. All I will say is that I kept all of my body hair and apart from Big Dave trying to attack me in my room after we had returned from the clubs, nothing else funny happened. I promise,

Emma xxx. After arriving back home in Leicester, time started ticking quickly towards one of the biggest days of my life.

A few weeks before our wedding, my brother got up to his good old tricks again and stole my sister's bike. So after contacting him, I demanded to know what the hell he was doing. I went on to tell him that I didn't need any shit at my wedding and if he didn't sort out the situation he had created with his foolish actions, there would be no way he was going to be welcome at the wedding. He promised he would sort everything out and started going on about how he had missed out on so much of our lives and that he didn't want to miss this.

When I came off the phone I was quietly confident that he would stick to his end of the bargain, but a phone call a few days later dashed any hopes of that. Big Dave had contacted me and told me that they still hadn't received the bike back and that he was going to go round and sort it out himself, but that he wanted to let me know his intentions first. I told him that Richard had had enough time to return the bike, so to do want he thought was right. But luckily for Richard, when Dave turned up to have it out with him, my Dad told Dave he wasn't there, even though it was clearly evident that he was. After this I rang Dad and told him to inform Richard when he saw him that he wasn't welcome at the wedding and if for some stupid reason he turned up, he would be quickly removed, with force if necessary.

Deep down, this was a very bitter pill to swallow, because after all these years I thought maybe we had turned a corner and moved on from this sort of crap, and maybe, just maybe we could have started to have a proper relationship, but thanks to him we never really did, and we still don't have one. But sometimes life is just weird like that. No matter how many times you give someone another chance, they think they can just keep messing up, just because you are related to them. But even though my anger for him still runs incredibly deep, I only want the best for him and for him to finally sort his bloody life out before it's too late. Whether that will ever happen, well, we will just have to wait and see, and if a miracle does somehow take place and he decides to finally change his ways, I will be there for him, like I have always been. Or maybe we will never get a chance to be proper brothers again. Who knows?

I woke the morning of the wedding, and it took me a minute to realise I was staying at my Mom's, back in my old room at the old house in Reddings lane. A place that held some happy memories, but mostly just shit ones that I have still not dealt with properly. Anyway, it was a beautiful May morning, but the weather forecast had scattered rain showers predicted for the best part of the day. But without a cloud in the picturesque skyscape, I couldn't have asked for a better start.

As you have probably worked out for yourself, I have been through a lot of shit during my life. Some great things and some bad, so I felt ready for anything the day could throw at me. Apart from the whole speech thing, I thought the day would just pass by without any nervous event. I thought I was easily mentally prepared for anything, but that day something did sneak up on me, like a ghostly figure. I'd just returned from the kitchen with a brew, I lit a Benson silver and took a deep long drag, something I had promised Emma I would eventually quit. My mind kept racing about how I had ended up here, about to marry the most amazing women I had ever met and how lucky I was. Never in a million years had I ever seen myself being in this position, but somehow, through all the crazy things, I was about to become a married man.

I arrived at the venue and started to sort out the only job that Emma had foolishly given me. Well, apart from just turning up, anyway. That was to rendezvous with my Auntie Liz, who had been kind enough to do the flowers for us, and to start to distribute the buttonholes to the wedding party. To be honest, I was more interested in getting a few swift beers down me before the ceremony started. So I ended up forgetting to hand them all out, which inevitably got me into Emma's bad books, so then she gave me some shit for my troubles. While sipping on a cool, crisp pint of Stella I was interrupted by the hotel's Master of Ceremonies, who informed me that I needed to take my place in the wedding room, as Emma was nearly ready to enter. But Emma, being Emma, was late, so I had to wait a further twenty minutes until she finally made an appearance.

Now usually I was able to keep my nerves and feelings under wraps, well, apart from maybe my sweaty palms, but suddenly from absolutely nowhere, I was completely overwhelmed with emotions, after hearing the first line of *Somewhere Over the Rainbow* playing from the music system as Emma elegantly walked towards me. My body tingled, and I shook from head to toe, as I struggled to keep my emotions under control. Apart from my best man, Dave, everybody was completely oblivious to my feelings and somehow, I finally got a firm grip of myself and snapped back into my usual cool, calm appearance. Now for the previous three years I had never said the words 'I Love You' to Emma. She had always known I did, but it wasn't until the wedding day that I finally said the three easy words that had somehow escaped me. To which she replied, 'You too'. That was usually my response to her.

Apart from a few missed words on my behalf, the ceremony went without a hitch, thankfully with no last minute crazy ex-girlfriends making a surprise appearance, and we were finally husband and wife. I couldn't believe it. How could someone like me with my crazy past have been lucky enough to marry someone like Emma?

We made our way outside and into the beautiful gardens that surrounded the magical building, and under a shower of glistening confetti, we took our first few steps as a married couple. It felt amazing, sharing that glorious memory with all our close friends and family. After the taking of a thousand photos, we settled down for the meal and speeches. I gobbled down my turkey roast, and then I had to conduct my speech, the thing that I had dreaded the most, which thankfully turned out to be a breeze. I've always loved a good drink and a few tunes, so the reception part of the wedding was always the bit I'd looked forward to the most. Well, apart from marrying Emma, of course.

The only thing was, just before the wedding we had been informed by the company who we had booked the DJ with that they had gone bust, and they had no record of the booking. The guy who I spoke to on the phone said he would do all he could to make it, but he had another event to cover that night. He couldn't promise anything. It meant that until the guy actually turned up, we had no clue whether we would have any music for the night, so we had taken an iPod that could be hooked up to the hotel's stereo system, just in case. Thankfully, I caught a passing glance of the DJ, as he ran past one of the windows half an hour late, but I didn't care. I was just chuffed he had turned up.

Every now and then in life, everyone will share a special moment with their partner and one such moment materialised during our first dance. With Lionel Ritchie's *Stuck on You* reverberating around the reception room, we stared into each other's eyes, just enjoying the moment together.

The night was absolutely epic, with everybody crammed on to the dance floor while the DJ pumped out some fantastic tunes. Granted, chosen by me of course, but every now and then a shitty Abba tune seemed to sneak on, thanks to my Mom, I think, and he then had to be warned about his future conduct. Usually the bride and groom are the first to leave, but not us; we stayed till the very end. Even when they closed our bar, we headed into the main one and continued drinking into the wee hours. It was about five in the morning when everyone left, and it was then we finally threw in the towel and headed for the bridal suite.

I was woken from my slumber a few hours later by the blinding sun that blasted through the crack in the curtains. The true effects of the previous night's drinking session were well and truly revealed. My head banged with every breath and you might know that when you're that bad, even the slightest movement will bring an urge for you to race to the toilet and deposit some of last night's alcohol. It's usually something like tequila, something that burns your nostrils when making a bid for freedom. The only thing you can do is try and make it to the shower and see if that eases any of the horrible side effects of excessive alcohol consumption.

The one thing I wasn't looking forward to that morning was the long hungover hour journey back to Leicester. As I had to collect our naughty dog, Lionel, from the kennels before one o'clock, I didn't have much time to recover before the journey started. After saying my goodbyes to everyone who had stayed the night, I climbed into my car and prepared myself for a soul-destroying journey home, when one whiff of my body odour or breath by a passing police officer would see me short of my driving licence.

Now, you know when there is no way you should be even thinking about driving, never mind actually driving. Apart from a couple of other times I would never usually have done it, but that day was one of those days. I found myself concentrating so hard on the driving that I kept making mistakes and if there had been a police car in my vicinity, it would have been so obvious that I was over the limit. But we finally arrived home in one piece, I unpacked the car and fell on the sofa, absolutely knackered.

It was then that I realised my wedding ring was missing from my finger, and I scrambled from my drunken state and frantically started to search the house for it, but to no avail. Then I thought that maybe I'd left it in the car, so I raced outside and across the road, narrowly avoiding being knocked down by a passing BMW, which seemed to be doing twice the speed limit. I searched the car from top to bottom, but my elusive ring was nowhere to be seen.

I'd almost given up all hope of finding it and started trying to think of a way of explaining to my new wife that I had lost my prized possession on only the second day of wearing it, but then I noticed something glistening on top of one of the many metal drains that was on our road. Unbelievably, as I got closer I could tell it was my ring. I was completely overwhelmed with joy and as the ring clearly did not fit my finger correctly, I wore it on the adjacent one for the next few years until I finally had it adjusted.

The next few years passed, and we started to try to sort out some of our debts. It was always in the back of our minds to start a family and at some point, to move back to Birmingham to be closer to loved ones. At that time, I'd also changed my job and had started working at a place called Stonecraft Paving, where the son of one of Emma's friends worked. From the get-go I thought there was no way I was going to last at that place, as I couldn't see myself getting along with one of the managers.

I have said this before, but when you've been in the Army there is no way you can take shit off anybody, especially some civilian idiot who has no clue. But somehow, I don't know how, I stuck it out. Even though I've had some unbelievably crazy arguments with the managers, arguments that at other places would definitely have got me my marching orders, up to this point in time, I am still here four and a half years later. I have to say I now have a good relationship with Rich, the manager, who I used to argue with like crazy.

Chapter twenty seven – Death and new beginnings

I remember this event like it was yesterday. It was a normal day at work and I'd been in the office just chewing the fat with Scott, something we always did, when I felt my phone ring inside my pocket. Phones were supposed to be banned, so I headed outside towards my car to answer it. It rang again, and I saw that it was Mom calling me. As soon I heard her voice I knew exactly what she was going to say.

"Hello, Jonathon. It's Nan, she has passed away." Now all I could think about was getting back to Birmingham and being with my Mom, because I knew this event was going to shake the family to its very core. After telling her I was on my way, I ran into the shop, and, trying my best not to show any emotions, I told Scott what had happened. I said that I was going, and I would call Rich later when I knew my plans. I jumped in the car and headed for the exit.

Now usually I can control my feelings, but that day was very different. Something I had never experienced before. It was as if someone had just turned a tap on in my head and thirty years of trapped and locked-away emotions came pouring out. I'm not ashamed to say that I pretty much cried the whole journey back to my house, where I got changed and headed to meet Emma, who was working in Coventry at the time. I rang and broke the news to Emma. Even though we had been together for years, I was still embarrassed to show my feelings and would just go quiet on the phone when trying to compose myself. I knew that she could tell I was absolutely devastated, but for some reason I was afraid to show any tears to her. I thought it was a sign of weakness. I met Emma at her work and we shared a quick conversation about what had happened, but at this point I was still none the wiser.

The whole journey back I kept finding myself bursting into tears and thinking I couldn't believe that Nan had gone. I hoped that she hadn't been in any pain at the end, because that was something she definitely hadn't deserved. We arrived at my Mom's where I'd planned to drop my car off, and we completed the rest of the journey in Emma's. Suddenly my phone rang, and it was Mom. She told me that she was still at the hospital with Auntie Liz, trying to get to the bottom of what had happened. She said that she hadn't told my sister Liz yet, and she wanted to know if I would get there for when she rang her. The car journey to my sister's house was now a horrible one, and knowing I was going to be the first person she would see when she was told of this horrible news made me extremely nervous

We parked on the drive and I unclipped my seatbelt, but before I went in, I took a deep breath and knocked. Liz opened the door and as soon as we looked at each other she burst into tears. This was the first time in years we'd hugged one another. We went inside and sat on the sofa. We quizzed each other to try to find out anything, trying to understand what might have happened, but she said that Mom was on her way and would explain everything then. A knock at the door brought us all from our deep thoughts, so Liz went and opened the door. From the cries I could tell Kathryn had turned up, so I headed to the hallway. Now, for some reason I just don't know how to be in these trying situations, so I just hugged them both. After a few minutes we returned to the living room and waited for Mom to arrive.

The wait for Mom was an agonising one and we were soon met with the reality of her arriving in tears with Auntie Liz. She started to explain what had happened. That morning Nan had been getting herself ready in the bathroom, when my Aunt Liz heard an almighty bang and rushed up the stairs to see what had happened. She went straight into the bathroom to find Nan face down on the floor, bleeding from her head. She telephoned for an ambulance and desperately tried to give first aid to her stricken Mom, but I think it was quickly evident that Nan had suffered something extremely serious.

The paramedics soon arrived and started to give life-saving treatment and removed her from the house and into the back of the ambulance. During this time Mom had been informed of what had happened and had left work for the hospital, but unfortunately when she arrived she learnt that Nan had already passed away. We found out later that it was from a pulmonary embolism. After a short time, Auntie Liz said she wanted to go back to the house and start cleaning up before my Auntie Helen turned up from Dorset. We all arrived at the house, and made our way in.

Now, every time I had been to my Nan's house, there'd always been a very welcoming feeling, but this time it was obviously very different. Saying that, I could still feel Nan's presence, and maybe she was still there. Auntie Liz was very adamant that she wanted to go and clean upstairs and remove any items that had been used by the ambulance crew during their battle to save Nan. I tried everything to convince her that she didn't need to see the scene, and that I would go and clean up so she didn't have to see what had been left, but she was having none of it and pushed by and climbed the stairs. I quickly followed, telling Emma to keep everyone else downstairs. As I entered the room where Nan had taken her last breaths, I was hit with extreme feelings of sadness and had to take a deep breath to try and compose myself.

The room was covered with bandages and lids from needles, which in their rush to leave the scene, the paramedics had left behind. Blood covered the floor from where Nan had hit her head, so the pair of us started to wipe away all the evidence of this heartbreaking event. It's very hard to try and describe my feelings of that moment. I think that maybe the years away spent in the Army, seeing some of the most utterly horrendous things you can see, might have prepared me for this day. That's the only way I can describe it. It was like I just went into some form of auto pilot, my brain not really registering what it was seeing. After we'd finished, we headed back downstairs, where the atmosphere was one of obvious sadness and despair. Deep down I'd always known this day would arrive and had kind of prepared myself mentally for it, but still it hurt terribly, although this was just a fraction of the pain Mom must have been feeling, and I think to be honest, a big piece of Mom died that day. It also made me think that there would be a day in the future, when we, as siblings, would experience the emotions of losing our Mom, something I know we all fear.

An hour or so later my Auntie Helen and Uncle Graham arrived, and straightaway they wanted to know what had happened. My Auntie went into great detail about the morning's events and told us all how she had tried in vain to get a response from Nan under the instructions from the person in the control centre. We all had no doubt that Auntie Liz had done everything she could, but it was clear that she never really stood a chance and Nan had already passed on. This conversation seemed too much for Graham, who left the room and went into the kitchen. Tears were now running freely from everyone's eyes, with us all probably mentally putting ourselves in Auntie Liz's position. It was something no one ever needs to go through. The memory would haunt anyone forever.

During this time, I felt as if Nan was still there with us, maybe even watching over us. I even felt like I'd seen a shadow through the crack between the door frame and the door, and every time I looked, whatever it was seemed to move to one side or the other. Maybe this was Nan looking in on us or maybe just my imagination playing tricks with me. Who knows? But I like to think it was her just checking on us.

After Emma returned to Leicester, Mom, Kathryn and I went back to my Mom's and tried to take in the day's tragic and life-changing events. As I went up to bed my thoughts were all about how the hell I would be able to sleep tonight. But, as ever, I was able to put the images of that day to the back of my mind and slowly drifted off to sleep. I woke a few times in the night and thought each time that everything had been a terrible nightmare, but once I realised I was still at my Mom's house I knew it hadn't been, and again tears would stream down my face, almost as if I was reliving the experience of losing my Nan all over again.

I was woken the following morning by the sound of wood pigeons calling out, and once I'd got my bearings, I headed downstairs to see if anybody else was awake. I found Mom just sitting there, locked in deep, dark thoughts, her eyes bloodshot, and it took a while for her to notice I was even standing in front of her. It looked as if she had aged ten years overnight, but I couldn't have blamed her for that after what she'd been through. Funny how life just drops things like this on you from completely out the blue. One minute you are going about your life with not even an inkling of worry. Then: Bang! The next thing you know, your life as you know it comes crashing down around you.

We started to talk about things and she asked whether I wanted to see Nan in the mortuary. I said that I would want to see her one last time. Later that day we all headed to the hospital where Nan was, and we went straight into reception to wait for further details of where we needed to go next. After a short wait, a kind woman came and told us to follow her. We walked across to the other side of the hospital in the pouring rain and were taken into an old building that was currently under reconstruction. The woman showed us into a small room, where we were told that they were just preparing Nan for us to see her

The wait was an agonising one, with everyone not really saying anything, but instead, just kind of trapped in our own deep thoughts of how we were about to deal with a very difficult moment in our lives. A door swung open and a woman approached us. She politely said that Nan was prepared for us, if we were ready. We cautiously made our way in and nervously headed towards a gurney which was set up in the middle of the room, where I could see Nan.

At first, I didn't want to look in too much detail, as I didn't want that to affect my last memory of her. Everyone around me was obviously devastated about what they were seeing, and tears were now pouring uncontrollably from everyone.

To repel my feelings, I started thinking about all the good memories I had shared with Nan from when I was a little boy staying the night at her house, she used to tell me that I would wriggle around in the bed and it was as if we were chasing each other around all night. I remembered how we always had long conversations about the future and how I should have made something out of my time in the Army. She was so right. She always was. I should have made more of my time there. Maybe I did waste a perfect opportunity. Everyone was distraught and held on to every last second with her, but it was soon time to leave her and so we headed back outside, but not before saying one last goodbye.

After going back to Mom's, I said my goodbyes and travelled back to Leicester. I parked the car, unlocked the door and sat on the sofa. The last forty eight hours had been truly eventful and it took me a minute to take in all that had transpired, but suddenly it was like the flood gates opened again and all my feelings and emotions came rushing out like an uncontrollable tidal wave. It wasn't long until Emma arrived home and we started talking about everything, but again I could feel the waves of emotions building up deep inside and before I knew it they came gushing out. I've never felt comfortable crying in front of Emma, it's as if I feel weak and then really embarrassed.

The funeral took place a couple of weeks later. So until then life for me just went back to normal, returning to work and just going back to the way things were before the tragic event. It's a pity that was not the case for the rest of the family. They were all still so close to it all and really struggled to get through such a difficult time. Whereas I, on the other hand, was able to just put it to the back of my mind and act as if it hadn't happened, something that I could always seem to do with ease. I have always been good at being able to put things in boxes in my mind and not really think about them until I wanted to deal with it.

The day of the funeral came, so Emma and I headed back to Birmingham and went straight to my Mom's. After we got changed, we drove to my Nan's and waited for the hearse and the rest of the funeral procession to arrive. I took this time to get my thoughts in check. I told myself that I had shed too many tears and would now keep my emotion buried within. Mom had been trying to contact Richard all morning. He was late and she was starting to get herself worked up, but luckily for him he rounded the corner and rushed by to get ready. We hadn't spoken for ages and shared an awkward reunion on the driveway, with the pair of us struggling to string more than a couple of words together for a conversation.

Then, out the corner of my eye I noticed the unmistakable sight of the black hearse turn into the road, and it slowly headed in our direction, finally stopping outside the house. We took a minute to regain our composure before climbing into the back of the black Mercedes limousine, and then we left for the crematorium. Earlier in the week Mom had asked me whether I would help carry Nan's coffin and before she'd got the words from her lips I said it would be a massive honour to do so. While we were in the car we started talking about how we should do this and as I was the only one that had experience in this sort of thing, I started to explain what the best way would be to carry out such a task.

When we arrived, we met up with the pall bearers and they told us that two of their guys would help with the coffin. The head bearer gestured over for us, so we headed in his direction and started to remove the coffin from the back of the hearse. One thing they hadn't made clear, was that they were only going to help us get Nan onto our shoulders. Then we would have to carry her the rest of the way.

Adam and Richard held the front and Dave and I took the head and carried her into the crematorium. Now, I'd done this before, but usually there are six men and another guiding you along and that's not easy, but with only four and the family watching on, this was very challenging. With my right hand gripping onto Dave's right shoulder, we pressed on, trying to keep in step with each other, which made it easier to negotiate the few stone steps that led us in.

Like a well-oiled machine we marched in and placed her carefully on the two wooden braces. As I retreated to the wooden benches, I placed my right hand on her coffin and under my breath I said goodbye. The funeral was an event that will stay with me forever, and sitting there listening to my Aunts, then my Mom talk about all their cherished childhood memories they had shared with her, it really made me think about my life and all the memories I also had shared with Nan, and instead of feeling sad and down, it brought a little smile to my face. Death shouldn't always be a sad event. Don't get me wrong, when I heard the news of Nan's passing I was devastated, but with death there needs to be a kind of celebration of their life and what they stood for, and also what they meant to you. I was just grateful that I had gone to see her in the hospital a week before she died. Miss you every day, Nan. Love you. Thanks for everything.

Not long after Nan's passing, Emma and I decided it was time to start a family and without going into too much detail we got on with things, but it took a further six months before I finally hit the jackpot. Emma had missed her period and had got herself one of those home pregnancy tests. To our shock and amazement, Emma was indeed pregnant. We just looked into each other's eyes and then hugged one another for what felt like forever. During the embrace I thought, *Shit! I'm actually going to be a Dad*, and on one hand that excited me, but on the other it scared the living shit out of me and I did my best to keep that hidden away.

Growing up, I had never really felt like I wanted to have kids or get married, really. I always liked the single life and to be really honest, I had a hell of a time being so. I'll admit now, it got me into a shedload of trouble, because I had this knack of always messing with the wrong women. If it wasn't married ones, it was friends of my sisters or mates' ex-girlfriends. Whoever! Whenever! I didn't really care. Once I had a drink in me, things would always just get crazy and there are so many stories that I could have included, but maybe the shit would have really hit the fan if I had added them all in. You know I'm talking about you, don't you? You know you meant a lot to me and still do. Just wrong time, wrong place. I don't know if I ever said, this but I'm sorry. Sorry for all the shit I caused you when I was acting like a prick. I hope you found your happiness, like I did mine.

Anyway, that's a different book, so back to this one. Yeah, what was I saying? I never saw myself as a family man. Maybe I was scared I would have been a failure like my Dad or Richard. Because, let's face the truth, I'm still a Wootton male deep down, but then maybe I could be like my Pop, a perfect example of a family man.

Life After the Book

Hello, everyone. Wow! A lot of things have happened since I finished this life-changing book. And to be honest with you, I'm not really sure where to begin. Clearly, I've been through some challenging and difficult times in my life, but I have to say the last eight or so months have rocked me to my core. I think I've cried more times in that period than any other point in my previous thirty plus years. The number of times I've nearly given up and disappeared has been unreal, but here I am still going strong.

Let's start with the birth of my second child, George Jonathon. I had to get my name in somewhere. I'm not going to bullshit here, ladies and gentlemen, but it wasn't easy, and it still isn't. But I'm getting there one day at a time. Sorry for the cliché. I'm not for one minute going to sit here and start lying my ass off, telling you I am the best parent in the world. Far from it. But one thing is for sure. I love my kids more than anything on this planet and God help anyone who ever tries to hurt them.

For some reason parenthood has never come easy to me. I have had to really work hard at being a father. I think maybe some people are more suited than others to raise their kids, and for me it's just difficult. It's probably because I expect too much of them too early and it frustrates me when they just don't get what I'm on about. Or maybe it comes from my childhood, when I had to grow up quickly. But rest assured, everyone, they are the only reason I'm still breathing. That's for certain. When I think about the dark and dangerous places my mind has visited recently, I thank God I have them in my life, keeping me going.

Watching George come into this world and holding him proudly for the very first time made me feel incredible. Truly happy, you could say. An unbelievably rare moment in my event-filled life that sadly hasn't really taken place too many times. Maybe one of a handful of times. I was thinking about this the other day and came up with some conclusions. I remember as I kid how really bad things seemed to follow really good things so quickly. So since then I never wanted to get too happy about anything, just in case bad situations quickly followed. If that makes any sense.

After George was born, things started to unravel slowly, like watching an hourglass gradually ticking away. That's what my life had become. Sometimes it felt as if I was watching my life from afar and seeing everything I had worked extremely hard for just effortlessly drift away. Maybe it was the pressure of being a parent again. Or maybe it was the pressure of living in that family bubble with way too many people having an opinion on something that had absolutely nothing to do with them. Or maybe it was the pressures of mortgages, debts, house renovations and mental health issues. Or maybe it was writing this book, but something had clearly changed deep inside me, and I had started to feel angry and claustrophobic all the time.

Everything in my life was making me angry and it had started to affect my marriage and my relationship with my amazing kids. I remember wanting to kill someone once with one of the golf clubs that I had in my boot, when this bloke cut me up on the drive to work. He made me so angry it felt like I was going to explode. The only thing that got me back in the car was the thought of what Emma would have said to me, and not the repercussions of caving in some poor bloke's skull. That guy never knew how close he came, I'm sure of it. I've always had a bad temper, but before it took me ages to lose it. At this time, though, it felt as if all my anger was bubbling just under the surface, waiting to burst through my skin.

I knew there was something seriously wrong and should have tried to tackle it head-on a lot sooner. And really, If I'm being completely honest with myself, I probably knew where it was coming from all along, although I did deny it every time I was questioned about it. But again, to be honest, I was absolutely petrified about dealing with all that, no matter how much people tried to push me into it. There was a reason why I didn't want to confront it all.

Writing the book had stirred up things from deep within my soul that I had never wanted to deal with from my past. All of a sudden, I was forced into dealing with difficult memories; from my childhood, from losing family members, stuff I had witnessed as a soldier, losing friends. And after all this time and all the pain, I knew I had to deal with the problems one by one. I tried for so long just to ignore them but after a massive argument with Emma around Christmas time, when I completely lost my temper, I knew

I had to seek expert help to get me through all of this and maybe save the marriage.

I started searching for someone through the internet that could help with my problems and maybe save my marriage. I'm not really sure why I called her, but one advert just stared out at me, and I seemed to be drawn to her. I rang Diana and after a brief conversation, we agreed that we should meet in person for an assessment and to talk about how I had been feeling for all those years. All the people who know me best would certainly testify that I'm not the easiest person to get to open up about my feelings, and everything that goes with that. But I knew if this was going to work, I really needed to unlock myself to her and let Diana truly understand what she was working with.

We met in the same place at the same time once a week for an hour and just talked. It was very awkward at first, but with her patience and her skillful approach, I slowly opened up, letting her in, and I revealed the pain that I had been hiding for as long as I can remember. She was shocked to hear what I had gone through and what I was still going through. I will always remember her crying through one of our sessions and her telling me how much my past moved her.

Now, I don't blame anyone or anything for the things that I have been through, and to be honest, how could I when I have made most of the choices that have directly affected me? Thankfully, I recently came to the conclusion that this was just how my life was meant to play out for me, and that we are all on a journey that needs completing. And during that journey we may have many highs and many lows along the way. So it's basically just about surviving the lows if you can and enjoying the highs when they present themselves. You know I always enjoyed those, don't you?

Even though I was starting to get through everything with Diana and we were making progress, things at home hadn't really changed that much. The arguments seemed to keep coming thick and fast, and now Isabella was starting to tell us off for shouting at each other. This was completely unacceptable and is something that I am very ashamed about. No matter how bad things become, you really should make sure the kids are not affected in any way.

I could feel that things were coming to a head and after one final painful argument with Emma, I decided it would be best for all involved if I moved back in with my Mom for a while to take stock of the situation and get my head straight. I knew things were bad between us but not for one minute did I think that we couldn't fix the situation. It was us. Our relationship was built on arguments and fallings out, but we had always managed to put things back together before it got to this situation. So what happened next shocked me.

That day will go down as probably the worst day of my life, filled with horrendous pain and the complete breaking of my heart. I will never forget it and still it haunts me now. Those images and conversations are scarred in my thoughts forever and sometimes I wish I could just erase them from my mind. Do you know one of those days that feels like a nightmare that you never wake up from? Well, it was one of those which you never get over; you just get used to it. Like losing a family member, I suppose.

Walking away from the life that we had built together was devastating and something that should only be done if you know it's definitely the right thing to do. Walking away from my kids, who are my absolute world; my house, my dreams. My whole world was in that house, but I knew I would never be truly happy. Well, if that's possible anyway. But, more importantly, I knew that if I stayed and things didn't change, I was only damaging the lives of Emma and the kids. And deep down I understood that I had to sacrifice myself for their long-term happiness.

Regardless of what people have said and thought about me, and trust me, it's been bad, I knew it was the only way. The person I had become was far worse than the situation I caused when I did leave, and I knew that far too well. It's crazy really because I sort of felt as if I was an imposter who never really belonged in that life. It was as if I suddenly woke up and thought, *Who am I, and why am I punishing my family?*

It takes a brave person to recognise the faults in oneself and make that truly awful life-changing choice. But no matter how many times I look back at that day, and trust me I do, it always feels as if I made the right decision, even though it still kills me.

The worst thing for me was saying good night every night to the pictures of Isabella and George that I have in my bedroom watching over me. It really breaks my heart that I can't say it in person. Sometimes I just break down and cry when I look at them. Like I said, leaving that house that day kind of killed me a little bit and in some ways, I feel I left a piece of my heart in there with the kids. I was such a wreck that day, just crying uncontrollably. I even burst into tears in the doctors as they were trying to sign me off work and make me take antidepressants. I said, hell no, to both of those suggestions.

I will always remember Emma's Dad consoling me when I was in a bad state. I had just said goodbye to the kids before I was due to leave, and Steve came into the house and put an arm round me, then kindly said that he was always there for me if I ever needed to talk about anything. Such a sad thing about what happened is that I sort of lost a father figure too that day. I really mean that, Steve. You have been more of a Dad to me than my own and I will miss that terribly. Sorry.

To my little monkeys, Isabella and George. I'm so sorry things worked out this way and I really hope that one day you will understand and forgive me for not being there with you all the time. You are the greatest thing that has ever come into my life, and without you two, who knows what would have become of me? You have made me feel so truly blessed and have enriched my life with happiness and joy. I so look forward to watching you grow up into the two amazing people that I know you can be. But not too quickly, I must add. Daddy doesn't want to grow old too quickly either. I really want to be given the time to walk you down the aisle, Isabella, and be your best man at your wedding, George. I would be the proudest Dad ever. I never thought I would be lucky enough to find the love that I feel for you both and it breaks my heart that I won't be there for you every day. But you know I will always be here for you no matter what, don't you? No one loves you as much as your Daddy.

I'm fighting back the tears writing this piece, because you mean everything to me and I will never forgive myself for the situation I have put you in. I, too, know how hard it is growing up in a one-parent family and it destroys me knowing that I am to blame for part of that, but you need to know that it doesn't mean I don't love you, because nothing could be further from the truth.

Tears are now free-falling from my eyes and I just want to say I'm sorry. Isabella, you make me so proud of the little girl you have grown into and I still can't believe that you came from me. You have so much love for everyone close to you and you're not afraid to show it. Please don't change that because it's the biggest quality a person can have. Don't be like your Dad, who for far too long has been petrified to even show a little of what's in his heart, as I always looked upon it as a weakness, which I now know is ridiculous.

Who would have thought the person I am and all the things I have been through could be scared of that? But it's true. Although with you two I find it more natural and I know you wouldn't judge me for showing a few tears. I promise that I am trying to change and will do everything to prove that, but it takes time. I've been doing it for as long as I can remember, and I know deep down the effects this has had on the people closest to me.

George, my little monkey, just thinking about you now brings a smile to my face and even through these tears I'm crying, you make me so happy. Your smile can light up any room and even when you have been really naughty, you have a way of just grinning and everything is forgotten. You will never know any different and think that the situation we have found ourselves in is normal. But I will always know what we did and how it could really affect your life. But I promise you, George, if I thought there was another way I would have done it.

After Emma and I broke up I went to see Diana for one last time and told her my intentions of not returning to continue our sessions, but instead I decided it was time to leave the past where it belongs. But with two conditions going forward. One was to try and make things better with my Dad and brother and try to build some form of relationship before it was too late. Well what do you expect? The jury is still out with that. Second, and probably more important, was to go and visit where Etch's ashes were scattered and after all those years, finally say my goodbyes.

I contacted Faz, an old Army friend and after getting the location of where I could find Etch, I travelled north up the M6 towards

Manchester. The whole journey I was so apprehensive and scared about the emotions I was about to experience, and really didn't know what to expect once I got there. I had always been prepared for this moment to arrive, but at times the very thought scared the shit out of me. I think when you hold onto something for so long, it's difficult to let it go. Sometimes I felt like I didn't want to, even though letting go was absolutely the right thing to do. It's funny how we hang onto those things that make us feel bad, isn't it? Maybe I felt as if once I let the pain go, I would lose the memory of him all together.

After leaving the motorway I followed the signs to Mossley, which is where Etch had been brought up. A really quiet and well-presented village and it was there where I first felt my emotions beginning to stir. Before getting to my final destination, I had to pull in to get some fags. I needed something to control my feelings. I continued my journey and finally after about ten minutes, I pulled in and parked.

The second I stepped out of the car I felt the first wave of raw and powerful emotions bursting through the trees on the breeze and hitting me. It was like even after all those years since he had been taken from his family, the wounds were still as fresh as they were that day. I somehow got myself together and wiped away a few tears, before moving off to explore the place. I looked across this absolutely beautiful, picturesque lake which is almost completely surrounded by gorgeous green mountains. I remember just standing there, cigarette in hand, just taking in the waves of emotion that seemed to be sweeping across the water now and hitting me head-on.

Some people nearby made me feel uncomfortable, which was nothing to do with them. I just don't like people seeing me that vulnerable. So I moved off and stumbled across somewhere a little more secluded to think about Etch and what he stood for as a man and a soldier. I found myself an uncomfortable, cold, wet rock and took a seat, and for the first time since the day he died, I finally let go of everything that had been building up inside of me.

I'm not ashamed to say it, but I cried so much that day and will always remember a couple coming around the corner with their little lad, minding their own business and finding me there crying my eyes out. All I could do was try and wipe away my soul-cleansing tears with the back of my sleeve, but I couldn't hide it. Even forgot to bring the tissues. What an idiot. Thankfully, saving me any further embarrassment, they gave me a wide berth. But just as they were leaving, the woman gave me a quick compassionate smile before they headed off in the opposite direction. It was as if they knew what all my tears were about.

After they left me to my emotional thoughts, I just sat there crying uncontrollably and for the first time in my life I didn't even try to stop the tears. It was like at that moment eight years of pain and regret came pouring out and mixed in with those tears for Etch, I'm sure my inner healing system attached some other emotions that I had been bottling up too.

I headed back to the car and just before I got in, a beautiful soul-fixing breeze hit me full on and it felt for just that moment that he was there with me. My body tingled, and it felt as if I had a moment in time to speak to him. So I told him that I was sorry it had taken me all these years, and that I would definitely be back to see him again one day. This sent me over the edge with another huge wave of emotions following shortly afterwards.

I put the car in gear and drove away from this beautiful location to set off home, but now the tears had become more like a torrent and were making it extremely difficult for me to drive. The more I cleared the tears, the more they poured from my sore eyes and ran down my stubbled cheeks. I remember sitting at a set of traffic lights with tears running down my face, and looking across at the car alongside me, and there looking directly at me was some bloke just staring at me with a worried look on his face. It wasn't until I got back on the motorway and was heading south that the tears finally stopped.

Thanks, Faz, for helping me with this. It really helped me to finally move on and leave the guilt where it belongs. In the past. Etch, you were a great soldier and a fantastic man and friend to everyone who knew you. Your family should be very, very proud of who you were, and I have no doubt that your memory will live on. I spoke to your sister not long ago about making sure I could use your name to try and carry on your memory. And I'm so grateful to them that they agreed.

It hasn't all been bad over the past eighteen months or so, because I also had the huge privilege and honour of walking both my sisters down the aisle. And unbelievably on the same day, just hours apart. It was such an event-filled and beautiful occasion that nearly had me in tears many times. Just want to say to you both, Liz and Kat, that it was absolutely one of the greatest days of my life, right up there with the births of Isabella and George. So, thank you so much from the bottom of my heart for giving me that great memory. I will always cherish it. You have really made me so proud to be your brother, and I love you both more than you will ever know.

To Emma. Where do I start? No matter what people say or think, I will always love you. No matter what. Because you were the person who saved me from myself when things were the hardest for me. You gave me years of happiness and a real purpose to my life. And, of course, you gave me our two amazing kids. Trust me, you will never understand the guilt and pain I carry around with me for how I made you feel when I left that day.

I will always look back at our time together with a smile and just think how lucky we really were to bring two unbelievably cheeky, smart and fantastic children into this world. I know I could have handled things differently when we split up, but that's all I knew. I'm truly so sorry for everything and hope that one day you can forgive me. We really had some magical times together and for me everything I ever did or ever said at the time was true.

I knew this bit was going to be difficult and that's why I saved it to do at the end. We really had something special, but somehow, we messed it up and were left with tears and regrets. And that's something I will never do again, because it nearly fucking killed me, leaving you and the kids. I was so close to giving up. I just really hope you find the person that you deserve to be with, who will treat you in the right way, but that person can never be me. After everything that we have said and done to each other over the past few months, I hope you get your happiness, Emma, I really mean that. Thanks for the good times and sorry for the bad.

I just want to say thank you to the people who have been there through everything. You know who you are. And to my Mom, who helped me with this book. I know it was a painful read at times. And for just taking me back in when I needed you the most.

Although it was a very difficult time for me, I really enjoyed reconnecting with you after all the years I had been away in different places. I know I never say it, but I love you, Mom.

This book nearly never happened, but thanks to a holiday in Benidorm and a chance meeting with Lee, things just seemed to come together. I had gone away for my mate Dave's birthday and it turned out that one of his mates was good friends with David, who published this book. Lee and David put the wheels in motion and the rest, they say, is history. So, thanks to everyone who made this possible. I will never forget it.

During the past few years while I have been struggling to write my story, I have been so disturbed by the number of times I have heard about ex-service men and women struggling to cope with a normal existence, and in some extreme circumstances, even taking their own life out of pure desperation and feeling like they had nowhere to turn. I think that most soldiers who have served in the past decade have lost members of their battalion in this terrible way, and I'm sadly no different.

The government really needs to work out a better way of looking after ex-forces people, and especially ones who have been struggling with post-traumatic stress disorder. It really brings tears to my eyes, knowing how many men and women are struggling to cope after serving their country.

Come on, guys, I know things can be difficult at times and sometimes we can feel that there is no way out.
But there is.
There is always someone to talk to. You never have to feel alone and scared. Just pick up a phone. Type a message. Knock at a door. Just reach out anyway you can. But remember, it's never too late and there is always someone there for you.
Never feel like you are alone.

We served our incredible country with pride and bravery, and as we scattered all over after leaving the service, we then got forgotten about by the very people we tried to protect, and whose way of life we tried to preserve. But together we can really help each other and maybe one day we can be fixed. Maybe not back to the person we once were, but at the very least, to a person who can move forward and function in this current society. Let's together try and put everything behind us, but not forget about the people that didn't get that chance.

The soldiers that never came home. Rest in peace, brothers.

Remember, when things get tough, and they always do, always look forward and never backwards. There is no point thinking of what's been, because you can't change it. Can you? Take it from someone who knows. But, finally after all these years of regret, pain, heartache and misery, I get it. I really do. Now. Sitting here today in front of my laptop, typing away, I feel liberated and understand what I have been doing wrong for way too long.

Sometimes you just have to let things go and move on with your life.

Printed in Great Britain
by Amazon